WISC III
COMPILATION

John Ruth Whitworth, PhD
Dorothy Lee Sutton, MEd

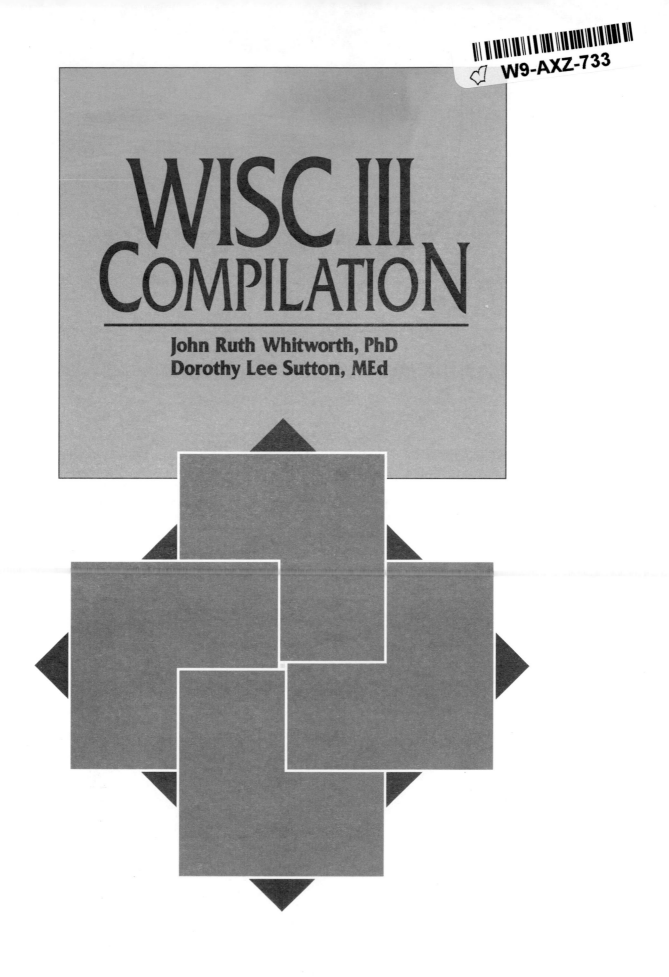

Academic Therapy Publications
20 Commercial Boulevard
Novato, California 94949-6191

International Standard Book Number: 0-87879-202-3-R

4 3 2 1 0 9
2 1 0 9 8 7 6 5 4

Contents

The Authors

DOROTHY LEE SUTTON is a counselor in the Goose Creek Consolidated Independent School District, Baytown, Texas. She received her Bachelor of Science degree in Speech and Hearing Therapy from the University of Houston and her Master of Education in Special Education from Lamar University. She has experience as a speech, hearing, and language therapist in both clinical and public school settings. She also served as an educational diagnostician, working with parents, regular education and resource teachers, and administrators in developing appropriate educational plans for handicapped children. She conducts inservice training for parents and teachers on the topics of Study Skills, Child Abuse, Dyslexia, and Learning Handicaps, and continues to serve as a consultant to regular and special education teachers.

JOHN RUTH WHITWORTH is a supervisor for the Balcones Special Services Cooperative Program in Austin, Texas. She received her Bachelor of Science in Elementary Education and her Master of Education in Special Education from Lamar University. Her PhD in Curriculum and Instruction with a minor in Neuropsychology was received from The University of Texas at Austin, Texas. She has teaching experience in both regular and resource classrooms. Her duties include interpreting neuropsychological assessment results for educational planning and supervision of resource teachers and programs. Dr. Whitworth conducts workshops on the following topics: Learning Styles, Teacher Effectiveness Training, Learning Disabilities, and Brain-Behavior Relationships.

For the children . . .

God, why did you make a kid like me?
I don't hear and I don't see—
I can't read a word like "at,"
And I can't spell a word like "cat."
My writing is messy and can't be read—
Sometimes I wish I were dead.
School's so hard I don't want to go;
They won't let me do what I know.
Let me stay home and fix my bike instead
I'd sure like to paint it a real bright red.
I can hit a ball with a baseball bat,
But I can't read a word like "at."
I don't hear and I don't see—
God, why did you make a kid like me?

by Dorothy L. Sutton

Introduction

As new tests are created and existing tests are revised, the need for up-to-date assistance for educational planning and implementation increases. The WISC III is one such revision and may replace the WISC-R as the instrument of choice in determining deficit areas related to learning. The *WISC III Compilation* provides updated assistance for educators in planning remediation of the identified deficits (based on WISC-III results) and in the writing of individual educational plans (IEPs).

While the WISC III is similar to the WISC-R, some basic differences are noted. The twelve subtests of the WISC-R have been retained and a thirteenth subtest, Symbol Search, has been added. In addition to the three IQ scores that were derived on the earlier Wechsler tests, one may now also compute factor-based index scores. These factors include Verbal Comprehension (VCI), Perceptual Organization (POI), Freedom from Distractibility (FDI), and Processing Speed (PSI). The first three factors were identified in the WISC-R but were used informally by diagnosticians and educational specialists in the gathering of assessment information. The addition of the Symbol Search subtest, along with the Coding subtest, introduced the fourth factor, Processing Speed. Norms are available for all four factors and their use has been substantiated by research results.

The *WISC III Compilation* is arranged in accordance with the subtest groupings that produce the four factor-based index scores, rather than in order of administration. In this manner, activities can be easily located for development or strengthening of a factoral deficiency as well as for specific subtest skill needs. Otherwise, the format for the *WISC III Compilation* is similar to that of the *WISC-R Compilation*. An introductory page for each subtest is provided before each group of subtest activities. On this page can be found (1) the purpose of the subtest, (2) factors influencing the student's performance on the subtest and in academic areas, (3) educational significances dealing with behavior and management techniques, and (4) the "Long-Term Goal" for remedial planning. **It is important to note that a single weakness reflected in a subtest score should not be held responsible for an academic deficiency, but should be considered in relation to other subtest and assessment results.**

Activities are written in behavioral terms under "Short-Term Objectives" with the lead-in phrase "The learner will be able to . . . ." The "Instructional Levels" are grouped by grade levels in an effort to provide sequential continuity to parallel the student's stages of growth and development. The levels are (1) kindergarten through third grade (K-3), (2) third through sixth grades (3-6), (3) sixth through ninth grades (6-9), and (4) ninth through twelfth grades (9-12). Skills for kindergarten learning actually begin development at a much earlier age and the activities for each K-3 level reflect those early developmental stages. Similarly, each grade group overlaps the instructional level before it to ensure that students who fall within a certain group will have the activities necessary to develop the readiness skills needed to progress in learning. Exceptions in the grouping for instructional levels are noted in Coding, Digit Span, and Symbol Search where the 6-9 and 9-12 levels are combined to form the 6-12 instructional level.

The Arithmetic subtest is the only academically specific subtest with activities listed according to the scope and sequence of mathematical learning. Many activities that deal with various subject matter are listed throughout the book in an effort to show how deficit remediation can be incorporated into academic teaching.

The activities listed in this book have been gathered from many sources and the authors do not claim originality for any of them. These are only suggestions and only a sample of all the activities that likely exist in the field of education. Educators using the *WISC III Compilation* should not feel limited to the activities or materials listed herein, but should feel free to add other activities and materials that are available but not listed.

The materials found in this book were all available during the 1991-92 school year based on catalogues from the publishing companies listed and/or from school supply houses such as Cole, Beckley-Cardy, Heffernan, Lakeshore, etc. But it must be noted that publishers discontinue materials, change addresses, merge with other companies, or go out of business altogether. As a result, some of the materials listed in the *WISC III Compilation* may cease to be available at any time. In that case, look for other materials that will provide the same assistance or be creative and develop something new.

One additional word of caution: **One testing instrument alone is not conclusive in establishing the educational needs of a child.** Any assessment should include both formal and informal testing procedures, observations of behavior in and out of school and information regarding physical development, home and family influences, and cultural and language background. The development of the *WISC III Compilation* is not predicated on the belief that the WISC III is the answer to an educator's prayers. Rather, it has been written to provide assistance to those using the WISC III as one tool in the total assessment of a student in need.

Suggested Resources

Blanco, R.F. 1972. *Prescriptions for children with learning and adjustment problems.* Springfield, IL: Charles C Thomas.

Bost, D., and Wills, C. 1976. *Assistance in diagnostics and educational planning through testing (monograph).* Beaumont, TX: Adept.

Chaney, C.M., and Miles, N.R. 1974. *Remediating learning problems: A developmental curriculum.* Columbus, OH: Charles E. Merrill.

Crain, J.F., and Gudeman, H.E. 1981. *The rehabilitation of brain functions.* Springfield, IL: Charles C Thomas.

Farrald, R.R. *A remedial diagnostic handbook for children with learning disabilities.* Sioux Falls, SD: Adapt Press.

Farrald, R.R., and Schamber, R.G. 1973. *A diagnostic and prescriptive technique: Handbook I.* Sioux Falls, SD: Adapt Press.

Hammill, D.D., and Bartel, N.R. 1975. *Teaching children with learning and behavior problems.* Boston, MA: Allyn and Bacon.

Hester, G.A., and Dominquez, O.A. 1976. *A second look at math.* Tulsa, OK: Educational Progress.

Kephart, N.C. 1971. *The slow learner in the classroom.* Columbus, OH: Charles E. Merrill.

Lowry, D.W., Ockenga, E.G., and Rucker, W.E. 1986. *Pre-Algebra.* Lexington, KY: Heath and Co.

Moore, P. 1973. *Suggested remediation techniques for the Detroit Tests of Learning Aptitude.* Longview, TX: Pine Tree Independent School District.

Reitan, R.M. 1985. *Aphasia and sensory-perceptual deficits in children.* South Tucson, AZ: Reitan Neuropsychology Laboratory.

Reitan, R.M. 1986. *Traumatic brain injury. Volume 1: Pathophysiology and neuropsychological evaluation.* South Tucson, AZ: Reitan Neuropsychology Laboratory.

Reitan, R.M., and Wolfson, D. 1985. *Neuroanatomy and neuropathology.* South Tucson, AZ: Reitan Neuropsychology Laboratory.

Reitan, R.M., and Wolfson, D. 1988. *Traumatic brain injury. Volume 11: Recovery and rehabilitation.* South Tucson, AZ: Reitan Neuropsychology Laboratory.

Reynolds, C.R., and Mann, L. 1987. *Encyclopedia of special education.* New York, NY: John Wiley & Sons.

Sattler, J.M. 1982. *Assessment of children's intelligence and special abilities.* Boston, MA: Allyn and Bacon, Inc.

Valett, R.E. 1967. *The remediation of learning disabilities.* Belmont, CA: Fearon.

Wallace, G., and Kauffman, J.M. 1973. *Teaching children with learning problems.* Columbus, OH: Charles E. Merrill.

Wechsler, D. 1991. Manual for the *Weschler intelligence test for children-third edition.* San Antonio, TX: The Psychological Corporation.

Publishers

Academic Communication Associates	P.O. Box 566249 Oceanside, CA 92056
Academic Therapy Publications (ATP)	20 Commercial Blvd. Novato, CA 94949-6191
Activity Resources	P.O. Box 4875 Hayward, CA 94540
Addison-Wesley Publishing Co.	Jacob Way Reading, MA 01867
Advocacy Press	P.O. Box 236 Santa Barbara, CA 93102
American Guidance Service (AGS)	4201 Woodland Rd. P.O. Box 89 Circle Pines, MN 55014-1796
American Teaching Aids	P.O. Box 1406 Covina, CA 91722
Ann Arbor Publishers (A division of Academic Therapy Publications)	20 Commercial Blvd. Novato, CA 94949-6191
Apple Computer, Inc.	20525 Mariani Ave. Cupertino, CA 95014
Barnell/SRA	P.O. Box 5380 155 N. Wacker Chicago, IL 60606-5380
Bell & Howell	7100 McCormick Rd. Chicago, IL 60645
Bemiss-Jason Corp.	P.O. Box 11486 Palo Alto, CA 94306
BLIP Productions	P.O. Box 38146 Minneapolis, MN 55433
Borg-Warner Educational System	600 W. University Dr. Arlington Heights, IL 60645
Milton Bradley (A division of Hasbro)	443 Shaker Rd. E. Longmeadow, MA 01028

Cambridge Career Products

P.O. Box 2153, Dept. CC9
Charleston, WV 25328-2153

Cambridge Development
Laboratory, Inc.

214 Third Ave.
Waltham, MA 02154

Cambridge Video

P.O. Box 2153
Charleston, WV 25328-2153

Carson-Dellosa

3514 Arlington St.
Akron, OH 44319

Chaselle, Inc.

9645 Gerwig Ln.
Columbia, MD 21046

Childcraft

20 Kilmer Rd.
P.O. Box 3081
Edison, NJ 08818-3081

Childswork/Childsplay

441 N. 5th St., Third Floor
Philadelphia, PA 19123

Communication and Therapy Skill
Builders

3830 E. Bellevue
P.O. Box 42050
Tucson, AZ 85733

Communication Skill Builders

3830 E. Bellevue
P.O. Box 42050-E91
Tucson, AZ 85733

Community Playthings

P.O. Box 901
Rifton, NY 12471-0901

Comprehension Games Corp.

6283 Woodhaven Blvd.
Rego Park, NY 11374

Constructive Playthings

1227 E. 119th St.
Grandview, MO 64030

Continental Press

520 Bainbridge St.
Elizabethtown, PA 17022-9989

Creative Publications

5040 West 111th St.
Oak Lawn, IL 60453

Creative Teaching Associates

P.O. Box 7766
Fresno, CA 93747

Creative Teaching Press

P.O. Box 6017
Cypress, CA 90630

Cuisenaire Co. of America

12 Church St., Box D
New Rochelle, NY 10802

Curriculum Associates	5 Esquire Rd. North Billerica, MA 01862-2589
Davidson & Associates	P.O. Box 2961 Torrance, CA 90509
Delta Education	P.O. Box 950 Hudson, NH 03051
T.S. Denison	9601 Newton Ave. S., Suite 8200 Minneapolis, MN 55431
Didax Educational Resources	One Centennial Dr. Peabody, MA 01969
Disney Educational Productions	500 S. Buena Vista St. Burbank, CA 91521
DLM	One DLM Park P.O. Box 4000 Allen, TX 75002
EBSCO Curriculum Materials (A division of EBSCO Industries)	P.O. Box 1943 Birmingham, AL 35201
Edmark Associates	P.O. Box 3218 Redmond, WA 98073-3218
Educational Activities	P.O. Box 392 Freeport, NY 11520
Educational Design	47 West 13th St. New York, NY 10011
Educational Impressions	210 Sixth Ave. P.O. Box 77 Hawthorne, NJ 07507
Educational Insights	19560 So. Rancho Way Dominguez Hills, CA 92020
Educational Reading Services	P.O. Box 219 Stevensville, MI 49127
Educational Teaching Aids	199 Carpenter Dr. Wheeling, IL 60090
Encyclopedia Britannica Educational Corp.	422 N. Michigan Ave. Chicago, IL 60611
Enrich/Ohaus	760 Kifer Rd. Sunnyvale, CA 94086
ESP	P.O. Box 5050 Jonesboro, AR 72403

Essential Learning Products (A division of Highlights for Children)	2300 West Fifth Ave. P.O. Box 2607 Columbus, OH 43216-2607
Eye Gate Media	3333 Elston Ave. Chicago, IL 60618-5898
Fas-Track Computer Products	7030 C Huntley Rd. Columbus, OH 43229
Fearon Teaching Aids	P.O. Box 280 Carthage, IL 62321
Field Publications	4343 Equity Dr. P.O. Box 16618 Columbus, OH 43285
Fingermath International	Educational Center Box 92 Poughquag, NY 12570
Follett Publishing Co.	1010 W. Washington Blvd. Chicago, IL 60607
Gamco Industries	P.O. Box 310 Big Spring, TX 79721
Glencoe/McGraw-Hill (A MacMillen/McGraw-Hill Co.)	15319 Chatsworth St. P.O. Box 9609 Mission Hills, CA 91346-9609
Globe Book Company (A Simon & Schuster Co.)	4350 Equity Dr. P.O. Box 2649 Columbus, OH 43216
Good Apple	1204 Buchanan St. Carthage, IL 62321-0299
Hartley Courseware, Inc.	P.O. Box 419 Dimondale, MI 48821
Hayes School Publishing Co.	321 Pennwood Ave. Wilkinsburg, PA 15221
Heffernan (A division of Cole)	P.O. Box 5309 San Antonio, TX 78201-0309
High Noon Books (A division of Academic Therapy Publications)	20 Commercial Blvd. Novato, CA 94949-6191
Highlights for Children	2300 W. Fifth Ave. P.O. Box 269 Columbus, OH 43216-0269

Houghton Mifflin Co.

One Beacon St.
Boston, MA 02108

Hubbard

P.O. Box 104
Northbrook, IL 60062

Ideal School Supply

11000 S. Lavergne Ave.
Oak Lawn, IL 60453

Imperial International Learning Corp.

P.O. Box 548
Kankakee, IL 60901

Incentives for Learning

111 Center Ave., Suite I
Pacheco, CA 94553

Instructional Fair

P.O. Box 1650
Grand Rapids, MI 49501

Instructor/Scholastic, Inc.

730 Broadway
New York, NY 10003

Judy/Instructo

4325 Hiawatha Ave., S.
Minneapolis, MN 55406

Kenworthy Educational Service

P.O. Box 60 Dept. E
Buffalo, NY 14205

Kid's Stuff/Incentive Publications

3835 Cleghorn Ave.
Nashville, TN 37215-2532

Kimbo Educational

P.O. Box 477
Long Branch, NJ 07740

Lakeshore Curriculum Materials Center

2695 E. Dominguez St.
P.O. Box 6261
Carson, CA 90749

Lauri Enterprises

Phillips-Avon, ME 04966

Learning Resources

151 Pfingsten Rd., Unit M
P.O. Box 467
Deerfield, IL 60015

Learning Tree Publishing

P.O. Box 4116
Englewood, CO 80155

Learning Well

P.O. Box 3759, Dept. 8
New Hyde Park, NY 11040-1042

Learning Works

P.O. Box 6187
Santa Barbara, CA 93160

LEGO Systems

P.O. Box 2273
Enfield, CT 06082

LinguiSystems, Inc.	3100 4th Ave. P.O. Box 747 East Moline, IL 61244
Little, Brown and Co.	34 Beacon St. Boston, MA 02108
Love Publishing Co.	6635 E. Villanova Pl. Denver, CO 80222
Marshmedia	P.O. Box 8082 Shawnee Mission, KS 66208
Marvel Education Co.	200 Fifth Ave. New York, NY 10010
Media Materials	2936 Remington Ave., Dept. E98 Baltimore, MD 21211
Melody House Publishing (A.B. LeCrone Co.)	819 N.W. 92nd St. Oklahoma City, OK 73114
Charles E. Merrill Publishing Co.	1300 Alum Creek Dr. Columbus, OH 43216
Midwest Publications	P.O. Box 448 Pacific Grove, CA 93950
Milliken Publishing Co.	1100 Research Blvd. St. Louis, MO 63132
Mission Publications	P.O. Box 549 El Toro, CA 92630
National Geographic Society	Educational Division Dept. 90 Washington, DC 20036
Novo Educational Toy & Equipment	585 Avenue of the Americas New York, NY 10011
Nystrom	3333 Elston Ave. Chicago, IL 60618
Ohio Art Co.	One Toy St. New York, NY 10010
Opportunities for Learning (FSC Educational)	905 Hickory Ln. Mansfield, OH 44905
Parker Brothers (A division of Tonka)	50 Dunham Rd. Beverly, MA 01915
Playskool (A division of Milton Bradley)	Springfield, MA 01101

Prentice-Hall Learning Systems	P.O. Box 527 San Jose, CA 95106
Pro-Ed Publishers	8700 Shoal Creek Blvd. Austin, TX 78758
Psychological Corporation	555 Academic Court San Antonio, TX 78204-2498
Rand McNally and Company	P.O. Box 7600 Chicago, IL 60680
Reitan Neuropsychology Laboratory	2920 South 4th Ave. Tucson, AZ 85713
Remedia Publications	P.O. Box 1788 Scottsdale, AZ 85252
Frank Schaffer Publications	1028 Via Mirabel, Dept. 630 Palos Verdes Estates, CA 90274
Scholastic, Inc.	P.O. Box 7502 Jefferson, MO 65101
The School Co. (A division of Career Development Software)	5600 Randolph St. N. Little Rock, AR 72116
Science Research Associates (SRA) (A division of IBM)	155 North Wacker Dr. Chicago, IL 60606
Selchow & Righter Co.	Bayshore, NY 11706
Dale Seymour Publications	P.O. Box 10888 Palo Alto, CA 94303
Social Studies School Service	10200 Jefferson Blvd., Room 58 P.O. Box 802 Culver City, CA 90232-0802
Steck-Vaughn Co. (A division of National Education Corp.)	P.O. Box 26015 Austin, TX 78755
Summit Learning	P.O. Box 493 A Ft. Collins, CO 80522
Sunburst Communications	39 Washington Ln. P.O. Box 40 Pleasantville, NY 10570-3498
Sunburst Communications (software)	101 Castleton St. Pleasantville, NY 10570-3498
Texas Instruments	13500 N. Central Expressway P.O. Box 5012, M/S 54 Dallas, TX 75222

Trend Enterprises	P.O. Box 43073 St. Paul, MN 55164
Troll Associates	100 Corporate Dr. Mahwah, NJ 07430
Tupperware Educational Services	Dept. 1 P.O. Box 2353 Orlando, FL 32802
Ungame Co.	P.O. Box 6382 Anaheim, CA 92806
United States Government Printing Office	Division of Public Documents Washington, DC 20360
Varis Associates	P.O. Box 893 Hicksville, NY 11802
Weber Costello	1900 N. Narrangansett Ave. Chicago, IL 60639
Western Publishing Co.	Racine, WI 53404
H.W. Wilson Company	950 University Ave. Bronx, NY 10452
Wings for Learning	1600 Green Hills Rd. P.O. Box 660002 Scotts Valley, CA 95067-0006
Wonder Books (A division of Grosset & Dunlap)	51 Madison Ave. New York, NY 10010
Zaner-Bloser	2200 W. Fifth Ave. P.O. Box 16764 Columbus, OH 43216-6764

FACTOR I—VERBAL COMPREHENSION

INFORMATION

Information

I. **Purpose of the Subtest**
    To measure the student's knowledge of particular facts

II. **Factors Affecting Subtest and Academic Performance**
    A. Educational exposure
    B. Interest and motivation
    C. Memory
    D. Cultural and environmental background
    E. Associative thinking ability
    F. Anxiety
    G. Language skills, both receptive and expressive

III. **Educational Significance**
    A. The student should be exposed to a variety of experiences, both direct and vicarious, by being provided books, pictures, interest centers, field trips, guest speakers, magazines, etc., with ample time and opportunities available for assimilation. The teacher should encourage the student to use inferential thinking.
    B. In order to develop self-confidence and motivate the student to learn, the teacher should provide a system of tangible and intangible rewards.
    C. Family activities should be encouraged that will contribute to the expansion of the student's acquisition of facts.
    D. The teacher should structure learning activities to allow more individual attention and additional explanations for the student. Opportunities for oral expression by the student should be presented.
    E. The teacher should conduct periodic review of basic concepts that could be correlated to newly learned ideas.

IV. **Long-Term Goal**
    The learner will be able to remember particular facts from prior learning experiences.

Information

Short-Term Objectives

The learner will be able to

Instructional Level: K-3

Materials

1. participate in "Show and Tell" activities.

1. *Show and Tell*
   (Creative Teaching Press)
   Toys, other items from home

2. state on demand his full name, address, telephone number, and parent's name(s).

3. identify body parts as to names, locations, and functions.

3. *Body Parts Floor Puzzle*
   (Frank Schaffer)
   Mark-On/Wipe-Off Body Imagery
   Flannel Board Body Parts
   (Milton Bradley)
   My Face and Body
   (Judy/Instructo)
   *Peabody Language Development Kit-
   (Revised) Level P*
   (AGS)
   Body and Self-Awareness Big Box
   (DLM)

4. draw pictures of self, family, and environment.

5. record, on a chart, the date and his height at periodic intervals.

5. *Watch Us Grow Up*
   Gorilla Growth Chart
   (Judy/Instructo)
   Grow Chart
   (Trend)
   Growth Chart
   (Frank Schaffer)

6. recreate a bedroom, family seating arrangements at the dinner table, etc., using small toys and/or doll house furniture.

6. *Doll House Furnishings*
   (Marvel)
   DUPLO Family Workers
   LEGO People
   (LEGO)

7. discuss and/or describe trips made by the student's family to specified locations (e.g., grocery store, post office, etc.).

Information

Short-Term Objectives

The learner will be able to

Instructional Level: K-3

Materials

8. draw pictures or verbally describe field trips, films, etc., to community agencies (e.g., fire station, zoo, police station, hospital, courthouse, etc.).

8. *Community Helpers and Workers Unit*
   (Judy/Instructo)
   We Learn All About: Community Helpers
   (Fearon)
   Community Helpers/Community Workers
   (American Teaching Aids)
   Community Helpers—filmstrip/casette
   Let's Visit Read-Along Units
   (Troll)
   My Community
   (Marvel)

9. use toy and/or flannel board figures to identify the various roles of policeman, mailman, fireman, etc., by answering specific questions (e.g., "Who brings letters to your home?" or "Who helps when you are lost?").

9. *LEGO Community People*
   LEGO Community Vehicles
   (LEGO)
   Community Careers
   (Judy/Instructo)
   People Who Work Listening Lab
   (Troll)
   Who Am I? Career Characters
   (Carson-Dellosa)
   Community Helpers Flash Cards
   (Trend)
   Community Helpers/Community Workers
   (American Teaching Aids)
   Home and Community Helpers (K-3)
   (Marvel)

10. discuss self-understanding in relation to family, friends, school, and community.

10. *Me—That's Who! (Awareness)*
    Who Are You?—filmstrip
    (Troll)
    Being Friends—filmstrip
    A Kids' Guide to Getting Along with Others—videocassette
    (Learning Tree)
    Early Learning Skills
    (Nystrom)

Information

Short-Term Objectives

The learner will be able to

Instructional Level: K-3

Materials

11. respond appropriately to a prepared tape on which is recorded questions requiring specific answers (e.g., "Which day of the week is today?" or "How old are you?").

12. prepare an individual calendar for each month of the year marking each current day with an appropriate symbol such as stars, seals, numbers, etc., giving special emphasis to holidays and their meanings.

12. *Calendar Activity Fun*
    Days, Months, Seasons
    The Biggest Holiday Book Ever!
    Super Seasonal Reproducibles
       (Carson-Dellosa)
    Big Book
       (Fearon)
    Today's the Day
    Day By Day Calendar
       (Milton Bradley)

13. select a particular subject of interest and find appropriate pictures or objects for class presentation.

13. Magazines
    Catalogs
    Newspapers
    Various objects

14. retell stories, poetry, rhymes, etc., read by the teacher or presented on records or tapes.

14. *Overhead Transparencies for Creative Dramatics*
       (Creative Teaching Press)
    The Story Teller Presents . . .
       (American Teaching Aids)
    Chall-Popp Reading Books
       (Continental Press)
    Primary Reading Series
       (Educational Insights)

15. answer specific questions regarding the elements of position, quantity, identification, and time, using pictures and objects (e.g., "What is under the table?" "How many children are in the picture?" "Is it daytime or nighttime?" "What is the season?").

15. *Spatial Relationship Puzzles*
       (Ideal)
    Resource Guide for Basic Concept Teaching
       (Psychological Corporation)
    K-Talk
    Opposites Power
       (Communication Skill Builders)

Information

Short-Term Objectives
The learner will be able to

Instructional Level: K-3

Materials

Wooden Inlay Puzzles: Seasons
(Judy/Instructo)
Teacher-prepared questions

16. relate the events of a TV show to the class.

17. recognize a verbal statement as being absurd and explain why.

17. *Ready, Set, Listen!*
The Word Kit
BESST
   (LinguiSystems)
Think Spots I: Absurdities
SkillKeepers Levels B and C
   (Remedia)
Semantically Speaking—For Early Intervention
Sentence Improbabilities/Sentence Rhymes and Definitions
   (Communication Skill Builders)

10. graph time and temperature daily.

18. *We Dress for Weather*
Weather Station
   (Judy/Instructo)
Educational Thermometer
   (Milton Bradley)
The Weather Club
   (Educational Insights)
Time Skills, Gr. 1-2, 2-3
   (Carson-Dellosa)
Tell Time Quizmo
   (Milton Bradley)

19. recognize and discuss jobs, skills, and use of tools necessary for familiar occupations.

19. *Elementary Career Series*
   (Media Materials)
Our Helpers
   (Milton Bradley)
Community Helpers Lotto
   (Trend)
Stepping Out with Language
   (Community Skill Builders)

INFO.

27

Information

Short-Term Objectives

The learner will be able to

20. discuss the facts of good nutrition and the basic food groups.

Instructional Level: K-3

Materials

20. *Eat Right/Feel Right*
      (Trend)
    Jumbo Nutrition Yearbook, Gr. 1, 2, 3
      (ESP)
    Food and Nutrition Teaching Pictures
      (Marvel)
    Good Nutrition . . . Good for You!
      (Troll)
    Goal: Beginning Health and Nutrition
      (Milton Bradley)

Information

Short-Term Objectives

The learner will be able to

Instructional Level: 3-6

Materials

1. draw a picture of an individual classroom. (Expand this activity to include the organization of the school structure.)

2. demonstrate personal understanding of different cultural backgrounds through the discussion of stories, filmstrips, etc.

2. *World Cultures*
   (Hayes)
   Ethnic Pride
   Americans, Too!
   (Good Apple)
   Communities Around the World
   (Continental Press)

3. locate specific places on a map or globe.

3. *Map Skills*
   (Continental Press)
   Map Skills for Today
   Map Skills Games
   (Field)
   Project Earth
   Geo-Safari
   (Educational Insights)
   Global Flash Cards
   Game of the States
   (Milton Bradley)
   United States Map Skills
   Maps Unfold the World, Pt. 1 & 2
   (Milliken)
   Map Skills
   (Frank Schaffer)

4. review a selected TV program by participating in class discussions and answering predetermined questions.

4. Teacher-prepared questions

5. make a science notebook by cutting out magazine pictures depicting a particular season of the year (e.g., winter). (This procedure should be followed to include each of the other three seasons.)

5. *The Learn-About Reading Center: Wonder of the Seasons*
   Venture Read-Alongs: Seasons Unit
   (Troll)
   Magazines

Information

Short-Term Objectives

The learner will be able to

Instructional Level: 3-6

Materials

6. select and complete a science project (e.g., planting a seed and charting its growth or hatching a fertilized egg in a chick-u-bator).

6. *Science Shelf Activities*
(Ideal)
Scienceworks
(Addison-Wesley)
Science Projects
(Fearon)

7. present current events information to the class from a TV news program or newspaper.

8. draw a picture or discuss interesting aspects of a film or filmstrips pertaining to a community, state, or nation.

9. report in a paper or a class discussion the reason for the establishment of a particular holiday.

9. *Let's Celebrate Holidays*—filmstrips
(Troll)

10. cut out pictures from magazines illustrating the way people live in different countries.

10. Magazines

11. draw a map showing the way from school to home.

11. *Finding Your Way*
(Fearon)
Map Skills for Today
(Field)
Map Skills
(Milliken)
Map Skills
(Frank Schaffer)
Building Primary Maps
(Judy/Instructo)

12. make a simple book report on a book of his choice.

13. identify accurate pictures of musical instruments.

13. *Science Picture Library: Musical Instruments*
(Educational Insights)

Information

Short-Term Objectives	Instructional Level: 3-6
The learner will be able to	**Materials**

14. identify the instruments heard in recorded instrumental music.

14. Instrumental music albums

15. recognize objects by understanding clues and descriptors in games (e.g., "I Spy," "Twenty Questions," etc.).

15. *Password*
   Educational "Password" Game
   Clue
      (Milton Bradley)
   Hidden Treasure/Context Clues—
      software
   Categorizing: Detective Games—
      software
   Snooper Troops Case #2: The Disappearing Dolphin—software
      (Troll)

16. answer questions concerning presidential facts after listening to a discussion about them.

16. *Presidents*
      (Good Apple)
   Presidents of the United States Flash Cards
      (Trend)
   The Presidency, the Men and the Office
      (Instructional Fair)

17. distinguish fact from fiction.

17. *Fact or Opinion/Smart Shopper*
      (Learning Well)
   Fact or Opinion—software
      (Communication Skill Builders)

18. relate facts about the symbols of America.

18. *Symbols of Our Heritage*
      (Instructional Fair)
   I Am an American
      (Frank Schaffer)

19. find specific points on a map according to longitude and latitude.

19. *Map Skills for Today*
      (Field)
   Developing Map Skills: Book 2
   Outline Maps of the USA
      (Hayes)
   Exploring Your World Geography Games: Hemisphere Hunt
      (Media Materials)

Information

Short-Term Objectives

The learner will be able to

20. relate facts about various occupations.

Instructional Level: 3-6

Materials

20. *Learning About Careers Teaching Pictures*
       (Marvel)
    Elementary Career Series
       (Media Materials)
    Working Choices
       (Milton Bradley)
    Careers Bulletin Board Set
       (Frank Schaffer)
    A Day in the Life of Reading Modules
    Career Insights
    Career Days
    Young Careers: What's It Like to Be Book Bag
       (Troll)
    Career Activity Books
       (Opportunities for Learning)

Information

Short-Term Objectives

The learner will be able to

Instructional Level: 6-9

Materials

1. prepare a personal data sheet giving pertinent information (e.g., name, address, telephone number, parents' names, occupations, etc.).

2. prepare a class scrapbook reporting current events.

2. Newspapers
   Magazines

3. prepare a bulletin board illustrating a favorite story.

3. *Reluctant Readers Collections*
   (Scholastic)

4. describe verbally selected pictures.

4. *Peabody Language Development Kit (Revised)-Level 2*
   (AGS)
   Storytelling Pictures
   (DLM)

5. discuss and/or demonstrate prevocational aspects involved in job selection after viewing pertinent filmstrips (e.g., filling out application forms, preparation for interviews, etc.).

5. *Understanding Jobs and Careers—* filmstrips
   (Learning Well)
   Career Exploration Video Series
   Getting a Job Series
   Me and Jobs
   Work-a-Day America
   (Opportunities for Learning)
   How to Get a Job—A Handy Guide for Jobseekers
   (U.S. Government Printing Office)
   Careers and Values
   (Social Studies School Service)

6. play games requiring the understanding of clues and descriptors such as "Clue" and "Twenty Questions."

6. *Clue*
   (Parker Brothers)
   Password
   Educational "Password" Game
   (Milton Bradley)

Information

Short-Term Objectives

The learner will be able to

7. present to the class a report on a famous person, either written or verbally.

8. discuss with class members folk tales, mythology, and legends of America and other lands.

9. draw a map in relation to his home of the community demonstrating locations of important buildings (e.g., courthouse, churches, post office, grocery store, etc.).

10. report and/or discuss a selected group of school rules as stated in the school handbook. (If no handbook is available, have the student list and discuss the known rules.)

Instructional Level: 6-9

Materials

7. *Research Teasers and Pleasers,*
   Gr. 3-6, 6-8
      (Opportunities for Learning)
   50 Great Americans
      (Incentives for Learning)
   Famous American Bulletin Board Set
   Famous Black American Bulletin
      Board Set
      (Frank Schaffer)
   Famous Friends Series
      (Good Apple)

8. *20 Questions:*
      Classical Mythology
      American Folklore
      (Instructional Fair)
   Scholastic Literature Filmstrips:
      Mythology
      Folklore and Fables
   Scholastic Literature Anthologies:
      Myths and Legends
      (Scholastic)
   Rib-Tickling American Folktales
      Filmstrip Library
   Myths and Legends of Ancient Greece
      Filmstrip Library
      (Troll)

9. *Finding Your Way*
      (Fearon)
   Building Primary Maps
   Building a Community
      (Judy/Instructo)

10. School handbook

Information

Short-Term Objectives

The learner will be able to

Instructional Level: 6-9

Materials

11. list the cities through which one should pass when traveling from a given point to a specific destination.

11. *Taking a Trip*
    (Fearon)
    Various state maps

12. recognize individual states, their capitals, abbreviations, and their neighboring states.

12. *State Flash Cards*
    U.S. Bingo
    (Ideal)
    States, Capitals, & Abbreviations
    Wrap-Ups
    U.S. Travel Game
    United States Map Game
    (Oportunities for Learning)
    Games of the States
    (Milton Bradley)
    50 Nifty States
    (Good Apple)
    United States Flash Cards
    (Media Materials)

13. answer questions after researching a selected topic in a reference book (e.g., an encyclopedia).

13. Encyclopedia
    Almanac
    Atlas
    Teacher-prepared list of topics

14. explain the step-by-step procedure from the beginning of a project to its completion (e.g., planting flower seeds, etc.).

15. prepare a scrapbook by utilizing all available reference media on holidays, discussing their dates and significance.

15. *Written Language Skills: Holidays*
    and Celebrations
    (Love)
    Holidays and Seasons
    Let's Celebrate Holidays
    (Troll)
    Encyclopedia

16. act as a newscaster and report on four news items.

Information

Short-Term Objectives

The learner will be able to

Instructional Level: 6-9

Materials

17. answer questions after viewing film-strips about living in America today.

17. *Regions of the United States*—filmstrips
    One Nation: Exploring the United States—filmstrips
    (Troll)

18. discuss how federal and state laws are enacted.

18. *How a Bill Becomes a Law*
    (Opportunities for Learning)
    You and the Constitution
    (Addison-Wesley)
    Our Government in Action
    United States Government
    (Creative Teaching Press)

19. discuss and answer questions concerning the presidency and presidents.

19. *Presidents of the United States*
    Presidential Posters: Washington to Bush
    (Opportunities for Learning)
    Presidents
    (Good Apple)
    Famous Presidents Bulletin Board Set
    (Frank Schaffer)
    The Presidency, the Men and the Office
    (Instructional Fair)

20. investigate and discuss factors regarding specific types of careers.

20. *Exploring Careers*
    Career Exploration Kit
    Career Capers
    Computer Career Planning Series:
     Career Exploration Series
    (Opportunities for Learning)
    Career Lab
    (Ideal)
    Working Choices
    (Milton Bradley)
    Choosing a Job You'll Like
    (Incentives for Learning)
    Entering the World of Work
    Career Skills
    (Glencoe/McGraw-Hill)

Information

Short-Term Objectives	Instructional Level: 6-9

The learner will be able to

Materials

Prepare Yourself—filmstrip
Careers Without College
Exploring Careers
The Quick Job-Hunting Map
   (Social Studies School Service)

21. identify landforms and water bodies using maps.

21. *Developing Skills with Maps and Globes*
   (Nystrom)
3-D Landforms
   (Educational Insights)

22. discuss factors involved in good nutrition.

22. *Intermediate Science Transparencies: Nutrition*
Intermediate Science Duplicating Master: Nutrition and Health
Intermediate Science Diagrammatic Posters: Nutrition
   (Milliken)
Jumbo Nutritional Yearbook, Gr. 6
   (ESP)

Information

Short-Term Objectives

The learner will be able to

1. share with the class information regarding local industries.

2. gather names of the mayor, city manager, council members, etc.

3. discuss various vocational occupations after viewing filmstrips and/or reading books, pamphlets, etc.

4. list and discuss the necessary requirements for vocational preparation (e.g., applying for a Social Secuity number, filling out an application, etc.).

5. participate in role-playing activities involving applying and being interviewed for a job.

Instructional Level: 9-12

Materials

1. Information from the local Chamber of Commerce

2. Information from the local Chamber of Commerce

3. *Career Exploration Video Series*
   Work-a-Day America Video
      (Opportunities for Learning)
   The Job Box
   Job Sheets
   The Career Box
   Career Sheets
      (Fearon)
   Vocational Reading
      (Imperial International)
   The Right Job—software
   The Choice is Yours—software
      (Sunburst)
   What Color Is Your Parachute?
   The Three Boxes of Life
      (Social Studies School Service)

4. *How to Get a Job—A Handy Guide for Jobseekers*
      (U.S. Government Printing Office)
   Janus Job Application File
      (Fearon)
   Finding a Job
      (Steck-Vaughn)
   Getting a Job—filmstrip
   Preparing for Your Career
      (Opportunities for Learning)
   Real Life Reading Program
      (Scholastic)

5. *Your Appearance on the Job Interview*—video
   Don't Call Us, We'll Call You
      (Lakeshore)
   Job Interview Skills
   Getting a Job Series—filmstrip
      (Opportunities for Learning)

Information

Short-Term Objectives

The learner will be able to

Instructional Level: 9-12

Materials

6. list and discuss personal attributes and qualifications necessary to find and maintain a job.

6. *Finding a Job*
     (Steck-Vaughn)
   LifeSchool: Occupations and
     Interpersonal Skills
     (Fearon)
   On-the-Job Skills Series—filmstrips
   Getting a Job Series—filmstrips
   On the Job
   Job Survival Series
     (Opportunities for Learning)
   Entering the World of Work
   Career Skills
     (Glencoe/McGraw-Hill)
   You Are the Boss
     (High Noon Books)

7. plan a week-long vacation trip, accounting for routes, cities to visit, length of stay in cities, and points of interest.

7. *Facts About the Cities*
   Facts About the States
     (H.W. Wilson)
   Various state road maps

8. prepare a report for class presentation on a famous American person.

8. *Champions of Change*
     (Steck-Vaughn)
   50 Famous Americans
     (Incentives for Learning)
   Famous People Flash Cards
     (Media Materials)
   Famous American Bulletin Board
     Set
     (Frank Schaffer)
   Facts About the Presidents
     (H.W. Wilson)

9. relate general knowledge about cities and states.

9. *Facts About the Cities*
   Facts About the States
     (H.W. Wilson)
   Game of the States
     (Milton Bradley)
   Fun-to-Know Flash Cards: States and
     Capitals
     (Trend)

Information

Short-Term Objectives

The learner will be able to

Instructional Level: 9-12

Materials

I.Q. Games: U.S. Geography
(Educational Insights)
Various travelogues and state maps

10. prepare a written or oral report regarding the importance and effect of a newspaper item of current significance.

11. list the state congressional representatives and senators.

11. World Almanac
State Almanac
State Congressional Record

12. report and discuss with the class a specific set of school rules.

12. School handbook

13. discuss with the class teenage relationships and responsibilities.

13. *Decision-Making for Success in Life*
(Educational Insights)
Choices
Challenges
(Advocacy Press)
Just for Teens—filmstrip
(Opportunities for Learning)
Teenage Problems: How to Survive the Teenage Years—videocassette
Friendship and Dating
Relationships and Personal Choices
(Social Studies School Service)
What's Right, What's Wrong? You Decide
(Sunburst)

14. discuss the realities of dealing with money.

14. *Managing Your Money*
Handling Your Money
All About Money Box
(Incentives for Learning)
Money Management and Banking Series—software
Money! Money!—software
(Opportunities for Learning)
Using Dollars and Sense
(Fearon)

Information

Short-Term Objectives

The learner will be able to

Instructional Level: 9-12

Materials

15. complete written worksheets concerning safety rules and regulations related to driving.

15. *Life Skills Driving Workbook*
    In the Driver's Seat Workbook
      (Opportunities for Learning)
    Driver Education: Behind the Wheel
      (Hayes)
    Get That License
      (Fearon)
    Road Signs of the Times
      (Ideal)
    You Are the Driver
      (High Noon Books)
    State driver's manual

16. recite general terms necessary to understanding map reading.

16. *Map and Globe Skills, Vol. 2*
      (Weber Costello)
    Exploring Your World Geography
    Games:
    City Limits
    State Race
    Hemisphere Hunt
    World Wiz
      (Milton Bradley)
    Developing Map Skills with Maps and Globes
      (Nystrom)
    Intermediate Social Studies Transparency/Duplicating Books, Gr. 5-9
      (Milliken)
    Practicing Map Skills, Book 2
    Learning Map Skills, Book 2
      (Hayes)

17. discuss the selection of the president and the responsibilities of the office.

17. *Presidential Quiz*
    Presidential Rummy
      (Educational Insights)
    American Citizenship Program:
    The Presidency, Congress, and the Supreme Court
      (Scholastic)

Information

Short-Term Objectives

The learner will be able to

Instructional Level: 9-12

Materials

Civics and Citizenship
  (Hayes)
The Presidency, the Men and the Office
  (Instructional Fair)
The American Government Series: Book 2
  (Opportunities for Learning)

18. discuss how the growth of the U.S. is affected by the decisions made by various presidents while in office.

18. *The Presidency, the Men and the Office*
  (Instructional Fair)
Presidents of the United States
Presidential Posters
  (Opportunities for Learning)
Famous People Flash Cards: Presidents of the United States
  (Milton Bradley)
Presidential Posters
  (Ideal)

19. relate the names of inventors of significant inventions.

19. *Invention Time Line*
Inventions
  (Creative Teaching Press)
Mind Bogglers: Book 3
  (Fearon)
BrainBoosters: Inventions and Discoveries
  (Educational Insights)

20. discuss the effects of diet and exercise upon body growth and health.

20. *Science Activity Centers: The Nutrition Box*
Exploring the Human Body: Nutrition Box
  (Educational Insights)

SIMILARITIES

Similarities

I. **Purpose of the Subtest**
    To measure the ability to think and reason associatively and logically at concrete and abstract levels.

II. **Factors Affecting Subtest and Academic Performance**
    A. Verbal concept formation—specifically, sameness and differences
    B. Cultural background
    C. Interests
    D. Memory
    E. Associative thinking
    F. Receptive and expressive language skills
    G. Visualization

III. **Educational Significance**
    A. Before analogical thinking can develop, it is necessary that the student understand the concept of "sameness."
    B. All sensory modalities should be utilized in the teaching of the "sameness-difference" concepts.
    C. Concrete instructions should be emphasized and given in a specific manner by the teacher until the student is able to understand abstractions.
    D. Relate various learned concepts to new material to strengthen skills in associative thinking and thus provide the student with a pattern for recognizing similarities and differences.
    E. Provide visual aids where possible. Make sure the student is close enough to the teacher so that an association can be formed between the spoken words and the visual aid used.
    F. The overall view of an idea should be presented in as concrete a manner as possible in order to insure understanding.

IV. **Long-Term Goal**
    The learner will be able to demonstrate the ability to think and reason logically at both concrete and abstract levels in terms of verbal concept development, analogous, associative, and semantic relationships.

Similarities

Short-Term Objectives	Instructional Level: K-3

The learner will be able to

Materials

1. sort and match identical objects in a box.

2. complete simple matching of color, using same-sized paper, cut-outs, sticks, cubes, etc.

3. interpret the concept of likeness by using matching and sorting exercises (e.g., red beads, white buttons, etc.).

4. sort geometric shapes and objects according to color, size, and shape. (Expand this activity to include differences within like groups, such as different shapes within like color groups.)

---

1. *Attribute Sorting Set*
   (Ideal)
   Box
   Identical toys

2. *Colored Inch Cubes*
   Using Colored Cubes for Cognitive
   Skills
   (DLM)
   Building Thinking Skills
   Primary Book
   (Midwest)
   Attribute Sorting Set
   (Ideal)
   Attribute Desk Blocks
   (Judy/Instructo)
   Attribute Blocks
   (Didax)

3. *Alike Because*
   (DLM)
   Learning Readiness Set
   (Continental Press)
   Attribute Sorting Set
   Plastic Beads
   Plastic Disks for Lacing
   Wooden Beads
   (Ideal)
   Lauri's Build-a-Skill
   (Lauri)

4. *Shapes & Similar Shaped Objects*
   (AGS)
   Jumbo Classifying Clues
   (Ideal)
   The I'm Ready to Learn Series:
   Visual Perception
   (Kids' Stuff)
   Lauri's Build-a-Skill
   Color and Shape Sorter
   Shape Squares

Similarities

Short-Term Objectives

The learner will be able to

Instructional Level: K-3

Materials

Fit-a-Shape
  (Lauri)
Attribute Tiles
  (Educational Insights)
Building Thinking Skills: Primary Book
  (Midwest)
Attribute Blocks
  (Didax)
Sort & Stack
  (Constructive Playthings)
Shape Sorting Box
  (DLM)
*Sorting Box Combination for
  Counting and Color*
  (Marvel)

5. recognize likenesses and differences among pictures of animals, shapes, and numbers in games.

5. *Differences Game*
  (Constructive Playthings)
Symbol Discrimination Series
  (Ann Arbor)
Association Picture Cards: Sets I-IV
  (DLM)
Learning Same & Different
  (Milliken)
Same or Different Wipe-Off Cards
  (Trend)
Animal Dominoes
Color & Shape Dominoes
  (Frank Schaffer)
Pick Pairs Game
Original Memory
Match & Move
Animals Families Memory
  (Milton Bradley)

6. distinguish between categorization of groups into broad classification, using picture cards (e.g., pets, toys, food, furniture, etc.).

6. *Categories*
Association Picture Cards: Sets I-IV
  (DLM)
The Classification Game
Classification Picture Cards

Similarities

Short-Term Objectives
The learner will be able to

Instructional Level: K-3
Materials

Lotto Games:
  Rooms (in the house)
  Colors
  Seasons
  Familiar Settings
  Geometric Shapes
Early Learning Curriculum Units:
  Animals
  Transportation
Body Parts & Senses
  (Judy/Instructo)
Learning to Classify
  (Milliken)

7. interpret the concept of difference using picture cards which reflect differences (e.g., tall, short, big, little).

7. *Opposites*
  (DLM)
Peabody Picture Collection: Opposites
  (AGS)
Same or Different Wipe-Off Cards
  (Trend)
Stickybear Opposites—software
  (EBSCO)
Primary Concepts II
  (Troll)
Alike and Not Alike
Size Proportion Cards
Proportion Picture Cards
  (Ideal)

8. describe differences within a single category such as dogs by looking at pictures (e.g., size, color, type, etc.).

8. *Association Picture Cards: Sets I-IV*
  (DLM)
Classification Picture Cards
Sorting Boxes with a Reading
  Curriculum Focus: Same & Different
Attribute Set: Shapes, Sizes, Colors
  (Judy/Instructo)
Alike and Not Alike
  (Ideal)

Similarities

Short-Term Objectives The learner will be able to	Instructional Level: K-3 Materials

9. complete puzzles and games involving sets and classification.

   9. *Pick Pairs Game*
     Picture Card Games I and II
     Spin and See Games
       (Milton Bradley)
     Lauri's Build-a-Skill: Beginning
      Classification and Sorting
      (Lauri)
     Charlie: Math Readiness,
      Classification Skills
      (Educational Insights)
     Commercial card games such as
     Old Maid, Fish

10. recognize similarities and differences among letters of the alphabet.

  10. *Symbol Discrimination Series*
      (Ann Arbor)
     Alphabet Flip Charts
      (Zaner-Bloser)
     b, d, p, q
      (Incentives for Learning)

11. recognize and circle the same letter or symbol which appears on a given line of a worksheet.

  11. *Visual Sequential Memory Exercises*
      (DLM)
     Symbol/Letter Tracking
     Letter Tracking
     Symbol Discrimination Series
      (Ann Arbor)

12. select all of a predetermined group of letters, such as all *a*'s, *b*'s, etc., from sets of cards of different colors and sizes on which are printed letters of the alphabet in upper- and lower-case forms.

  12. *Avalanche of Letters*
      (Lauri)
     Letter Fun
     Letter Cards
      (Ideal)
     Teacher-made cards

13. select pairs of words on a list that are alike (or different) (e.g., fat-cat, car-car, pin-pen, etc.).

  13. Teacher-prepared list of words

14. recognize and circle the same numerals 1-10 which appear on a given line on a worksheet.

  14. Teacher-prepared worksheet

Similarities

Short-Term Objectives	Instructional Level: K-3

The learner will be able to

Materials

15. match numerals 1 to 10 with cards having the correct number of objects, dots, etc. (This should first be done in numerical order, then in random order.)

15. *Sorting Box and Accessories*
    (DLM)
    Peg-It Number Boards
    Locking Numbers
    (Incentives for Learning)
    Numbers Lotto
    Flip Books: Numbers
    (Trend)

16. identify hidden or covered pairs of objects as same or different by feeling with both hands. (Difficulty of the activity may be increased by allowing use of only one hand at a time.)

16. *Feel and Match Textures*
    (Lauri)
    Small objects
    Screen, cloth or shoe box with
    cut-out and covered with cloth

17. differentiate between pairs of sounds according to likeness or difference.

17. *Sounds Lotto*
    (Milton Bradley)
    Listening Discrimination Blocks
    Listening Lotto-ry, Sets A & B
    (Educational Insights)
    Auditory Perception Program:
    Auditory Discrimination
    Sound Matching
    (Incentives for Learning)

18. differentiate between pairs of words with same and different consonant sounds in initial and final positions.

18. *Match Me Flash Cards*
    (Trend)
    CVC Picture-Word Program
    (Incentives for Learning)
    Bearamores Go to the Big City:
    A Game of Beginning and Ending
    Sound Recognition
    (Milton Bradley)
    Teacher-prepared tape and
    tape player

19. complete pictures of faces showing likenesses and differences of mood changes such as happy, sad, etc.

19. *Moods and Emotions Teaching*
    Pictures
    Face Matching Plaques
    Sorting Box Combination for Counting
    and Color: Expressions/Produce
    (Marvel)

Similarities

Short-Term Objectives

The learner will be able to

20. circle or match correctly letters, words, rhyming sounds, color, size, and shape in Bingo or Lotto activities.

Instructional Level: K-3

Materials

20. *Lotto Games:*
   Colors
   Geometric Shapes
     (Judy/Instructo)
   Disney Light & Learn
   Sesame Street Light & Learn
   Original Memory
   Match & Move Memory
     (Milton Bradley)
   Colors & Shapes Lotto
   Alphabet Lotto
   Numbers Lotto
   Rhyming Bingo
     (Trend)

SIMIL.

Similarities

Short-Term Objectives

The learner will be able to

1. classify objects or pictures according to broad general categories (e.g., transportation, food, shelter, etc.).

2. describe the object that is different in pictures of four objects, three being the same and one different.

3. complete sorting and grouping exercises according to color, number, shape, etc.

4. make a scrapbook using his choice of subject content based on likenesses or broad classification.

Instructional Level: 3-6

Materials

1. *Categories*
   Functions
   Associations: Sets 1 & 2
      (DLM)
   Classifying Shapes
      (Constructive Playthings)
   The Classification Game
   Lotto Games:
      Rooms (in the house)
      Colors
      Seasons
      Familiar Settings
      Geometric Shapes
   Early Learning Curriculum Units
      Animals
      Transportation
   Classification/Flannel Board Set
      (Judy/Instructo)
   Becoming a Strategic Learner
      (Curriculum Associates)

2. *Association Picture Cards: Sets I-IV*
      (DLM)

3. *Sorting Box and Accessories*
      (DLM)
   The Frostig Remediation Program
      (Follett)
   Attribute Sorting Set
   Shellsorts
      (Ideal)
   Attribute Logic Blocks
   Attribute Logic Block Activities
      (Dale Seymour)
   Sorting Box Combination for
      Counting & Color
      (Marvel)

4. Pictures from magazines, etc.

Similarities

Short-Term Objectives

The learner will be able to

5. group pictures of objects which have an identical use (e.g., saw-scissors, vacuum-broom, etc.).

6. match one- to four-letter words to discriminate likenesses and differences.

7. identify likenesses and differences in design and detail of pictures.

8. match a random arrangement of geometric shapes or pictures on a card to another card with the same shapes or pictures arranged in a design.

9. match pictures of objects with their printed names.

10. identify words as same or different after listening to recorded words having like and unlike consonant or vowel sounds in initial, medial, or final positions.

Instructional Level: 3-6

Materials

5. *Categories*
    (DLM)
   Pictures from magazines, catalogs, etc.

6. *See It-Do It*
    (DLM)
   *Symbol Discrimination and
    Sequencing*
   Word Tracking: High Frequency Words
   Sentence Tracking
    (Ann Arbor)

7. *Honey Bear, Funny Bear*
    (Frank Schaffer)
   Association Picture Cards: Sets I-IV
    (DLM)
   Teacher-made cards (some alike and some slightly different)

8. *Visual Recall Cards*
    (Incentives for Learning)
   Creature Factory
    (Educational Insights)
   *Sorting Box Combination for
    Counting & Color:
    Beginning Geometric Designs
    Advanced Geometric Designs
    Advanced Color Matching*
    (Marvel)

9. *Verb Puzzles; Noun Puzzles*
    (DLM)
   *Spin and See Games
   Match & Memory Memory
   Pairs Word Game*
    (Milton Bradley)

10. *Language Master*
     (Bell & Howell)
    SPARC
     (LinguiSystems)

53

Similarities

Short-Term Objectives

The learner will be able to

Instructional Level: 3-6

Materials

11. recognize whether a word spoken by the teacher or another classmate is the same or different as the word on a specific printed card.

11. Vocabulary word cards or spelling lists

12. sort and match faces according to like moods from a group of six or more pictures displaying various facial expressions.

12. *Face Matching Plaques*
Sorting Box Combination:
Expressions/Produce
Mood and Emotions Teaching Pictures
(Marvel)
Pictures of faces from magazines, etc.

13. determine whether a pair of objects in a paper sack are the same or different. (This activity may be modified by the use of two sacks with one object in each requiring the student to use both hands to make a determination.)

13. *Feel & Match Textures*
(Lauri)
Different textures, sizes, and shapes of materials, objects, etc.

14. identify while blindfolded likenesses and differences in the tastes of various foods (e.g., sour and/or sweet pickles, candy, etc.).

14. *Teach Me About Taste*
(Mission)
Pieces of food reflecting sweet, sour, salty, bland, hot, cold

15. match words and pictures that have opposite meanings.

15. *Opposites*
(DLM)
Classifications-Opposites
Pictures for Peg Boards
(Ideal)
Opposites—software
(Hartley)
Opposites Picture Cards
(Judy/Instructo)
Easy Picture Word Opposites
Word Opposite Memory Match
Easy Word Opposites Flash Cards
(Frank Schaffer)
Charlie: Vocabulary Skills—Antonyms
(Educational Insights)

Similarities

Short-Term Objectives

The learner will be able to

Instructional Level: 3-6

Materials

Antonyms
  (Incentives for Learning)
Opposites
  (Milton Bradley)

16. match words to pictures illustrating the meanings of the words.

16. *Skill Drill Flash Cards:*
    Basic Picture Words
    More Picture Words
    (Trend)
    Picture-Word Dominoes
    (Frank Schaffer)
    CVC Picture Word Program
    (Incentives for Learning)

17. match printed letters to appropriately colored felt or wooden squares and rectangles, representing letter configuration.

17. *Pre-Writing Design Cards*
    (DLM)

18. match printed words to appropriately colored felt or wooden squares and rectangles, representing word configuration.

18. *Pre-Writing Design Cards*
    (DLM)

19. match printed words to configurative-shape cards.

20. complete a written list of things which are alike according to a descriptive category (e.g., things that are square, sour, etc.).

Similarities

Short-Term Objectives

The learner will be able to

1. recognize synonyms and antonyms using flashcards and activity sheets.

2. name the items on flashcards and describe the relationship between them.

3. classify musical instruments according to wind, brass, and percussion.

4. identify the class to which words belong (e.g., nouns, verbs, adjectives, etc.).

Instructional Level: 6-9

Materials

1. *Opposites*
    (DLM)
    Antonyms and Synonyms—software
       (Hartley)
    Incentonym Puzzles
    Synonym Puzzles
    Antonyms
       (Incentives for Learning)
    Word Benders—software
    Connector Vectors, Books A-1, B-1
       (Midwest)
    *Creature Features: Vocabulary
     Development*
       (Educational Activities)
    *Basic Thinking Skills:
     Antonyms & Synonyms
     Antonyms, Synonyms, Similarities,
     and Differences*
       (Opportunities for Learning)
    Synonyms Poster Card
    Antonyms Poster Card
       (Milton Bradley)

2. *Object Match*
    (Marvel)
    All-Purpose Photo Library: Set I
    (DLM)

3. *Merry Music Makers*
    (Eye Gate Media)
    Musical Instruments Bulletin Board Aid
    (Trend)

4. *Binders Keepers: Parts of Speech*
    *Basic Language Skills Spirit Master
     Books*
       (Educational Insights)
    *Creature Features: Vocabulary
     Development*
       (Educational Activities)

Similarities

Short-Term Objectives
The learner will be able to

Instructional Level: 6-9

Materials

Language for Writing: Books 1-5
(Curriculum Associates)
Naming Names
Naming Actions
(Ideal)

5. assemble all the shades of one color in varying intensities by using cut-up paint chips.

5. Varying shades of paint chips

6. list pictured objects that begin with certain sounds or contain certain vowel sounds.

6. *All-Purpose Photo Library: Set I*
(DLM)
Consonant Pictures for Pegboard
Vowel Pictures for Pegboard
(Ideal)
Photo STICKS
Library of Vocabulary Photographs
(SRA)

7. underline in a list of words only the words which apply to a certain subject (e.g., baseball).

7. Teacher-prepared lists

8. identify the words which show action in a list of words.

8. *All About Verbs*
(Incentives for Learning)
Creature Features: Vocabulary Development
(Educational Activities)

9. recognize, while blindfolded, various objects by feeling texture, temperature, etc.

9. *Feel & Match Textures*
(Lauri)

10. identify the tastes of foods as sweet, sour, bitter, etc.

10. Pieces of food

11. identify differences of students in the classroom as to taller-shorter, wider-narrower, longer-shorter, etc.

Similarities

Short-Term Objectives	Instructional Level: 6-9
The learner will be able to	**Materials**

12. classify pictures reflecting emotional qualities into appropriate groups.

12. *Moods and Emotions Teaching Pictures*
   Face Matching Plaques
   Sorting Box Combination: Expression/Produce
   (Marvel)

13. complete statements requiring opposites (e.g., "Babies are little; men are _____ .").

13. *Aids to Psycholinguistic Teaching: Auditory Association*
   (Charles E. Merrill)
   Word Thinkercises
   Discovering Logic
   Adventures with Logic
   (Dale Seymour)
   Basic Thinking Skills, Books A-D
   (Opportunities for Learning)
   Thinkanalogy Puzzles—software
   Building Thinking Skills, Books 2 & 3
   (Midwest)
   Cognitive Challenge Cards
   (ATP)
   Vocabulary Connections
   (Steck-Vaughn)
   BESST, Vol. 2
   Semantics for Teens
   (LinguiSystems)

14. repeat a series of four words in correct sequence and explain the relationship between them (e.g., hamster, goldfish, dog, cat-pet classification).

14. *Language Quicktionary*
   The Word Kit
   BESST, Vol. 1
   (LinguiSystems)
   Teacher-prepared lists

15. play TV games involving stimulus words and their synonyms (e.g., "Password," "Match Game," etc.).

15. *Password*
   Educational "Password" Game
   Concentration
   Upwords
   (Milton Bradley)

Similarities

Short-Term Objectives

The learner will be able to

Instructional Level: 6-9

Materials

16. match pictures relating to occupations and careers.

16. *Careers That Count*
    Career Capers
       (Opportunities for Learning)
    Working Choices Game
       (Milton Bradley)

17. identify the word that does not belong with the others in a series of four words (e.g., cat, horse, ball, dog).

17. Teacher-prepared lists

18. complete games and puzzles that require vocabulary pertaining to particular classifications (e.g., occupations, transportation, communications, etc.).

18. *Steady Job Game*
    Working Choices
    Employ Bingo
       (Milton Bradley)
    Crossword Puzzles-USA
       (Frank Schaffer)
    BESSST
    The Word Kit
    Language Quicktionary
       (LinguiSystems)
    Activities for Dictionary Practice
    Classification and Organization
       Skills—Developmental
       (Curriculum Associates)

19. match capital cities and abbreviations to the states of the United States.

19. *U.S. Bingo*
       (Ideal)
    I.Q. Games: U.S. Geography
       (Educational Insights)
    Outline Maps of the USA
    Geography of the United States of
       America
       (Hayes)

20. match appropriate answers to basic addition, subtraction, multiplication and division problems.

20. *Math Flash Cards:*
    Addition
    Subtraction
    Multiplication

Similarities

Short-Term Objectives

The learner will be able to

Instructional Level: 6-9

Materials

Gameboards:
  Addition
  Subtraction
  Multiplication with the Monsters
  (Frank Schaffer)
Division Flash Cards, Vertical
Horizontal Flash Cards:
  Addition
  Subtraction
  Multiplication
  Division
  (Ideal)
Addition/Subtraction Dominoes
Multiplication Dominoes
Division Dominoes
  (Judy/Instructo)
Mathfacts Game-Addition and
  Subtraction
Mathfacts Game-Multiplication and
  Division
  (Milton Bradley)

Similarities

Short-Term Objectives

The learner will be able to

1. write antonyms for words on a teacher-made list (e.g., hot-cold, wet-dry, slow-fast).

2. find synonyms for specific words by looking in a dictionary. (This activity could be expanded to include antonyms.)

3. discuss the likenesses and differences of homonyms and synonyms.

4. classify the different instruments in a band or orchestra according to wood-wind, brass, string, percussion.

5. classify pictures of animals according to mammals, reptiles, fowls, amphibians, insects, etc.

6. make a notebook of pictures reflecting the concept of opposite using pictures cut from magazines, mounted and labeled appropriately.

Instructional Level: 9-12

Materials

1. *Antonyms*
    (Incentives for Learning)
   Antonyms and Synonyms
    (Communication Skill Builders)
   Semantics for Teens
    (LinguiSystems)

2. Dictionary
   Teacher-made word list

3. *Homonyms*
    (Incentives for Learning)
   Scopes Visuals 2: Vocabulary Building
    (Scholastic)
   150 Skill Building Reference Lists
   Semantically Speaking (Advanced Edition)
    (Communication Skill Builders)

4. *Merry Music Makers*
    (Eye Gate Media)

5. *Science Picture Library*
   Science Safari
    (Educational Insights)
   Science Study Cards
    (Milton Bradley)
   The Animal Kingdom
   Understanding Biology
    (Hayes)
   Our Living World
    (Instructional Fair)

Similarities

| Short-Term Objectives | Instructional Level: 9-12 |
| The learner will be able to | Materials |

7. classify and list tools according to function.

7. Various tools and power tools

8. group letters, numbers, and varied-sized designs by length of number or letter series.

8. Student-made letters, numbers

9. recognize the absurdities among a list of statements some of which are absurd.

9. *BESST, Vol. 2*
   The Word Kit
      (LinguiSystems)
   Sentence Improbabilities
      (Communication Skill Builders)
   Silly Sounds Game
      (Ideal)

10. sort words according to tenses from a list of verbs reflecting tenses including present, past, and future.

10. *Language for Writing, Book 2*
       (Curriculum Associates)
    Scope Visuals 28: Parts of Speech
       (Scholastic)
    Build Basic Skills Set
    Binders Keepers: Parts of Speech
       (Educational Insights)
    Teaching Vocabulary Vol. 2
    Grammar for Teens
       (LinguiSystems)

11. name words within a given class (e.g., verbs, nouns, adjectives, adverbs, etc.).

11. *Scopes Visuals 28: Parts of Speech*
       (Scholastic)
    Parts of Speech Skill Box
       (Troll)
    Build Basic Skills Set
    Binders Keepers: Parts of Speech
       (Educational Insights)
    Teaching Vocabulary Vol. 2
    Grammar for Teens
       (LinguiSystems)

12. classify individual verbs according to present, past, and future forms of each verb (e.g., is, was, will be).

12. *All About Verbs*
       (Incentives for Learning)

Similarities

Short-Term Objectives	Instructional Level: 9-12
The learner will be able to	**Materials**

13. identify adjectives and the nouns they modify in sentences and paragraphs.

   13. *Language for Writing, Book 3*
       (Curriculum Associates)
       Grammar for Teens
       (LinguiSystems)
       What's the Word Game
       All About Adjectives and Adverbs
       (Incentives for Learning)

14. sort different shapes using games and races.

   14. *Attribute Block Desk Set*
       Attribute Block Activity Cards
       (Learning Resources)
       Pattern Blocks Activities
       Pattern Blocks
       (Dale Seymour)

15. sort various coins and paper money according to value, size, engraving, color, etc.

   15. *Coin and Paper Bill Sets*
       (Dale Seymour)
       Money in Action
       All About Money Box
       (Incentives for Learning)
       School Money Kit Class Set
       (Educational Insights)

16. develop a list of objects from school and/or home environment and, using the dictionary, locate appropriate synonyms.

   16. Dictionary
       Thesaurus

17. determine appropriate antonyms from a list of words expressing abstract concepts such as love, liberty, etc., and discuss the concepts involved.

18. demonstrate recognition of relationships through the use of comparison, cause-and-effect, and contrast in writing sentences.

   18. *Building Thinking Skills, Book 3:*
       Verbs
       (Midwest)
       Word Ways: Activities for Following
       Directions, Books A & B
       (Opportunities for Learning)
       Cause and Effect Card Games
       (Communication Skill Builders)

Similarities

Short-Term Objectives

The learner will be able to

Instructional Level: 9-12

Materials

19. sort and compare objects according to various attributes.

19. *Attribute Block Desk Set*
    Attribute Block Activity Cards
       (Learning Resources)
    PowerCards: Same/Different
       Power 1, 2, 3
    Talk T' Win
    Photo Cue Cards
    More Photo Cue Cards
       (Communication Skill Builders)

20. classify plants, animals, insects, etc., according to kingdom.

20. *The Animal Kingdom*
    The Plant Kingdom
       (Hayes)
    The Flash Card Collection: Animals
       (Trend)

VOCABULARY

Vocabulary

I. **Purpose of the Subtest**
   To measure the child's ability to define specific words

II. **Factors Affecting Subtest and Academic Performance**
   A. Cultural background
   B. Educational exposure
   C. Memory
   D. Conceptual development
   E. Verbal comprehension and expression
   F. Language development
   G. Auditory discrimination
   H. Attention

III. **Educational Significance**
   A. Introduce new words using first order statements and concrete examples such as presenting a block and saying, "This is a block."
   B. All presentations should be made using vocabulary understood by the student. The teacher should check frequently for the student's understanding.
   C. Encourage the student to use newly learned words when speaking by the use of rewards.
   D. Provide activities allowing opportunities for free expression of ideas.
   E. Reading material selections should be supervised by the teacher.
   F. Formal listening exercises should be included in vocabulary building experiences.
   G. Discuss how multiple meanings of specific words are dependent in usage upon context. Point out the minute differences among words of similar meaning.

IV. **Long-Term Goal**
   The learner will be able to define and appropriately use specific words.

Vocabulary

Short-Term Objectives
The learner will be able to

1. participate in show-and-tell activities.

2. write or tell an original story of direct or vicarious experiences such as field trips, visual aids, films, and filmstrips.

3. identify verbally all 26 letters of the alphabet.

4. manipulate blocks to distinguish between concepts: same-different, big-little, up-down, in front of-behind, first-last, etc.

Instructional Level: K-3
Materials

1. *Show and Tell*
   (Creative Teaching Press)

3. *Alphabet Mastery*
   (Ann Arbor)
   The Valett Perceptual-Motor Transitions to Reading Program
   (ATP)
   Lock-a-Letter
   Avalanche of Letters
   A-Z Panels
   (Lauri)
   Letter Games—software
   Charlie Brown's ABC's—software
   (Troll)
   Alphabet Flashcards
   (Milton Bradley)
   Wee Bee!
   Stickybear Alphabet—software
   (EBSCO)
   Q Is for Duck: An Alphabet Guessing Game
   (Houghton Mifflin)

4. *Spatial Relationship Puzzles*
   Where Is It? Spatial Relationship Cards
   (Ideal)
   Peabody Language Development Kit— Revised
   (AGS)
   Early Concepts Skillbuilders: What's Up—software
   (EBSCO)
   The Best Concept Workbook Ever
   The Best Concept Pictures Ever
   Follow Me!
   (LinguiSystems)

Vocabulary

Short-Term Objectives	Instructional Level: K-3

The learner will be able to

Materials

Primary Concepts
Milk Bottles—software
   (Troll)
Great Beginnings: Prepositions
The Flipbook: Prepositions, Sets 1 & 2
   (Communication Skill Builders)

5. classify words appropriate to his environment (e.g., food, furniture, clothing, etc.).

5. *MEER*
   MEER Images
      (LinguiSystems)
   Lauri's Build-a-Skill: Beginning
      Classification and Sorting
      Advanced Classification
      (Lauri)
   Vocabulary Skill Builder Series—
      software
      (EBSCO)
   Discrimination, Attributes, and Rules:
      Odd One Out—software
      (Sunburst)

6. name and discuss people who serve the community (e.g., policemen, firemen, postmen, etc.).

6. *Early Learning Curriculum Units:*
      Community Helpers and Workers Unit
      (Judy/Instructo)
   Community Helpers Lotto
      (Trend)
   Community Helpers
      (Troll)
   We Learn About Community Helpers
      (Fearon)

7. describe pictures or objects by color, size, shape, and use.

7. *Vocabulary To Go*
   Find Your Way with Words
   Games To Go
      (LinguiSystems)
   Attribute Sorting Set
      (Ideal)
   Gertrude's Secrets—software
   Gertrude's Puzzles—software
   Talking Picture Dictionary
      (Troll)

Vocabulary

Short-Term Objectives

The learner will be able to

Instructional Level: K-3

Materials

Early Concepts Skillbuilders: What's the Difference
Learning with Literature: Cinderella
 (EBSCO)
Discrimination, Attributes, and Rules: Gnees or not Gnees
 (Sunburst)
Pictures of objects
Small objects in classroom or from home

8. label and discuss a collection of items and be able to label and discuss the items (e.g., leaves, rocks, flowers, stamps, etc.).

8. *Rock Collection*
 Shells
 Butterflies
 (Ideal)
 Remarkable Rocks
 Colossal Fossils
 Super Seashells
 Genuine Gems
 (Educational Insights)
 Personal collections from home

9. play definition games within the vocabulary range of the student (e.g., "Can you think of another name for 'round'?").

9. *Working With Words*
 (Curriculum Associates)
 Wizard of Words—software
 (Troll)
 Vocabulary Quizmo: Synonyms
 Synonym Poster Cards
 (Milton Bradley)
 Spelling Four Square: Synonyms
 (Creative Teaching Associates)
 The Word Kit
 (LinguiSystems)
 Vocabulary Building/Starwords
 (Learning Well)

10. "buy" items of food from a play grocery store.

10. Empty cans, boxes, etc., that food comes in
 Pictures of food
 Play money

11. describe a hobby, trip, or a souvenir from a vacation.

Vocabulary

Short-Term Objectives

The learner will be able to

Instructional Level: K-3

Materials

12. make a word index, filing each newly learned word alphabetically with written definitions and appropriate pictures.

12. *Talking Picture Dictionary*
    (Troll)
    Angling for Words Dictionary
    Word Express: The First 2,500 Words of Spoken English—Illustrated
    (ATP)
    Index cards
    File box
    Magazines, catalogs, etc., for pictures

13. make up or learn riddles to ask classmates.

13. *Sound It*
    (Imperial International)
    Rhyming Riddles for Speech
    (ATP)
    Dr. DooRiddles A1
    Challenging Codes: Riddles and Jokes
    (Midwest)
    Razzle Dazzle Riddles
    Riddle Romp
    Riddle Round-Up: A Wild Bunch to Beef Up Your Word Power
    What's Mite Might?: Homophone Riddles to Boost Your Word Power
    What's a Frank Frank? Tasty Homophone Riddles
    Too Hot to Hoot: Funny Palindrome Riddles
    (Houghton Mifflin)

14. tell a story about an action picture, describing the people, action, etc., and how they relate to each other.

14. *Play Scenes Lotto*
    (Milton Bradley)
    Photopacks
    (Incentives for Learning)
    Cognitive Challenge Cards
    (ATP)
    Think It—Say It
    (Communication Skill Builders)

15. complete unfinished stories that require the listing of items (e.g., "I'm going on a trip and I will take . . . ").

Vocabulary

Short-Term Objectives
The learner will be able to

Instructional Level: K-3
Materials

16. explain meanings of words by drawing pictures or using objects.

17. play games that focus attention on size and shape of objects.

17. *Match Maker*—software
    (Troll)
    Discrimination, Attributes and Rules: Teddy's Background—software
    (Sunburst)
    Geometric Shape Lotto
    (Trend)
    Sequential Cards—By Color, Shape, Size
    (Incentives for Learning)
    Shape Squares
    Fit-a-Shape
    Fit-a-Size
    Fit-a-Circle
    Fit-a-Space
    Junior Fit-a-Space
    (Lauri)

18. name an object when asking for something before it is given.

19. answer simple questions requiring simple common sense answers (e.g., "Why do you have a mouth?"). (Have the student stand in front of a full length mirror and the teacher can point to the various body parts.)

19. *Answers to Questions*
    (ATP)
    Who, What, Where, When, Why—software
    (Troll)
    MEER
    MEER Images
    Ready, Set, Listen
    (LinguiSystems)
    Questions for Thinking Skills
    (Communication Skill Builders)

20. tell how to do things (e.g., how to make a bed, brush teeth, etc.).

Vocabulary

Short-Term Objectives

The learner will be able to

Instructional Level: K-3

Materials

21. use a picture dictionary to put a selected list of vocabulary words in alphabetical order.

21. *Talking Picture Dictionary*
    (Troll)
    Talking Picture Dictionary of More New Words
    (Opportunities for Learning)
    Houghton Mifflin Picture Dictionary
    (Houghton Mifflin)
    Word Express: The First 2,500 Words of Spoken English—Illustrated
    (ATP)

22. complete puzzles which are designed to help in the visualization of words by showing the number of spaces needed for each word.

22. *The Word Kit*
    Teaching Vocabulary Worksheets
    (LinguiSystems)
    Crossword Puzzles
    Word Works I: Wordcross—software
    (EBSCO)
    Word Puzzles, Gr. 1-2, 2-3
    (Instructional Fair)
    Michigan Programmed Spelling, Levels 1, 2, 3
    (Ann Arbor)
    Crossword Puzzles & Word Hunts, Sets 1, 2, 3
    Crossword Puzzles, Gr. 2-3
    (Frank Schaffer)

23. identify pictures of things mentioned in nursery rhymes read to the class by the teacher.

23. *Nursery Rhymes Teaching Pictures K-3*
    (Marvel)
    Oral Language Posters K-2
    (Houghton Mifflin)
    Mother Goose Rhymes Flannelboard Aids
    Mother Goose II and III Flannelboard Aids
    (Judy/Instructo)
    Rhymes for Learning Times
    Nursery Rhyme Time
    (T.S. Denison)
    Mother Goose Rhymes
    (Hayes)

VOCAB.

Vocabulary

Short-Term Objectives

The learner will be able to

24. identify and define vocabulary words by listening to records and tapes.

Instructional Level: K-3

Materials

24. *Learning Basic Skills Through Music: Building Vocabulary* (Educational Activities)
    Make The Right Choice
    Journey into Space (Kimbo)

Vocabulary

Short-Term Objectives

The learner will be able to

Instructional Level: 3-6

Materials

1. demonstrate his ability to use the dictionary by writing the definitions of selected words.

1. *Using the Dictionary, Gr. 3-6*
   (Field)
   Webster's Dictionary Game
   (Dale Seymour)
   Angling for Words Dictionary
   (ATP)
   Alphagrab
   (Houghton Mifflin)
   Activities for Dictionary Practice
   Working with Words
   Lessons for Vocabulary Power
   (Curriculum Associates)
   Dictionary Skills—software
   (Troll)

2. find words in the dictionary that pertain to various subject areas.

2. *Activities for Dictionary Practice*
   Working with Words
   (Curriculum Associates)
   Master Match—software
   Go to the Head of the Class—software
   (Troll)

3. prepare a vocabulary notebook categorizing the words according to subject areas or some other appropriate classification. (Pictures may be included.)

3. *The School Speller*—software
   (Sunburst)
   The Vocabulary Box
   (Educational Insights)
   Vocabulary Boosters 2 & 3
   (Remedia)

4. describe a story seen on television or in a movie.

5. describe what is seen while looking through an empty picture frame.

5. Empty picture frame or one made of tag board or poster board

6. play "I'm going on a trip and I'm taking . . ." (e.g., "a pair of shoes."). (The next child says the same thing and adds one more item. Each child repeats all the items named and adds one more thing.)

6. *Aids to Psycholinguistic Teaching:*
   Auditory Reception
   (Charles E. Merrill)

Vocabulary

Short-Term Objectives

The learner will be able to

Instructional Level: 3-6

Materials

7. introduce people such as classmates, teachers, parents, etc.

8. read rebus stories.

8. *Spellagraph*—software
(Troll)
Muppet Slate—software
(Sunburst)
Perceptual Development Activities: Rebuses, Signs, and Symbols
(Opportunities for Learning)
Rebus Reading: Beginning Sentence Building
Clark Early Learning Program
(DLM)
Rebus Stick-Ons
Standard Rebus Glossary
(AGS)
Stamp-It!
(Communication Skill Builders)
Rebus Writer—software
(Cambridge Development Library)
Catchword: A Rebus Galore Blackline Masters Book
(High Noon Books)

9. work crossword puzzles.

9. *Michigan Programmed Spelling, Levels 4, 5, 6*
(Ann Arbor)
Spelling Puzzler—software
(Houghton Mifflin)
Crossword Reading, 1, 2, 3
(Remedia)
Word Works 1: Word Cross—software
Crossword Puzzles
(EBSCO)
Crossword Magic—software
(Troll)

10. make a list of words using only the letters in a particular word (e.g., how many words can be made from the letters that make up the word "Christmas?").

10. *Word Detective*—software
(Sunburst)

Vocabulary

Short-Term Objectives

The learner will be able to

11. describe a classmate until another can guess who is being described.

12. repeat stories, nursery rhymes, etc., told by the teacher.

13. describe various objects according to size, color, shape, materials made from, what can be done with them, who might use them, and other characteristics (e.g., hard-soft, long-short, "I spy something . . .").

14. act out stories with puppets or marionettes, saying the various parts for them.

Instructional Level: 3-6

Materials

11. *Guess Who?*
     (Milton Bradley)
     The Question Collection: Who Am I?
     (Communication Skill Builders)

12. *Storytelling To Go*
     (LinguiSystems)

13. *Who Am I? Package*—software
     (Troll)
     Primary Concepts II—filmstrip
     (Educational Reading Services)
     Objects in the classroom, from home,
     toys, etc.

14. *Family Puppets:*
     Hispanic
     Black
     White
     (Learning Resources)
     Puppet Playmates:
     Community Helpers
     Members of the Family
     Hand-Held Puppets:
     Happy Faces
     Animal Faces
     (Judy/Instructo)
     Houghton Mifflin Puppet Kits
     (Houghton Mifflin)
     The Missing Prince and Other
     Primary Plays for Oral Reading
     The Lost Cat and Other Primary Plays
     for Oral Reading
     The Reader's Theater Series of
     Classic Plays
     (Curriculum Associates)

VOCAB.

Vocabulary

Short-Term Objectives

The learner will be able to

15. play vocabulary games.

16. tell the rules of a game to be played by a group of people.

17. create and/or read riddles to the class.

Instructional Level: 3-6

Materials

15. *Computer Scrabble*—software
    (Cambridge Development Laboratory)
    Scrabble
    Scrabble Junior
    (Selchow and Righter)
    Boggle
    Boggle Junior
    (Parker Brothers)
    Vocabulary Challenge—software
    Magic Castle/Vocabulary Building—
    software
    (Troll)
    Sight Word Bingo
    Word Yahtzee
    (Milton Bradley)
    Vocabulary Building/Starwords
    (Learning Well)
    Vocabulary Builder, Level 1
    (Creative Teaching Associates)

17. *Jokes & Riddles*
    (Wonder Books)
    Funny Jokes and Foxy Riddles
    (Western)
    Dr. DooRiddles, A1, B1
    Challenging Codes: Riddles and Jokes
    (Midwest)
    Peter Puzzlemaker
    The $1.00 Word Riddle Book
    (Dale Seymour)
    Razzle Dazzle Riddles
    Riddle Romp
    *Riddle Round-Up: A Wild Bunch to
    Beef Up Your Word Power*
    *Too Hot to Hoot: Funny Palindrome
    Riddles*

Vocabulary

Short-Term Objectives

The learner will be able to

Instructional Level: 3-6

Materials

*What's Mite Might? Homophone
Riddles to Boost Your Word Power*
*What's a Frank Frank? Tasty
Homograph Riddles*
(Houghton Mifflin)

VOCAB

18. write sentences using vocabulary words presented to him in stories or activities.

18. *Vocabulary Development: Words,
Words Words*
(Educational Reading Services)
Vocabulary Connection
(Remedia)
Words to Remember 1 & 2
Cloze Vocabulary and More, Gr. 2-5
(Opportunities for Learning)
The Cloze Line
(High Noon Books)

19. classify words according to their appropriate parts of speech (e.g., nouns, verbs, adjectives, etc.).

19. *Reading Creature Features:
Vocabulary Development*
(Educational Activities)
Name That Word
(Creative Teaching Associates)
Vocabulary Connections
(Steck-Vaughn)
Basic Language Skills
(Educational Insights)
Usage: Parts of Speech, Gr. 4-6
(Milliken)
Activities for Dictionary Practice
Language for Writing
Word Analysis Kit
(Curriculum Associates)
Mastering Basic Parts of Speech
(Incentives for Learning)
*Word Express: The First 2,500 Words
of Spoken English—Illustrated*
(ATP)
Parts of Speech Skill Box
(Troll)
No-Glamour Grammar
(LinguiSystems)

Vocabulary

Short-Term Objectives

The learner will be able to

20. demonstrate meanings of prefixes and suffixes by listing the definitions of root words and how these meanings are modified.

Instructional Level: 3-6

Materials

20. *Morph-Aid: A Source of Roots, Prefixes, and Suffixes*
    (Dale Seymour)
    Improving Your Vocabulary Skills
    (Opportunities for Learning)
    Reading Creature Features: Structural Analysis
    (Educational Activities)
    Working with Words
    Activities for Dictionary Practice
    (Curriculum Associates)
    Cues and Comprehension (Reading)
    (Ann Arbor)
    Prefixes/Suffixes/Syllables
    (Frank Schaffer)
    Charlie: Prefixes and Suffixes
    (Educational Insights)
    Elements of English 4-5
    (Milliken)
    Phonics IIB
    (Hayes)
    The Game Drawer Series: Decoding Games, Drawers 9 & 10
    (Ideal)
    Vocabulary Boosters
    (Fearon)
    Pursuit
    Escape
    (Creative Teaching Associates)
    English Language (Prefixes/Suffixes)
    (Troll)

Vocabulary

Short-Term Objectives	Instructional Level: 6-9
The learner will be able to	**Materials**

1. use the index and table of contents of the dictionary when completing written assignments.

    1. *Fearon New School Dictionary*
        (Fearon)
    Study Skills: Strategies and Practice
        (Curriculum Associates)
    The Dictionary Skill Box
        (Troll)
    Intermediate Dictionary
        (Houghton Mifflin)
    Using Dictionary Skills
        (Instructional Fair)
    Dictionary Skills
        (Milliken)
    Developing Dictionary Skills
        (Good Apple)

2. make a vocabulary chart to display words used in different subject areas.

3. make a word file, alphabetizing each new word learned. (Include abstract words such as *like, love, good, bad, thought,* etc.)

    3. *Vocabulary Development: Words, Words, Words*
        (Educational Reading Services)
    Alphagrab
    Vocabulary for Achievement
        (Houghton Mifflin)
    Activities for Dictionary Practice
    Working with Words
        (Curriculum Associates)
    Vocabulary Challenge—software
    Wizard of Words—software
        (Troll)
    Vocabulary Builder, Levels 1 & 2
    The Word Game
        (Opportunities for Learning)
    File box and index cards
    Notebook

4. participate in discussions concerning science projects, TV programs, movies, and cultural influences of different persons.

Vocabulary

Short-Term Objectives

The learner will be able to

Instructional Level: 6-9

Materials

5. utilize specific vocabulary in adventure and sports topics.

5. *Codebusters, Sets 1, 2, 3*
Adventure Reading Series
Sports Reading Series
The World of Reading: The World of Sports
(Educational Insights)
On Their Own—Series
(High Noon Books)

6. take part in skits that utilize functional vocabulary (e.g., when applying for a job; when introducing friends, parents, or speakers; when asking parents for special privileges; when persuading a friend to do a favor, etc.).

6. *On My Own at Home*
On My Own with Language
Problem Solving for Teens
FILE
(LinguiSystems)
Talk T' Win
(Communication Skill Builders)
On the Job
Getting A Job
Vocabulary for the World of Work
Persuasive Speaking—video
Developing Social Skills: Learning Conversational Techniques—filmstrips
(Opportunities for Learning)

7. orally describe people, places, and things.

7. *The Question Collection*
150 Skill-Building Reference Lists
(Communication Skill Builders)

8. explain a project (e.g., how to play a game, how to build a birdhouse, how to construct a model, etc.).

9. present reviews of books, plays, or newspaper articles.

10. participate in group discussions about dress codes, smoking, drugs, and other teenage concerns.

10. *Incomplete Plays*
(Dale Seymour)
Learning to Say No
What Would You Do?

Vocabulary

Short-Term Objectives
The learner will be able to

Instructional Level: 6-9
Materials

Thinking About Feelings
  (Opportunities for Learning)
Drugs: What You Need to Know
Saying No to Drugs
Understanding Values, Gr. 6
  (Field)
Stop, Think & Go Game
You Can Say No: Here's How—video
Let's Talk About . . . Responsibility—
  video
  (Sunburst)

11. locate and define unknown words found in the newspaper.

11. Newspapers
    Dictionary

12. dramatize job interviews that require a list of ten words to be used in the interview.

12. *Job Interview Guide*
    (Opportunities for Learning)
    Interviewing for a Job—video
    (Cambridge Career Products)

13. recognize functional word cards (e.g., *Exit, Posted, No Trespassing, Yield, Walk, Do Not Walk, Entrance,* etc.).

13. *Survival Signs*
    (Ideal)
    More Vocabulary To Go
    (LinguiSystems)
    Survival Sign and Symbols Bulletin Board Set
    (Trend)
    Survival Words—software
    Survival Signs—software
    (Opportunities for Learning)

14. play and teach synonyms to one's classmates with the "Synonym Rummy" game. (Deal six cards to each of two or three players. Place remaining cards face-down and turn the top card face-up beside the stack. The object is to collect sets of synonyms (four). Player Number One opens by drawing either the face-up card or the top card from the stack.

14. Thirteen sets (four cards each) of synonyms (e.g., cheerful, happy, joyous, elated)

Vocabulary

Short-Term Objectives

The learner will be able to

He discards one card by placing it on the face-up pile. Player Number Two may then draw Player Number One's discard or the top card on the stack. The one with the most sets wins.)

15. play and teach antonyms to one's classmates with the "Antonym Rummy" game. (See the instructions for activity #14 above. Students should match three antonyms to one synonym card, e.g., happy-sad, unhappy, morose.)

16. dramatize poems, short stories, fairy tales, etc., with verbal interaction and manipulation of puppets or stand-up figures. (This activity can be performed before a young audience.)

17. demonstrate working vocabulary knowledge for each academic area (history, science, math, etc.) by listing five words for each subject.

Instructional Level: 6-9

Materials

15. Thirteen sets (four cards each) of antonyms as described above.

16. *Fingerplay Story Mitt*
 Plush Animal Puppets
  (Constructive Playthings)
 Let 'Em Talk: Oral Language
  Activities for the Classroom
  (Dale Seymour)
 Animal Handpuppets
 Family Handpuppets
 Marionette Theater Set
  (Childswork/Childsplay)
 Wooden Stand-Up Figures:
  White Family
  Black Family
  Hispanic Family
  Asian Family
  Families
  Animals
  Community Helpers and Workers
 Hand-Held Puppet Masks:
  Family Faces
  Animal Faces
  (Judy/Instructo)

17. *Go to Head of the Class*
  (Milton Bradley)
 Go to the Head of Class—software
  (Troll)

Vocabulary

Short-Term Objectives	Instructional Level: 6-9
The learner will be able to	**Materials**

HELP 3 & 4 Language Game
HELP 5
Teaching Vocabulary Worksheets
  (LinguiSystems)

18. locate and define words hidden among groups of letters.

18. *Wizard of Words*—software
    Wordzzzearch—Hidden Word
      Puzzles—software
      (Troll)
    Word Tracking: High Frequency Words
    Word Tracking: Proverbs
    Word Tracking: Limericks
      (Ann Arbor)
    Word Puzzles, Grades 5-6, 6-7, 7-8
      (Milliken)
    Word Search Puzzles: Categories (5-12)
    Holidays
    Sports
    Word Puzzles, Books 1-7
      (Remedia)

19. present riddles to the class.

19. *The $1.00 Word Riddle Book*
    Peter Puzzlemaker
      (Dale Seymour)
    More Vocabulary To Go
      (LinguiSystems)
    Dr. DooRiddles
    Challenging Codes: Riddles and Jokes
      (Midwest)
    Riddles Galore Code Book
      (High Noon Books)

20. define words learned in context of high interest low reading levels stories.

20. *The Reading Scene*
    Talewinds Books
      (Continental Press)
    Adventure Reading Series
    Sports Reading Series
    The World of Reading Series
      (Educational Insights)
    Superstars
    Superstars in Action

Vocabulary

Short-Term Objectives	Instructional Level: 6-9
The learner will be able to	**Materials**

Spotlight
The Great Series
  (Steck-Vaughn)
New Directions in Reading
  (Houghton Mifflin)
Top Shelf Literature: High Interest
 Independent Reading
  (Barnell/SRA)
Legal Eagle Series
9-5 Series
Life Line Series
Perspectives, Sets 1 & 2
High Adventures, Sets 1 & 2
High Five Series
Great Trials in History
Classics Then and Now
  (High Noon Books)

21. complete crossword puzzles.

21. *Crossword Magic*—software
  (Cambridge Development Laboratory)
The Word Works—software
Crossword Puzzles
  (EBSCO)
Crossword and Word-Search Wizard
Crozzzwords—Crossword Puzzles
  (Troll)
Classroom Toolbox—software
  (Sunburst)

Vocabulary

Short-Term Objectives

The learner will be able to

1. demonstrate working vocabulary knowledge by listing ten words for each academic area in which he is enrolled.

2. read for enjoyment and then discuss what is read.

3. recognize and "read" a word after listening to a magnetic tape of the word.

4. describe the events on a specified TV program.

5. use a dictionary to trace word origins and development of meanings.

6. complete crossword puzzles, scrabble games, and analogy games.

Instructional Level: 9-12

Materials

1. *Vocabulary Connections*
   (Steck-Vaughn)
   HELP 5
   Teaching Vocabulary Worksheets
   (LinguiSystems)
   Go to the Head of the Class
   (Milton Bradley)
   Go to the Head of the Class—software
   (Troll)

2. *Read On!*
   The World of Reading Series
   (Educational Insights)
   Library book of student's choosing

3. *Language Master: Word Picture Program*
   (Bell & Howell)

5. *Fearon New School Dictionary*
   (Fearon)
   Syllabo: Vocabulary Builder—software
   Vocabulary Power
   (Curriculum Associates)
   Vocabulary Connections
   (Steck-Vaughn)

6. *Cognitive Challenge Cards*
   (ATP)
   Word Puzzles
   (Milliken)
   Word Analogy/Word Classifying
   Crossword Puzzles
   Word Works 1, 2, 3—software
   (EBSCO)
   More Vocabulary To Go
   Teaching Vocabulary Worksheets
   (LinguiSystems)

Vocabulary

Short-Term Objectives	Instructional Level: 9-12
The learner will be able to	**Materials**

Short-Term Objectives

The learner will be able to

Instructional Level: 9-12

Materials

Crossword Reading
  (Remedia)
Hangman
Upwords
Word Yahtzee
  (Milton Bradley)
Scrabble
  (Selchow and Righter)
Crossword Magic—software
  (Troll)
Peter Puzzlemaker
  (Dale Seymour)

7. make up word games and crossword puzzles.

7. *Crossword and Word-Search Wizard*—
  software
Word Works, 1, 2, 3—software
  (EBSCO)

8. locate and define words hidden in a group of letters.

8. *Word Search Puzzles—Categories*
  (Remedia)
Wordzzzearch—Hidden Word Puzzles
  (Troll)
Word Tracking: Proverbs
Word Tracking: Limericks
  (Ann Arbor)

9. play-act different characters or book titles, etc., from required readings.

10. report on a chosen hobby, interest, or ambition.

11. group words according to category, concept order, and contrasts and opposites.

11. *On My Own at Home*
Teaching Vocabulary Worksheets
FILE
Language Quicktionary
  (LinguiSystems)

12. tell how prefixes change the meaning of root words.

12. *Prefix-Suffix Puzzles*
  (Incentives for Learning)
Pursuit
  (Creative Teaching Associates)

Vocabulary

Short-Term Objectives

The learner will be able to

Instructional Level: 9-12

Materials

Activities for Dictionary Practice
Syllabo: Vocabulary Builder—software
   (Curriculum Associates)
Morph-Aid: A Source of Roots,
  Prefixes, and Suffixes
   (Dale Seymour)
Vocabulary Development
Structural Skills Quizmo
   (Milton Bradley)
Vocabulary Skills—Prefixes, Suffixes,
  and Root Words—software
   (Troll)

13. change prepared sentences by using a word that means just the opposite of a designated word in each sentence.

13. *Connections: Working with Analogies*
   (Continental Press)
The Basic Book of Synonyms and
  Antonyms
   (Dale Seymour)
Building Thinking Skills, Book 3:
  Verbal
Basic Thinking Skills: Analogies A-D
Thinkanalogy Puzzles
   (Midwest)
FILE
   (LinguiSystems)
Word Thinkercises
   (Good Apple)
Analogy Match-Ups
   (Incentives for Learning)

14. discuss subjects dealing with social and health issues (e.g., drugs, smoking, dress codes, etc.).

14. *AIDs Answers for Teens*
Drug Questions and Answers
   (Learning Works)
"Coping With" Books-Revised, Set 3:
  Coping with Facts and Fantasies
   (AGS)
Teenagers and Tough Decisions—video
   (Cambridge Career Products)
Making Decisions
   (Remedia)

Vocabulary

Short-Term Objectives

The learner will be able to

Instructional Level: 9-12

Materials

Can of Squirms (High School)
If It Were You
  (Opportunities for Learning)

15. complete exercises designed to develop an extensive vocabulary by use of commercial manipulative materials.

15. *System 80*
  (Borg-Warner)
Language Master: Word Picture Program
English Development Program
  (Bell & Howell)
Upwords
Word Yahtzee
  (Milton Bradley)
Vocabulary Builder Level II
  (Creative Teaching Associates)
Teaching Vocabulary Worksheets
Teaching Vocabulary Vol. 2
  (LinguiSystems)

16. relate how suffixes change the meaning of root words.

16. *Spellex Word Finder*
Syllabo: Vocabulary Builder—software
  (Curriculum Associates)
Vocabulary Development
Structural Skills Quizmo
  (Milton Bradley)
Escape
  (Creative Teaching Associates)
Vocabulary Skills—Prefixes, Suffixes, and Root Words—software
  (Troll)
Prefix-Suffix Puzzles
  (Incentives for Learning)
Morph-Aid: A Source of Roots, Prefixes, and Suffixes
  (Dale Seymour)

17. utilize vocabulary associated with vehicles and driving while reviewing phonics in game activities.

17. *In the Driver's Seat*
  (Opportunities for Learning)
Life Skills Driving
  (Educational Insights)
Driver Education: Behind the Wheel
  (Hayes)

Vocabulary

Short-Term Objectives

The learner will be able to

Instructional Level: 9-12

Materials

18. demonstrate imaginative usage of words in prose and poetry.

18. *Create-a-Story Series*
      (Dale Seymour)
    I Believe in Unicorns
    Hippogriff Feathers
      (Good Apple)
    Poetry Express—software
    That's My Story/Creative Writing—
      software
      (Troll)
    Story Starters
      (Educational Insights)

19. utilize vocabulary associated with sports activities.

19. *Talewinds Books: Sports Biographies*
    The Reading Scene
      (Continental Press)
    The World of Reading: The World of Sports
    Sports Reading Series
      (Educational Insights)
    Champions of Change
    Mastering Basic Reading Skills
      (Steck-Vaughn)
    On Their Own—Series
      (High Noon Books)

20. participate in word-building games.

20. *Boggle*
      (Parker Brothers)
    Upwords
    Word Yahtzee
      (Milton Bradley)

COMPREHENSION

Comprehension

I. **Purpose of the Subtest**

To measure the ability to evaluate properly a situation typical of real life and determine the appropriate set of responses.

II. **Factors Affecting Subtest and Academic Performance**
   A. Experiential and environmental background
   B. Cultural exposure
   C. Moral values
   D. Reasoning
   E. Practical information and judgment
   F. Social awareness

III. **Educational Significance**
   A. Many classroom discussions regarding cause and effect relations are essential to promote understanding.
   B. Encourage the student to ask and respond to "why" and "if" questions.
   C. The rationale for assignments should be explained so that the student will understand the goals to be accomplished.
   D. Assist the student in understanding moral and social requirements of society through class discussions and group activities. Encourage parental participation.
   E. Provide visual clues to assist in the understanding and performance of commands.

IV. **Long-Term Goal**

The learner will be able to evaluate and appropriately respond to real-life situations.

Comprehension

Short-Term Objectives

The learner will be able to

1. execute simple commands (e.g., "Jump," "Bend over," "Sit down," etc.) gradually increasing complexity.

2. perform specific body movements in games (e.g., "Simon Says," "Mother, May I," etc.).

3. demonstrate comprehension of basic concepts of up, down, behind, before, first, last, etc. utilizing manipulative objects.

4. answer specific "why" questions (e.g., "Why do we have houses?" "Why do we have policemen?").

Instructional Level: K-3

Materials

2. *Aids to Psycholinguistic Teaching: Manual Expression*
   (Charles E. Merrill)

3. *Spatial Concept Picture Book*
   Language Activities for Kindergarten and First Grade
      (Academic Communications)
   Concepts Take Shape
      (Communication Skill Builders)
   Boehm Resource Guide for Basic Concepts
      (Psychological Corporation)
   Where Is It? Spatial Relationship Cards
      (Ideal)
   Children's Video School House: Up & Down, In & Out, Big & Little
      (Kimbo)
   Primary Concepts, I and II
      (Troll)
   Follow Me!
   The Best Concept Pictures Ever
   The Best Concept Workbook Ever
   Preschool To Go
   Listening To Go
      (LinguiSystems)
   Small toys and objects

4. *Why—Because*
      (Ideal)
   Answers to Questions
      (ATP)
   Who, What, When, Where, Why—
   software
      (Communication Skill Builders)

96

Comprehension

Short-Term Objectives
The learner will be able to

Instructional Level: K-3
Materials

MEER
MEER Images
Help 2
  (LinguiSystems)

5. supply missing details or invent the next thing happening in a story told with frequent pauses by the teacher.

5. *What's Missing Set, 4 Books*
  (Judy/Instructo)

6. discuss the logical and/or illogical happenings in folklore.

6. *American Folk Heroes and Tall Tales*
  (Troll)
American Indian Folk Tales
Aesop's Fables: I Can Read, Parts I, II
  (Eye Gate Media)

7. discuss problems or social situations presented in pictures, filmstrips, books or games.

7. *If It Were You*—filmstrip
What Would You Do?—video
  (Educational Insights)
What Do You Think? (Values)
  (Troll)
Friendship Theme Units: Everyday Situations
  (Milliken)
Aggressive Behavior Books and Cassettes
Passive Misbehavior Book and Cassettes
  (Mission)
Talking, Feeling, and Doing
  (Childswork/Childsplay)
Once Upon a Color: Thinking Skills
  (Eye Gate Media)
Understanding Values, Grades 1, 2, & 3
  (Field)

8. discuss social situations (e.g., "What if" or "What would you do if" questions) and state consequences for one's own behavior.

8. *Talking, Feeling, and Doing*
Mad, Sad, Glad
  (Childswork/Childsplay)
Revised Developing Understanding of Self and Others—DUSO-R
  (AGS)

Comprehension

Short-Term Objectives

The learner will be able to

Instructional Level: K-3

Materials

Understanding Values, Grades 1, 2, & 3
   (Field)
*Winnie The Pooh and The Right
   Thing To Do*
Let's Talk With Winnie The Pooh
*Good Citizenship With Winnie
   The Pooh*
   (Disney Educational Products)

9. explain the rules and steps involved in playing a selected game.

10. describe one's parent's job or a job that he would like to have.

10. *Young Careers*
   (Troll)

11. discuss general school safety rules and the reasons for obeying them.

11. *A Kid's Guide to School Safety*
   (Troll)
*Safety At School With Winnie
   The Pooh*
Pooh's Great School Bus Adventure
   (Disney Educational Products)
School Bus Manners for Primaries
   (Eye Gate Media)

12. describe or demonstrate the use of objects in show-and-tell activities.

12. *Show and Tell*
   (Creative Teaching Press)

13. complete unfinished stories.

13. *You Decide/Open-Ended Tales*
   (Troll)
*Adventures in Pragmatic Problem-
   Solving: Stories and Language
   Activities for Children*
   (Academic Communications)
Stamp A Story
   (Childswork/Childsplay)

14. participate in games requiring skill in logic (e.g., checkers, dominoes, Monopoly, etc.).

14. *Monopoly*
   (Parker Brothers)
Chess
Checkers
Chinese Checkers
   (Milton Bradley)

Comprehension

<table>
<tr><td>

Short-Term Objectives
The learner will be able to

</td><td>

Instructional Level: K-3
Materials

</td></tr>
<tr><td>

15. create verbal or written stories using pictures or filmstrips for stimulation.

</td><td>

15. *Storytelling Pictures*
      (DLM)
   Fundamentals of Seeing for Primaries
      (Eye Gate Media)
   Getting Ready to Write Creatively
      (Troll)
   Stamp A Story
      (Childswork/Childsplay)
   *Peabody Language Development Kit
    Revised-Level P*
      (AGS)

</td></tr>
<tr><td>

16. solve simple riddles.

</td><td>

16. *The $1.00 Word Riddle Book*
      (Dale Seymour)
   Little Riddles, Sets A and B
      (Educational Insights)
   Dr. DooRiddles, Book A1
      (Midwest)
   Razzle Dazzle Riddles
   Riddle Romp
   Rhyming Riddles for Speech
      (Pro-Ed)
   *Riddle Roundup: A Wild Bunch to
    Beef Up Your Word Power*
      (Houghton Mifflin)
   *Aids to Psycholinguistic Teaching:
    Auditory Reception*
      (Charles E. Merrill)

</td></tr>
<tr><td>

17. identify words that do not belong in sentences.

</td><td>

17. *Aids to Psycholinguistic Teaching:
    Auditory Reception*
      (Charles E. Merrill)
   GammaRummy
      (Educational Insights)

</td></tr>
<tr><td>

18. answer yes or no to simple questions.

</td><td>

18. *Aids to Psycholinguistic Teaching:
    Auditory Reception*
      (Charles E. Merrill)

</td></tr>
</table>

COMP.

Comprehension

Short-Term Objectives
The learner will be able to

Instructional Level: K-3
Materials

19. identify the days of the week before and after a specific day.

19. Calendar

20. act out various nursery rhymes and fairy tales.

20. *Flannelboard Storytelling Combos 1, 2, and 3*
    Disney Face Puppets
    (Judy/Instructo)

Comprehension

Short-Term Objectives

The learner will be able to

1. discuss appropriate behavior during various activities and in various situations.

2. discuss reasons for having policemen, firemen, doctors, dentists, nurses, etc.

3. discuss a specific local or world event and what could be done to prevent or help the situation.

4. discuss cause-and-effect relationships.

5. discuss personal responsibilities in various situations.

Instructional Level: 3-6

Materials

1. *Telephone Manners for Primaries*
   Library Manners for Primaries
   School Cafeteria Manners for Primaries
   Table Manners for Primaries
   Conversational Manners for Primaries
      (Eye Gate Media)

2. *Community Helpers Puppet Playmates*
      (Judy/Instructo)
   Young Careers: What's It Like to Be
      Book Bags
   Community Helpers
      (Troll)

3. Local newspapers or magazines

4. *Cause and Effect: What Makes It*
      Happen—software
   Think . . . Listen and Learn
   American Tall Tales Listening Lab
      (Troll)
   Language Card Decks: Cause
    and Effect
      (AGS)
   Cause and Effect/Mountain Climbing
      (Learning Well)

5. *Revised Developing Understanding of*
      Self and Others—DUSO-R
      (AGS)
   What Now? Deciding What's Right
      (Educational Insights)
   Making Choices
      (Eye Gate Media)
   Aids to Psycholinguistic Teaching:
      Auditory Association
      (Charles E. Merrill)
   What Do You Think? (Values)
      (Troll)

COMP.

Comprehension

<table>
<tr><td>

Short-Term Objectives
The learner will be able to

</td><td>

Instructional Level: 3-6
Materials

Can of Squirms
Is Anyone Listening? A New Look at Peer Pressure
  (Opportunities for Learning)

</td></tr>
<tr><td>

6. discuss the concepts of savings planning for the future.

</td><td>

6. *Revised Developing Understanding of Self and Others—DUSO-R*
   (AGS)

</td></tr>
<tr><td>

7. teach the members of the class the rules of a game in correct sequential order.

</td><td></td></tr>
<tr><td>

8. perform specific directions with increasing complexity.

</td><td>

8. *Aids to Psycholinguistic Teaching; Auditory Sequential Memory*
   (Charles E. Merrill)
   Follow Directions Carefully, Gr. 2-3, 4-5
   Following Written Directions, Gr. 4-7
   (Opportunities for Learning)
   Following Directions, Gr. 2-4, 3-5, 4-6
   (Frank Schaffer)
   Following Directions . . . Step by Step
   Listening and Following Directions
   (Educational Insights)

</td></tr>
<tr><td>

9. collect and interpret pictures for a situations notebook.

</td><td>

9. Magazines
   Newspapers

</td></tr>
<tr><td>

10. discriminate between stories that are fact or opinion, true or false.

</td><td>

10. *Fact or Opinion*—software
    (Hartley)
    Fact or Opinion—software
    (Communication Skill Builders)
    Comprehension Games: Fact or Opinion/Smart Shoppe
    (Learning Well)

</td></tr>
<tr><td>

11. identify and explain verbal or pictorial absurdities.

</td><td>

11. *Junior Thinklab*
    (SRA)
    What's Wrong Cards
    (Ideal)

</td></tr>
</table>

Comprehension

Short-Term Objectives

The learner will be able to

Instructional Level: 3-6

Materials

What's Wrong Here?
  (DLM)
Fundamentals of Seeing for Primaries
  (Eye Gate Media)
Ready, Set, Listen!
Question the Direction
The Word Kit
BESST
  (LinguiSystems)

COMP.

12. answer "why" questions in all academic areas to demonstrate comprehension.

12. *Answers to Questions*
    (ATP)
    Why—Because
    (Ideal)
    Who, What, When, Where, Why—
    software
    (Communication Skill Builders)

13. demonstrate appropriate responses in emergency situations (e.g., when to call a policeman, the fire department, fire drills, weather emergencies, etc.).

13. *Safety Patrol: Danger Busters—*
    software
    (Troll)

14. answer the following questions regarding cubes of sugar, butter, wood, and ice.
    If you were to put all these cubes into a pan of boiling water at the same time:
    a. Which would sink first?
    b. Which would sink last?
    c. Why? Why not?
    d. Which would not float?
    e. Which would float?
    f. Which would melt first?
    g. Which would not melt at all?

14. Cubes of sugar, butter, wood, ice

15. identify an advertising message and match it to the appropriate picture.

15. Printed ads from magazines and newspapers

Comprehension

Short-Term Objectives	Instructional Level: 3-6
The learner will be able to	**Materials**

16. decide from a list of sentences and adages which are logical and illogical and discuss his decision.

16. Teacher-prepared list of sentences and adages

17. discuss the meanings of Aesop's Fables.

17. *Aesop's Fables: I Can Read, Parts I, II*
    (Eye Gate Media)
    Fables I
    (Creative Teaching Press)
    Readalong Aesop's Fables
    The World of Reading: The World of Fables
    (Educational Insights)
    Fables, Myths, and Poems
    (Educational Designs)

18. list in a brainstorming session many possible uses for a single object (e.g., a pencil, a ball, a piece of paper, etc.).

19. describe in detail to the class an embarrassing experience.

20. discuss the necessity for rules in various sports and games.

Comprehension

Short-Term Objectives

The learner will be able to

1. develop notebook or bulletin board units such as "Dressing for the Occasion," "Planning Meals and Selecting Foods," etc., using pictures, articles, etc.

2. participate in discussions regarding appropriate behavior in specific social situations (e.g., sports activities, classroom activities, home and family life, etc.).

3. discuss local and world events, their social implications, and cause-and-effect relationships.

4. role-play situations in which judgment and appropriate behavior must be demonstrated.

Instructional Level: 6-9

Materials

1. Pictures and articles from newspapers and magazines.

2. *Can of Squirms*
     (Opportunities for Learning)
   What's Right, What's Wrong?
     You Decide—video
     (Sunburst)
   Kids Deal with Divorce
   My Dad's an Alcoholic
   Values
     (Eye Gate Media)
   Personal Development Video Series
     (The School Co.)
   Better Communication Skills for Teens
     (Childswork/Childsplay)
   You Are the School Counselor
     (High Noon Books)

3. *Cause and Effect Card Games*
     (Communication Skill Builders)
   Newspaper articles
   Reports based on television shows such as "20-20"

4. *Values*
     (Eye Gate Media)
   Can of Squirms
     (Opportunities for Learning)
   Let's Talk about Responsibility—
     video
   Yes? No? Maybe? Decision Making Skills—video
     (Sunburst)
   You Are the Judge I and II
     (High Noon Books)

COMP.

105

Comprehension

Short-Term Objectives

The learner will be able to

5. decide if behavior was appropriate in role-playing situations.

6. answer questions beginning with "Why" and "If" (e.g., Why is June 21st the longest day of the year? If June 21st is the longest day of the year, when is the shortest day?).

7. select a topic of controversy in the local area and discuss what he would do if he were the mayor, police chief, doctor, etc.

8. participate in games requiring skill in logic and strategy.

9. identify absurdities in sentences and stories.

Instructional Level: 6-9

Materials

5. *Me & Others*
   (Opportunities for Learning)
   Values
   (Eye Gate Media)
   You Are . . . Series
   (High Noon Books)

6. *Who, What, When, Why*—software
   (Hartley)
   Answers to Questions
   (ATP)
   Study Skills Essentials
   (Eye Gate Media)
   Teacher-prepared list

7. *You Are the Mayor*
   (High Noon Books)
   Local newspaper

8. *Stratego*
   Chess
   Checkers
   Chinese Checkers
   (Milton Bradley)
   Monopoly
   (Parker Brothers)
   Let's Play Detective
   (Childswork/Childsplay)
   Mind Benders
   Mind Benders Software
   (Midwest)
   Word Thinkercises
   Logic Thinkercises
   (Good Apple)

9. *Thinking, Listening, and Communicating*
   (Eye Gate Media)

Comprehension

Short-Term Objectives

The learner will be able to

Instructional Level: 6-9

Materials

The Word Kit
BESST
  (LinguiSystems)
Sentence Improbabilities
  (Communication Skill Builders)

10. describe and discuss absurdities in pictures.

10. *Aids to Psycholinguistic Teaching: Visual Association*
  (Charles E. Merrill)
What's Wrong Here?
  (DLM)
What's Wrong Card Sets 1 & 2
  (Communication Skill Builders)

11. discuss folklore and Aesop's fables (e.g., their meanings, logical or illogical events, social implications).

11. *Rib-Tickling American Folktales*
  (Troll)
Fables, Legends, and Folktales
  (Hayes)
Myths and Fables Workbook
  (Opportunities for Learning)
Aesop's Fables, Part II
  (Eye Gate Media)

12. participate in games that require verbal expression and comprehension skills (e.g., "Twenty Questions," "The OK Game," and "The Ungame," etc.).

12. *The OK Game*
The Ungame
  (Ungame Co.)
The Self-Esteem Game
The Stop, Relax, and Think Game
  (Childswork/Childsplay)
Go to the Head of the Class
Game of Life
  (Milton Bradley)

13. describe a hobby or a game, progressing through a step-by-step process.

13. *How a Picture is Made*
  (Eye Gate Media)

14. discuss "choice and consequences," cause-and-effect relationships.

14. *Language Card Deck: Cause and Effect Cards*
TAD: Toward Affective Development
Transitions
  (AGS)

COMP.

107

Comprehension

Short-Term Objectives
The learner will be able to

Instructional Level: 6-9
Materials

Tales for Thinking, Levels 2 and 3
(Curriculum Associates)
Consequences
(DLM)
Aids to Psycholinguistic Teaching:
Auditory Association
(Charles E. Merrill)

15. provide captions for cartoons or pictures.

15. *Creative Writing Skills, Grades 6-8*
(Instructional Fair)
Cartoon Comprehension
(Frank Schaffer)
Cartoons from newspapers and magazines

16. discuss the need for laws and rules in daily living.

16. *Why Follow the Rules*—video
(Sunburst)
Living Skills: Every Kids Guide to
Laws that Relate to Kids in the
Community
(Mission)
Your Rights and the Law
You and the Law
(Opportunities for Learning)
Mind Bogglers, Book 3
(Hayes)

17. present a report on the meaning of the "Golden Rule."

18. discuss the changes a person experiences as he ages.

19. discuss the various religious beliefs of man.

20. explain to his classmates how to use the card catalogue to locate a book, find the book on the shelf, and check the book out of the library.

20. *Using Today's Library*
Library Skills
(Eye Gate Media)
Using the Library
(Opportunities for Learning)
Using Library Skills, Gr. 4-6
(Instructional Fair)
How to Use a Library
(Milliken)

Comprehension

Short-Term Objectives

The learner will be able to

1. discuss problem situations using pictures.

2. discuss the concepts of saving "for a rainy day" and planning ahead for the future.

3. complete unfinished stories appropriately.

4. discuss "choice and consequences," cause-and-effect relationships.

5. list answers to questions such as "Why do we have policemen?" "Why do we have houses?" etc.).

Instructional Level: 9-12

Materials

1. *What's Right, What's Wrong?*
   You Decide
   (Sunburst)
   Consequences
   (DLM)

3. *Open-Ended Stories*
   (Globe)
   Story Sparkers
   Write On!
   Cliffhangers
   (Educational Insights)

4. *Cause and Effect Card Games*
   (Communication Skill Builders)
   Comprehension Games: Cause and
   Effect/Mountain Climbing
   (Learning Well)
   A Matter for Judgment
   (Globe)
   Inductive Thinking Skills: Cause
   and Effect
   (Midwest)
   Reading for Understanding 3
   (SRA)

5. *On My Own At Home*
   (LinguiSystems)
   Answers to Questions
   (ATP)

COMP.

Comprehension

Short-Term Objectives

The learner will be able to

Instructional Level: 9-12

Materials

6. outline simple paragraphs by finding the main idea or topic and subtopics or ideas.

6. *Reading Comprehension Series:*
   Getting the Main Idea
     (Educational Insights)
   Game Drawer Comprehension Games:
   Drawer 6
     (Ideal)
   The Outlining Kit
   Thirty Lessons in Outlining
     (Curriculum Associates)
   Sentences and Paragraphs
   Paragraph Skills
     (Eye Gate Media)
   Outlining, Note Taking, and Report
   Writing
     (Hayes)

7. complete a science project that can be presented and described to the class.

7. *Search: A Research Guide for Science*
   Fairs and Independent Study
     (Dale Seymour)
   Science Projects
   Science Experiments with Everyday
    Things
   Science Activities with Simple Things
     (Fearon)

8. answer questions in all learning areas that begin with how or why.

8. *Who, What, When, Where, Why*
     (Communication Skill Builders)
   Tell Me Why:—videos
    Flowers, Plants, and Trees
    Gems, Metals, and Minerals
    Pre-Historic Animals, Reptiles, and
     Amphibians
    Water and Weather
    Space, Earth and Atmosphere
    A Healthy Body
    Anatomy and Genetics
     (Summit Learning)

Comprehension

Short-Term Objectives

The learner will be able to

Instructional Level: 9-12

Materials

9. write a story to go with a title from a selected list.

9. *Story Sparkers*
   Write On!
      (Educational Insights)
   Creative Writing, Gr. 6-8
   Story Starters, Gr. 6
      (Milliken)
   Writing for Fun
   Everyday Writing
      (Eye Gate Media)
   Creative Newspaper, Film and Novel
   Activities
      (Opportunities for Learning)
   Storytelling Pictures
      (DLM)
   Springboards for Writing
      (ATP)
   Teacher-prepared list of titles

10. provide captions for cartoons or pictures.

10. *Creative Writing Skills, Gr. 6-8*
      (Instructional Fair)
    Storytelling Pictures
      (DLM)
    Cartoons and pictures from
      newspapers or magazines

11. discuss world events, why they might have occurred, and how they might effect the rest of the world, the local area, and the students themselves.

11. Newspapers
    News magazines

12. participate in role playing social situations, stopping before the solution to the problem is enacted. Have other students offer suggestions of possible solutions. Then let role players complete the skit to see who knew the correct ending. Discussion may be allowed as to the rightness or wrongness of the solutions.

12. *Open-Ended Plays*
      (Globe)
    Interpersonal Skills Worktexts
    Can of Squirms (High School)
      (Opportunities for Learning)
    Yes? No? Maybe? Decision Making
    Skills
      (Sunburst)
    Incomplete Plays
      (Dale Seymour)

COMP.

111

Comprehension

Short-Term Objectives

The learner will be able to

13. participate in games that require thinking and planning ahead (e.g., chess, checkers, Monopoly, etc.).

14. discuss behaviors appropriate to various situations that could arise in daily living.

15. describe the skills involved in obtaining a job.

16. present a report on first aid procedures and treatment.

Instructional Level: 9-12

Materials

13. *Monopoly*
    (Parker Brothers)
    Chess
    Checkers
    Chinese Checkers
    Connect Four
    (Milton Bradley)

14. *Understanding and Preventing AIDS*
    (Eye Gate Media)
    I Don't Know What to Do: Decision Making Skills
    Can of Squirms (High School)
    Understanding Your Feelings
    (Opportunities for Learning)
    You Are the Banker
    (High Noon Books)

15. *RX4LD—How to Join the Job Club*
    Vocational Entry Skills for Secondary Students
    (ATP)
    Career Exploration
    Jobs for the 90's
    (Sunburst)
    Action 2000: Jobs in Your Future
    (Scholastic)
    You Are the Boss
    (High Noon Books)

16. *First Aid: Newest Techniques—Series A, B, C*
    (Sunburst)
    *First Aid: Emergencies Mean Action—*software
    *First Aid Basics—*software
    (Marshmedia)
    Emergency Action: Know What to Do Before the Ambulance Arrives
    Dr. Heimlich's Home First Aid
    CPR: The Way to Save Lives
    (Cambridge Video)

Comprehension

Short-Term Objectives

The learner will be able to

Instructional Level: 9-12

Materials

17. discuss the inalienable rights guaranteed every individual.

17. *Civics and Citizenship: Puzzles, Games, and Individual Activities*
(Hayes)
U.S. Constitution in Plain English
(Eye Gate Media)
American Citizenship—filmstrip
Living Law
(Scholastic)
American Archives: Collections A & B
(Educational Insights)
Your Rights and the Law
Student's Rights: Focus on the First Amendment
(Opportunities for Learning)
You Decide! Applying the Bill of Rights to Real Cases
Critical Thinking in U.S. History: Book 1—Colonies to Constitution
(Midwest)

18. participate in a class project developing and planning a model community.

18. *Building a Community*
(Judy/Instructo)

19. discuss myths and mysteries that exist in today's world.

19. *Scope Skills Books: Strangely True*
(Scholastic)
Myths, Magic, and Monsters: Comprehensive Reading Skills
(Opportunities for Learning)

20. write creatively about moods or feelings stimulated by pictures and music.

20. *Photos for English Composition Classes*
(Opportunities for Learning)
Photo Library II
(Incentives for Learning)

FACTOR II—PERCEPTUAL ORGANIZATION

PICTURE COMPLETION

Picture Completion

I. **Purpose of the Subtest**

To measure the ability to identify visually a relevant part that is missing within a picture.

II. **Factors Affecting Subtest and Academic Performance**
   A. Visual conceptualization
   B. Perceptual organization
   C. Memory
   D. Visual discrimination
   E. Cultural experiences and background
   F. Time element
   G. Concentration and attention

III. **Educational Significance**
   A. All learning situations should include emphasis on helping the student to learn to recognize the essential details in visually presented material.
   B. Provide visual experiences or opportunities to involve the student in active learning, utilizing everyday occurrences stressing the recognition of relevant parts of the learning experience. For example, one such experience could be brushing one's teeth, recognizing that a toothbrush, toothpaste, and water are essential parts of this activity.
   C. Structure the student's environment so that visual attention will be focused upon the selected stimulus by eliminating excessive visual detail within his working area. A carrel for studying may prove beneficial.
   D. The student's desk should be free of any material that does not relate to the task that is at hand.
   E. Work with the auditory-vocal channel of communication combined with the visual mode of presentation. When visual presentations are made, use only the number of visual items that the student can successfully comprehend.
   F. All homework assignments and directions should be written and checked by the teacher to make sure all details are included.
   G. Encourage the student to take more time in checking his own work, examining tasks and instructions, etc.

IV. **Long-Term Goal**

The learner will be able to visually identify relevant parts that are missing in pictures.

Picture Completion

Short-Term Objectives

The learner will be able to

1. find objects hidden in the classroom.

2. match accurately geometric shapes and designs.

3. select the appropriate choice, biggest, smallest, etc., from geometric shapes, objects, etc., of differing size.

Instructional Level: K-3

Materials

1. Concrete objects such as chalk, eraser, pencils, small toys

2. *Shape Sorting Peg Board*
   Geometric Pegboard
      (Constructive Playthings)
   Geometric Shape Sorter
   Shape Form Board
   Geometric Color Clown
      (Learning Resources)
   Fit-a-Shape
   Shape Squares
      (Lauri)
   Math Big Box
   Math Manipulatives Big Box
      (DLM)
   Geometric Shape Lotto
      (Judy/Instructo)
   Shape Sorter and Stacker
      (Playskool)
   Bearamores Learn Colors & Shapes
      (Media Materials)
   Half 'n Half Design and Color
      (Ann Arbor)

3. *Montessori Cylinder Blocks with Knobs*
   Knobbed Difference Puzzles
      (Constructive Playthings)
   Size Form Boards
      (Ideal)
   Shape Templates
      (DLM)
   Fit-a-Size
      (Lauri)
   Concept Understanding Program
      (Incentives for Learning)
   Patchworks:
     Size and Shape Recognition
     Size Perception
      (Milton Bradley)

Picture Completion

Short-Term Objectives
The learner will be able to

4. recognize shapes in pictures of common objects.

5. complete figure-ground exercises.

6. complete jigsaw puzzles appropriate for grade level.

Instructional Level: K-3
Materials

4. *Paper Shapes Projects*
   (Judy/Instructo)
   Let's Learn: Shapes
   (Carson-Dellosa)
   Basic Shapes Cut and Paste
   (Frank Schaffer)
   Geometric Shapes Lotto
   (Judy/Instructo)
   Shapes in Things
   Curves and Corners
   (Ideal)

5. *Figure-Ground Activity Cards*
   See It—Do It
   (DLM)
   'M' Is for Mirror: Find the Hidden Pictures
   (Dale Seymour)
   Programmed Spelling: Levels 1, 2, and 3 with Cassette Tapes
   Perceptual Activities
   (Ann Arbor)
   Hidden Pictures, Grades K-1, 1-2
   (Frank Schaffer)

6. *Visual Perception Big Box*
   (DLM)
   Ani-Space
   Fit-a-Space
   (Lauri)
   Knobbed Differences Puzzles
   Houses Perception Puzzles
   (Constructive Playthings)
   Animal Parents and Babies Inlay Puzzles
   Transportation Inlay Puzzles
   Fairy Tales and Nursery Rhymes Beginning Woodboard Inlay Puzzles
   Beginners Inlay Puzzles
   Occupations Puzzles

PICT.
COMP.

Picture Completion

Short-Term Objectives

The learner will be able to

Instructional Level: K-3

Materials

Dinosaurs Beginning Woodboard
Inlay Puzzles
(Judy/Instructo)

7. identify body parts in games and puzzles.

7. *Mix and Match Bears*
(Milton Bradley)
Body and Self-Awareness Big Box
(DLM)
Body Parts Puzzle
Boy Puzzle
Girl Puzzle
Teddy Bear Puzzle
(Judy/Instructo)
Body Parts Floor Puzzle
(Frank Schaffer)

8. discriminate among shapes, symbols, letters, etc.

8. *Symbol Discrimination Series*
Symbol Discrimination and Sequencing
Symbol/Letter Tracking
(Ann Arbor)
Cassette Activity Books: Reading
Readiness Series
(Media Materials)
b, d, p, q
(Incentives for Learning)
Alpha Match
(Judy/Instructo)
Classifying Shapes
Shapes and Color Abacus
(Constructive Playthings)

9. complete alphabetical letters which have some part of each letter missing.

9. *Alphabet Practice Cards*
Practice the Alphabet
(Ideal)
Teacher-made alphabetical letters

10. identify what is missing in pictures.

10. *Missing Parts Lotto*
(Milton Bradley)
What's Missing Set
(Judy/Instructo)

Picture Completion

Short-Term Objectives

The learner will be able to

Instructional Level: K-3

Materials

Finish the Picture Wipe-Off Cards
   (Trend)
Floppy Teacher: What Is Missing?—
   software
   (Cambridge Development Library)

11. sort specific letters made out of felt, foam, rubber, sandpaper, etc.

11. *Alpha Tiles*
      (Educational Insights)
   Avalanche of Letters
   A-Z Panels
      (Lauri)
   Tactile Alphabet Cards
      (Learning Resources)
   Super Alphabet Pack
      (Judy/Instructo)
   Foam Letters
      (Ideal)
   Alphabet Motor Activities Book
      (DLM)
   *Vallett Perceptual-Motor Transitions
      to Reading Program*
      (ATP)

12. match letter sounds to pictures of familiar objects.

12. *Sound/Picture Match-Ups*
      (DLM)
   *Toy Chest of Beginning Sounds
      Flannelboard Aid*
      (Judy/Instructo)
   Consonant Pictures for Pegboard
   Vowel Pictures for Pegboard
      (Ideal)
   Easy Vowels Flash Cards
   Easy Consonants Flash Cards
   *Initial Consonants K-2: Fun with
      Initial Consonants*
      (Frank Schaffer)
   One of a Kind—software
   Reader Rabbit—software
      (EBSCO)
   Initial Consonants—Set A
   Consonant Puzzles
   ABC Book: Alligators to Zippers
      (Zaner-Bloser)

Picture Completion

Short-Term Objectives
The learner will be able to

Instructional Level: K-3
Materials

13. identify missing letters in known words.

13. *Boxed Activity Cards: Short and Long Vowels*
    (Frank Schaffer)
    Instant Spelling Words for Writing
    (Curriculum Associates)
    M-ss-ng L-nks—software
    (Sunburst)
    Teacher-prepared lists

14. complete simple pictures that have missing lines or parts.

14. *Visual Closure Cards*
    (Ideal)
    Teddy Bear Alphabet Dot-to-Dot
    (Frank Schaffer)
    Front/Back and Missing Parts Lotto
    (Milton Bradley)
    Paths, Patterns, & Letters
    Visual-Motor Readiness Set
    Learning Readiness Set
    (Continental Press)
    Perceptual Activities Packets
    (Ann Arbor)

15. read rebus stories.

15. *Catchword: The Rebus Galore Activity Book*
    (High Noon Books)
    Perceptual Development Activities; Rebuses, Signals, & Symbols
    (Opportunities for Learning)
    Game Drawer Comprehension Games: Drawer 1
    (Ideal)
    Clark Early Language Program
    (DLM)
    Big Book Programs for Early Childhood and Special Education
    (Dale Seymour)
    Magic Slate—software
    Magic Slate Poster
    (Sunburst)

16. create an original rebus story.

16. *Magic Slate*—software
    (Sunburst)

124

Picture Completion

Short-Term Objectives	Instructional Level: K-3
The learner will be able to	**Materials**

<table>
<tr><td></td><td>

Perceptual Development Activities:
Rebuses, Signs, & Symbols
  (Opportunities for Learning)
Standard Rebus Glossary
Rebus Stick-Ons
  (AGS)
Rebus Reading: Beginning Sentence
  Building
  (DLM)
Catchword: The Rebus Galore
  Activity Book
  (High Noon Books)

</td></tr>
</table>

PICT. COMP.

17. play games that require recognition of clues, like "Twenty Questions" or "Password."

17. *Password*
    Educational "Password" Game
    Concentration
      (Milton Bradley)
    I.Q. Games Set
      (Educational Insights)
    Field Trip Mysteries
      (Judy/Instructo)
    Treasure Hunter—software
      (Houghton Mifflin)

18. construct compound words using pictures from magazines and newspapers such as a picture of a fire and a picture of a man.

18. Magazines
    Newspapers

19. construct compound words from a master list using word cards and/or word puzzles.

19. *Compound Word Puzzles*
      (Ideal)
    Compound Word Puzzles
      (Incentives for Learning)
    Peabody Picture Collection—
      Compound Word Puzzles
      (AGS)

Picture Completion

Short-Term Objectives

The learner will be able to

20. find objects hidden in pictures.

Instructional Level: K-3

Materials

20. *Hidden Pictures K-1, 1-2*
(Frank Schaffer)
Graphing Hidden Pictures
(Carson-Dellosa)
Teddy Bear Search
(Milton Bradley)
Listening Language Laboratory Series
(SRA)
Mystery Letters
(Love)
Learning with Literature: Pinocchio
(EBSCO)

Picture Completion

Short-Term Objectives

The learner will be able to

1. sort objects according to color, size, and shape.

2. recall specific objects, words, and actions presented in pictures and stories.

3. complete jigsaw puzzles appropriate for age level.

4. perform matching exercises.

Instructional Level: 3-6

Materials

1. *Classifying Shapes*
   Shapes and Color Abacus
      (Constructive Playthings)
   Plastic Beads
   Large Colored Beads
   Colored Cubes
      (Ideal)
   Attribute Blocks Desk Set
   Classifying Counters
      (Learning Resources)

2. *Memory: What's in a Frame?*—
      software
      (Sunburst)
   Look and Learn—software
      (EBSCO)
   Original Memory
      (Milton Bradley)
   Reading Readiness Picture Card Combo
   Consonant/Vowels Picture Card Combo
      (Judy/Instructo)

3. *U.S. Map Woodboard Puzzle*
      (Judy/Instructo)
   Dinosaurs Floor Puzzles, Sets 1 & 2
      (Frank Schaffer)
   Commercial jigsaw puzzles of all sizes

4. *Sight Word Memory Match*
      (DLM)
   Pick Pairs Game
   Play Scenes Lotto
   Original Memory
   Animal Families Memory
   Front/Back Memory
      (Milton Bradley)
   Memory: Memory Building Blocks—
      software
      (Sunburst)

PICT.
COMP.

Picture Completion

Short-Term Objectives
The learner will be able to

Instructional Level: 3-6
Materials

Early Concepts Skillbuilder: Match It—software
(EBSCO)

5. identify what is missing in drawings of common objects with one or more details missing.

5. *Front/Back Lotto*
Missing Parts Lotto
(Milton Bradley)
What's Missing Set
(Judy/Instructo)
Perceptual Activities Packets
(Ann Arbor)

6. find the hidden objects in pictures.

6. *"M" is for Mirror: Find the Hidden Pictures*
(Dale Seymour)
Figure-Ground Activity Cards
(DLM)
Graphing Hidden Pictures
(Carson-Dellosa)
Listening Language Laboratory Series
(SRA)
Mystery Letters
(Love)
Learning with Literature: Pinocchio
(EBSCO)

7. play games like "Bingo" and "Lotto" that require visual discrimination and matching skills.

7. *Color & Shape Bingo*
Basic Sight Words Bingo
USA Bingo
(Trend)
Bingo
Original Memory
Animal Families Memory
Front/Back Memory
(Milton Bradley)
Nature Lotto
(Constructive Playthings)
Shapes, Sizes and Shapes, Colors and Shapes
Shapes, Sizes, and Colors

128

Picture Completion

Short-Term Objectives

The learner will be able to

Instructional Level: 3-6

Materials

Lotto Games:
Rooms (in the house)
Seasons
Familiar Settings
Geometric Shapes
(Judy/Instructo)

8. recognize space, distance, and perspective differences.

8. *Spatial Relationship Puzzles*
Where Is It? Spatial Relationship Cards
(Ideal)
Spatial Relations Picture Cards
(DLM)

9. locate individual states on a map of the United States.

9. *United States Map Puzzle*
(Playskool)
United States Map floor Puzzle
U.S. Map Woodboard Puzzle
(Judy/Instructo)
U.S. Map Games
(DLM)

10. locate the capitals of each state on a United States map.

10. *United States Map Skills*
(Milliken)
Name That State Game
(Educational Insights)
U.S. Map Games
(DLM)

11. paint a picture either freehand or using commercial material.

11. Paint-by-number kits
Art supplies

12. identify written words appropriately describing pictures cut from magazines and pasted on one side of a poster board. (The written words may be glued beside the pictures.)

12. *Sound Matching*
(Incentives for Learning)
Pictures from magazines
Poster board

PICT.
COMP.

Comprehension

Short-Term Objectives

The learner will be able to

13. complete crossword puzzles and word hunt games appropriate for age level.

14. describe "how to" complete simple activities (e.g., make a bed, brush your teeth, etc.).

15. play games which require the student to remember what he sees such as matching playing cards turned face-down.

Instructional Level: 3-6

Materials

13. *Word Works 1, 2, 3*—software
Crossword Puzzles—software
(EBSCO)
Crossword Puzzles USA
(Frank Schaffer)
Vocabulary Connections
(Steck-Vaughn)
Spill & Spell
(Parker Brothers)
Scrabble, Jr.
Scrabble
(Selchow and Righter)
Word Searches, Grades 2-7
*Wordsearches: The Vocabulary
Builders*
*Basic Terms and Concepts:
Crosswords
Wordsearches*
(Instructional Fair)
Crossword Magic
Crossword Magic with Discs—software
(Opportunities for Learning)

15. *Sight Word Memory Match
Concentration*
(DLM)
Original Memory
Animal Families Memory
(Milton Bradley)
Memory: Memory Building Blocks—
software
(Sunburst)
Memory Jogger, Grades 1-3, 4-6
Memory Master—software
Touch 'N Match—software
Touch 'N See—software
(EBSCO)

Picture Completion

Short-Term Objectives	Instructional Level: 3-6

The learner will be able to

Materials

16. match similar objects such as sunflower seeds and watermelon seeds. (The level of difficulty can be controlled by the selection of objects.)

16. Seeds, beans, coins, buttons, etc.

17. answer correctly from memory questions concerning details in pictures that he studies for 60 seconds.

17. *Photo Libraries*
     (Incentives for Learning)
     Visual Memory Card Sets I, II, III, IV
     (DLM)
     Pictures from magazines

18. list from memory the objects viewed on a page for 60 seconds.

18. *Magic Slate Poster*
     (Sunburst)
     Visual Memory Card Sets I, II, III, IV
     (DLM)
     Teacher-prepared material

19. recognize likenesses and differences in words, phrases, and sentences.

19. *Sight Word Bingo*
     (Ideal)
     Sight Words Flash Cards
     GrammaRummy
     (Educational Insights)
     Sentence Builder
     (Kenworthy)

20. recognize and discriminate comparative and superlative forms of descriptive terms (e.g., taller, tallest, longer, longest, etc.).

20. *Comparison of Adjective Puzzles*
     (Incentives for Learning)
     Basic Language Skills: Adjectives and Adverbs
     (Educational Insights)
     Up With Language Series: Adjectives and Adverbs
     (Remedia)

PICT. COMP.

Picture Completion

Short-Term Objectives

The learner will be able to

1. complete grouping exercises by orally responding on a tape recording (e.g., "England, France, U.S. are all —————." "Beds, sofas, chairs are all —————.").

2. cut up a map and paste it onto cardboard and use it as a jigsaw puzzle.

3. list in detail the various steps necessary to complete a simple science experiment.

4. perform practice exercises of words or letters in cursive writing.

Instructional Level: 6-9

Materials

1. Tape recorder and tape
   Teacher-prepared lists

2. World and state maps
   Cardboard or poster board

3. *The Human Body*
   (Constructive Playthings)
   Magnetism and Electricity for Grades 5-9
   (Milliken)
   The Thomas Edison Book of Easy and Incredible Experiments
   Earth Science for Every Kid
   Chemistry for Every Kid
   (Summit Learning)
   Adventures in Science:
     Kitchen Science
     How Things Work
   (Educational Insights)
   Science Activity Labs: Basic Science Lab I
   (Weber Costello)
   Experiments in Energy
   Science Shelf Activities:
     Weather
     Sound
     Electricity
   Elementary Science Kit
   (Ideal)

4. *Handwriting: A Fresh Start*
   (Curriculum Associates)
   Handwriting Skills: Mastering Cursive Writing, Grades 5-8
   The 3-R Pack
   Write Better Kit
   (Zaner-Bloser)

Picture Completion

Short-Term Objectives

The learner will be able to

Instructional Level: 6-9

Materials

5. complete crossword and word hunt puzzles appropriate for age level.

5. *Lessons in Vocabulary Development*
   (Curriculum Associates)
   Vocabulary Puzzles: Word Puzzles,
   Gr. 5-6, 6-7, 7-8
   (Milliken)
   Cross-Number Puzzles
   (SRA)
   Crossword Cubes Game
   Crossword Dominoes
   Scrabble, Jr.
   Scrabble
   (Selchow and Righter)
   Wordsearches: The Vocabulary
   Builders
   Basic Terms and Concepts:
   Crosswords
   Wordsearches
   (Instructional Fair)
   Word Works 1, 2, 3—software
   (EBSCO)
   Word Quest—software
   Classroom Toolbox—software
   (Sunburst)

6. play games that provide an opportunity to supply missing parts of words.

6. *Syllable Safari*
   (Ideal)
   Syllable Puzzles
   (Incentives for Learning)
   Probe
   (Parker Brothers)
   M-ss-ng L-nks—software
   (Sunburst)

7. supply the titles and main ideas of written selections or stories heard on tapes.

7. *Exercises in Reading Comprehension:*
   Level 6
   (Hayes)
   Troll Listening Lab, Levels 5-6, 7-8-9
   (Troll)
   Reading-Thinking Series 2
   (Media Materials)

PICT.
COMP.

Picture Completion

Short-Term Objectives

The learner will be able to

8. measure objects within the classroom such as desk tops, etc., by use of a ruler or yardstick.

9. play games that require matching skills.

10. put together individual syllables to make words taken from a master list. (These words may first be mounted on tag board and cut into appropriate syllables.)

11. identify the word missing in a sentence written on the chalkboard by the teacher. (A master list of words may be provided.)

Instructional Level: 6-9

Materials

8. Ruler
   Yardstick
   Measuring tape

9. *Match & Move Memory*
   Bingo
   Old Maid
   Crazy Eights
      (Milton Bradley)
   Analogy Match-Ups
      (Incentives for Learning)
   USA Bingo
      (Trend)
   Memory Building Blocks—software
      (Sunburst)
   Memory Master—software
      (EBSCO)
   Make a Match—software
      (Troll)

10. *Syllabo: Vocabulary Builder*—
       software
    Activities for Dictionary Practice
       (Curriculum Associates)
    Syllable Safari
       (Ideal)
    Fun with Phonics: Syllable Fun
       (Media Materials)
    Syllable Puzzles
    Syllable Systems
       (Incentives for Learning)
    Skill Power Teaching Units:
    Syllables
       (Remedia)

11. Teacher-prepared list of words

Picture Completion

Short-Term Objectives

The learner will be able to

Instructional Level: 6-9

Materials

12. differentiate between real and nonsense words and sentences.

12. *Sentence Tracking*
     (Ann Arbor)
     GrammaRummy
     (Educational Insights)
     Question the Direction
     FILE
     BESST
     Grammar for Teens
     (LinguiSystems)
     Switchboard—software
     (Sunburst)
     Teacher-prepared words and sentences

13. describe in detail an object, person, or picture.

13. *Vocabulary To Go*
     More Vocabulary To Go
     Find Your Way With Words
     Language Quictionary
     (LinguiSystems)

14. play games such as "Twenty Questions" which require knowledge and description of detail.

14. *Educational "Password" Game*
     Password
     Go to the Head of the Class
     (Milton Bradley)

15. form words using different beginning consonants and blends with word patterns.

15. *Word Patterns*
     Blend Dominoes
     (Incentives for Learning)
     Word Family Flash Cards
     Consonant Pictures for Pegboard
     Blends and Digraphs Pictures for Pegboard
     Start Your Engines
     Blend Dominoes
     (Ideal)

16. complete commercial paint-by-number kits.

17. recognize words that develop through the progressive present**ion** of designs.

17. *Progressive Visual Perceptual Training Filmstrips: Levels 1 and 2*
     (Educational Activities)

PICT.
COMP.

Picture Completion

Short-Term Objectives

The learner will be able to

18. match shape cards to appropriately shaped words.

19. discuss the differences in word meanings caused by prefixes and suffixes.

20. add prefixes and/or suffixes to root words to match definitions provided by the teacher.

Instructional Level: 6-9

Materials

18. *Upgrade*
    (Educational Activities)

19. *Activities for Dictionary Practice*
    (Curriculum Associates)
    Game Drawer Decoding Games: Drawer 10
    (Ideal)
    Structural Skills Quizmo
    (Milton Bradley)
    Pursuit
    Escape
    (Creative Teaching Associates)
    Word Benders: Books B-1, C-1
    (Midwest)
    Prefix-Suffix Puzzles
    (Incentives for Learning)

20. *Structural Skills Quizmo*
    (Milton Bradley)
    Activities for Dictionary Practice
    (Curriculum Associates)
    Prefix-Suffix Puzzles
    (Incentives for Learning)
    Vocabulary Boosters
    (Fearon)
    Prefix Puzzles
    Suffix Puzzles
    (DLM)
    Pursuit
    Escape
    (Creative Teaching Associates)
    Word Benders: Books B1, C-1
    (Midwest)
    Teacher-prepared lists of definitions, root words, and affixes

Picture Completion

Short-Term Objectives

The learner will be able to

1. complete advanced puzzles appropriate for age level.

2. plot a route from one point to another on a map, noting each city passed through.

3. supply words or phrases for missing parts to form a complete sentence.

4. identify syllables within a word.

Instructional Level: 9-12

Materials

1. *Jigsaw Puzzles*
   Spatial Reasoning Puzzles
   Crossmatics: A Challenging Collection of Cross-Number Puzzles
      (Dale Seymour)
   Mind Benders: Books B-1, C-1
   Cross-Number Puzzles
      (Midwest)
   Crosswords and Wordsearches
      (Opportunities for Learning)
   Crozzzwords—Crossword Puzzles— software
   Wordzzzearch—Hidden Word Puzzles— software
   The Game Show—software
      (Troll)

2. *Taking a Trip*
      (Fearon)
   Mapping Your World
      (National Geographic)
   Road Atlas
      (Rand McNally)
   State maps

3. *GrammaRummy*
      (Educational Insights)
   Super Sentence
      (Creative Teaching Associates)
   Sentence Builder
      (Kenworthy)
   Sentence Builder
      (Milton Bradley)

4. *Syllable Safari*
      (Ideal)
   All About Reading Box: Syllable Puzzles
      (Incentives for Learning)
   Alphamaster
      (Educational Insights)

PICT.
COMP.

137

Picture Completion

Short-Term Objectives
The learner will be able to

Instructional Level: 9-12
Materials

Syllabo: Vocabulary Builder—
  software
Activities for Dictionary Practice
  (Curriculum Associates)

5. describe the actions which are reflected in pictures.

5. *Tricky Picture Stories: Set of 3*
    (Educational Insights)
   Contemporary Concerns of Youth
    (AGS)
   Storytelling Posters
    (DLM)
   Pictures, Please!
    (Communication Skill Builders)
   Photopacks
    (Incentives for Learning)

6. trace and/or cut out each state outline and paste it on a master map of the United States.

6. *United States Map, Outlines*
    (Milliken)
   State & World Map Outlines
   Blank Map Outlines
    (Opportunities for Learning)

7. identify misplaced phrases in sentences.

7. *Sentence Builder*
    (Kenworthy)
   GrammaRummy
    (Educational Insights)
   Sentence Improbabilities
   Language Activities Resource Kit
    (Communication Skill Builders)
   FILE
    (LinguiSystems)
   Teacher-prepared sentences

8. identify the sentence that does not belong in a short paragraph.

8. *Switchboard*—software
    (Sunburst)
   Teacher-prepared paragraphs

9. describe in detail objects, people, pictures, etc.

9. *Vocabulary To Go*
   Find Your Way with Words
   Language Quicktionary
    (LinguiSystems)

138

Picture Completion

Short-Term Objectives

The learner will be able to

Instructional Level: 9-12

Materials

Pictures from magazines, etc.
Objects and persons in the classroom

10. present verbal or written descriptions stressing details of TV programs, films, or trips.

11. recognize and verbally describe important details in a short story that leads to the conclusion.

11. *Sherlock Holmes Reading Center*
    (Troll)
    Tricky Picture Stories: Set of 3
    Reading Comprehension Series:
    Predicting Outcomes
    (Educational Insights)

12. ask questions regarding missing information in a short story read to him by the teacher.

12. Student-prepared questions

13. recognize missing details on a map drawn to show the way to go from the student's home to school or other location.

13. *Finding Your Way*
    (Fearon)
    Building Primary Maps
    (Judy/Instructo)

14. complete craft activities such as mosaic or ceramic tile projects, model kits, leatherwork kits, macrame kits, etc.

14. Commercial kits

15. identify a word which has one-third of the bottom of the word covered.

15. *Word and Phrase Sentence Builder*
    (Kenworthy)
    Economo Word Builder
    Sentence Builder
    (Milton Bradley)
    Teacher-prepared flash cards

16. identify the person in a partially covered photograph of a sports, TV, or film personality.

17. make a complete sentence using randomly selected words.

17. *Sentence Game for Juniors*
    (Selchow and Righter)

PICT.
COMP.

139

Picture Completion

Short-Term Objectives

The learner will be able to

Instructional Level: 9-12

Materials

GrammaRummy
   (Educational Insights)
Word and Phrase Sentence Builder
   (Kenworthy)
Sentence Builder
   (Milton Bradley)
Switchboard—software
   (Sunburst)

18. locate specific data on a table, TV schedule, bus or plane schedule, etc.

18. Various tables, arrival and departure schedules, sports schedules, etc. Teacher-prepared questionnaire

19. recognize the methods of representation of elevation on maps and globes.

19. *U.S. Relief Map*
   World Relief Map
   Raised Relief Globe
      (Opportunities for Learning)
   3-D Landforms
      (Educational Insights)

20. utilize the key provided for maps.

20. *Basic Map Skills*
      (Educational Insights)
   Maptime . . . USA
   Prime Time Maps
      (Good Apple)

21. identify objects when viewed from different distances and/or perspectives.

21. *Building Thinking Skills: Book 3, Figural*
   Roller Dog—software
      (Midwest)
   Visual Thinking Cards, Gr. 4-8, 8-12
   Perception
      (Dale Seymour)
   Up Close—Guess It! Card Sets:
      Nature-Made Things
      People-Made Things
      (Judy/Instructo)

PICTURE ARRANGEMENT

Picture Arrangement

I. **Purpose of the Subtest**

To measure the ability to place in correct sequence a series of pictures reflecting a real-life situation.

II. **Factors Affecting Subtest and Academic Performance**
   A. Visual attention
   B. Visual comprehension of a total situation
   C. Concentration
   D. Anxiety
   E. Cultural and environmental background
   F. Directionality
   G. Planning and organization
   H. Time element

III. **Educational Significance**
   A. Classroom activities should be arranged in a logical sequence so that the student may develop the concepts of temporal relationships and cause and effect.
   B. Encourage the student to participate in group activities presenting various social situations such as skits, plays, games, etc., in order to develop social awareness.
   C. Provide successful experiences that will motivate the student to make use of independent judgment.
   D. Present new material in an orderly, logical manner with explanations to insure student awareness.
   E. Proper order of letters and/or numbers should be reinforced with as many sensory modalities as possible—particularly the kinesthetic mode.

IV. **Long-Term Goal**

The learner will be able to place various learning materials in correct sequence reflecting real-life situations.

PICT. ARR.

Picture Arrangement

Short-Term Objectives

The learner will be able to

1. arrange pictures and objects in correct order.

2. select small objects and place them in sequential order to tell a story (e.g., small dolls and doll furniture).

3. put picture cards in the proper order from left to right to tell a story.

Instructional Level: K-3

Materials

1. *Sequence Cards, Groups I, II, III*
     (Educational Insights)
   Sequencor
     (Lauri)
   A Day at School, Logic Sequence Cards
   What Follows Next? Sequence Picture Cards
     (Ideal)
   Visual Sequencing
     (Frank Schaffer)
   Sequencing Beads and Design Cards
   Sequential Cards—By Color, Shape and Size
   Sequential Cards—Levels I, II, III
   Sequential Cards—From-To Series
   Sequential Cards—By Size
     (Incentives for Learning)

2. *Instructo Activity Kit: Let's Learn Sequence*
     (Judy/Instructo)
   Small or miniature toys or objects

3. *Sequence Picture Cards*
   Visual Big Box
     (DLM)
   Fairy Tale Sequencing
   Nursery Rhyme Sequencing
   Visual Sequencing
   Sequencing Cards
     (Frank Schaffer)
   Language Card Deck: Sequencing Cards
     (AGS)
   Sequencing Picture Cards
   Flannelboard Stories:
     Little Red Riding Hood
     Billy Goats Gruff
     Three Little Pigs
     (Judy/Instructo)

144

Picture Arrangement

Short-Term Objectives

The learner will be able to

Instructional Level: K-3

Materials

Sequential Cards—A Family's Day
Sequential Cards—Levels I, II, III
  (Incentives for Learning)

4. complete body puzzles by organizing or sequencing body parts into a whole.

4. *Body and Self-Awareness Big Box*
    (DLM)
   My Face and Body Flannelboard Aid
   Body Parts Puzzle, 6 Pieces
   Body Parts Puzzle, 12 Pieces
   Body Parts Puzzle, Girl
   Body Parts Puzzle, Boy
     (Judy/Instructo)
   Body Parts Puzzle
     (Lauri)

5. complete directional and sequential puzzles that develop cause-and-effect relationships.

5. *Sequencing Skills Boxed Activity Cards*
     (Frank Schaffer)
   Language Card Deck: Cause and Effect Cards
     (AGS)
   What Follows Next? Sequence Picture Cards
     (Ideal)
   Sequential Cards—From-To Series
     (Incentives for Learning)
   Visual Perception Big Box
   Sequence Picture Cards
   Seasonal Sequence Cards
     (DLM)

6. discuss the steps involved in good health habits.

6. *Health and Safety Listening Lab*
     (Troll)
   Choosing Good Health Habits
     (Steck-Vaughn)
   A Kid's Guide to Personal Hygiene— filmstrips, cassettes or video
     (Learning Tree)

PICT.
ARR.

145

Picture Arrangement

Short-Term Objectives

The learner will be able to

Instructional Level: K-3

Materials

7. arrange cartoon strips (four pictures) in the correct sequential order to tell a story.

7. *Sequencing Cards, 4-Scene Cards*
   (Frank Schaffer)
   What Follows Next? Sequence Picture Cards
   (Ideal)
   Teacher-made laminated cartoon strips from newspapers, comic books, etc.

8. place squares, triangles, and circles in progression of sizes from large to small and from small to large.

8. *Fit-a-Size*
   (Lauri)
   Sequencing Sizes—Which Is Big? Bigger? Biggest?
   (Ideal)
   Sequential Cards—By Color, Shape, and Size
   Sequential Cards—By Size
   (Incentives for Learning)
   Junior Thinklab
   (Scholastic)
   Patchworks: Size and Shape Recognition
   (Media Materials)

9. place wooden or plastic shapes in appropriately-shaped holes in a specified sequence.

9. *Form Fitter*
   (Playskool)
   Geometric Inset Board
   (Marvel)
   Coordination Board
   (Judy/Instructo)
   Fit-a-Shape
   Shape Squares
   (Lauri)

10. retell a story that has been read aloud by drawing or arranging simple pictures in proper sequence.

10. *Story Puzzlebooks:*
    A Day at the Park
    A Day at the Beach
    (Educational Insights)
    Flannelboard Stories:
    Goldilocks and the Three Bears
    Jack and the Beanstalk
    Cinderella

Picture Arrangement

Short-Term Objectives
The learner will be able to

Instructional Level: K-3
Materials

Rumplestiltskin
  (Judy/Instructo)
Library books
Children's magazines, etc.

11. demonstrate understanding of concepts of first, last, next to last, before, and after using flashcards or objects.

11. *Sequential Cards—Level I*
    (Incentives for Learning)
    The Game Bag Series: Game Bag I
    (Ideal)
    Visual Memory Cards: Sets I-IV
    (DLM)
    Follow Me!
    (LinguiSystems)

12. describe a meal by arranging pictures of food or play food in the order in which the food was eaten.

12. *Food and Nutrition Teaching Pictures*
    Lunch Food
    Breakfast Food
    Dinner Food, Sets 1 & 2
    (Marvel)
    Magazine pictures

13. follow specified directions in proper sequence.

13. *Following Directions*
    Sequencing
    (Milliken)
    Listening and Following Directions
    I Can Follow Directions, Grades K-1, 1-2, 2-3
    (Educational Insights)
    Following Directions—Reading with Zeebo
    (Frank Schaffer)
    Health and Safety Listening Lab
    People Who Work Listening Lab
    (Troll)

14. arrange in a specific sequence pictures of signs that must be recognized in everyday life.

14. *Functional Signs*
    (DLM)
    Safety Street
    Safety Signs
    (Bemiss-Jason)

PICT.
ARR.

147

Picture Arrangement

Short-Term Objectives	Instructional Level: K-3
The learner will be able to	**Materials**

<table>
<tr><td></td><td>

International Traffic Sign Set
Traffic Signs Teaching Picture Set
  (Marvel)
Traffic Safety Bulletin Board Set
  (Carson-Dellosa)
Fun-to-Know Flash Cards:
  Signs & Symbols
  (Trend)
Safety Signs and Symbols Desk Tape
  (Judy/Instructo)

</td></tr>
<tr><td>

15. begin, add to, or end a story appropriately.

</td><td>

15. *Disney Flannelboard Stories:*
  Peter Pan
  Bambi
  Snow White and the Seven Dwarfs
  Lady and the Tramp
  Winnie the Pooh and the Honey Tree
  Winnie the Pooh and the Blustery Day
  (Judy/Instructo)

</td></tr>
<tr><td>

16. circle the letters that are alike in a given row.

</td><td>

16. *Letter Tracking*
  Symbol/Letter Tracking
  Symbol Discrimination and Sequencing
  Symbol Discrimination Series
  (Ann Arbor)
  Visual Sequential Memory Exercises
  (DLM)
  Teacher-prepared worksheets

</td></tr>
<tr><td>

17. role play a story that has been read to the class.

</td><td>

17. *Giant Step Library*
  (Educational Insights)
  American Tall Tales Listening Lab
  (Troll)
  Disney Face Puppets:
  The Three Little Pigs
  Peter Pan
  Pinocchio
  Winnie-the-Pooh
  (Judy/Instructo)

</td></tr>
</table>

Picture Arrangement

Short-Term Objectives

The learner will be able to

Instructional Level: K-3

Materials

18. arrange in correct order from smallest to biggest, pictures of animals, objects, etc.

18. *Patchworks: Size Perception*
    (Media Materials)
    Sequential Cards—By Size
    Sequential Cards—By Color, Shape and Size
    (Incentives for Learning)
    Shellsorts
    (Ideal)

19. write the appropriate numerals or letters in blanks representing the missing items.

19. *Missing Numbers Kit*
    (Didax)
    Letter Perfect
    (Educational Insights)
    Teacher-prepared worksheets

20. count children or objects in a line in the ordinal positions of first, second, third, etc.

20. *The Game Bag Series: Game Bag I*
    (Ideal)
    Cardinal/Ordinal Puzzles
    (Incentives for Learning)

21. arrange color cards in shades from light to dark.

21. *Sorting Box Combination for Counting and Color*
    (Marvel)
    Paint chips from paint stores

22. follow simple sequential directions provided in a recipe.

22. *Following Directions: Intermediate Level*
    (Curriculum Associates)
    Cook and Learn
    (Addison-Wesley)

23. tell what would happen next in a story read by the teacher.

23. *Storybooks Plus*
    (Curriculum Associates)

PICT.
ARR.

Picture Arrangement

Short-Term Objectives

The learner will be able to

Instructional Level: 3-6

Materials

1. list road, street, and safety signs and match the proper sign to the written word (e.g., go, stop, walk, exit, etc.).

1. *Functional Signs*
   (DLM)
   Survival Signs
   Road Signs of the Times
   (Ideal)
   Fun-to-Know Flash Cards: Signs and Symbols
   (Trend)
   Safety Signs and Symbols Desk Tape
   (Judy/Instructo)

2. discuss Aesop's fables after hearing the stories read aloud.

2. *The World of Reading Series: The World of Fables*
   Read-Along Aesop's Fables
   (Educational Insights)

3. mount pages of comics on heavy cardboard, cut the pages into individual pictures, and read the story in proper sequence.

3. Newspaper comic strips
   Comic books, etc.

4. arrange in correct sequential order a scrambled alphabet.

4. *Avalanche of Letters*
   (Lauri)
   Letter Perfect
   Tub O' Letters Upper Case
   Tub O' Letters Lower Case
   (Educational Insights)
   Felt Letters Upper Case
   Felt Letters Lower Case
   (Judy/Instructo)

5. complete activity sheets which have blanks (e.g., ___ , d, ___ , f, ___ , h, i, ___).

5. *Letter Perfect*
   (Educational Insights)
   Teacher-made worksheets

6. arrange dominoes in order by numbers (e.g., six-blank, six-one, six-two, etc.).

6. *Jumbo Dominoes*
   (Ideal)
   Tactile Domino Blocks
   (Childcraft)
   Dominoes
   (Milton Bradley)

Picture Arrangement

Short-Term Objectives

The learner will be able to

7. prepare a monthly class calendar and chart class activities on it.

8. identify differences among objects or pictures of objects that are found in the same category (e.g., airplane-helicopter, car-truck, chair-bed, etc.).

9. list the steps involved in completing a health activity (e.g., brushing teeth, washing hair, bathing, dressing, etc.).

10. role-play with other members of the class the proper social behavior that should take place in a given situation (e.g., a trip to the zoo, shopping with baby sister, going to the grocery store for mother, etc.).

11. lead the class in performing a series of physical exercises that is imitated by other students in correct sequence.

12. reproduce block designs according to size, shape, and color.

Instructional Level: 3-6

Materials

7. *Day by Day Calendar*
   (Media Materials)
   Judy Calendar
   (Judy/Instructo)

8. *Find Your Way with Words*
   FILE
   (LinguiSystems)
   Concept Understanding Program-CUP
   Photo Libraries I and II
   (Incentives for Learning)

9. *Personal Skills: Nutrition and*
   Health Care
   (Mission)
   Health and Safety Listening Lab
   (Troll)
   The Health Parade
   (Hayes)

10. *Revised: Developing Understanding of*
    Self and Others—DUSO-R
    (AGS)
    A Kid's Guide to:
    Getting Along with Others
    Manners
    Friendship
    (Learning Tree)
    Social Skills
    (Mission)

12. *Design Blocks and Patterns*
    (Ideal)
    Cubes in Color
    Cubes in Color Design Cards

PICT.
ARR.

151

Picture Arrangement

Short-Term Objectives

The learner will be able to

Instructional Level: 3-6

Materials

Sequential Cards—By Color, Shape, and Size
  (Incentives for Learning)
Colored Inch Cube Designs
  (DLM)

13. place design cards into the proper sequential steps needed to obtain a given final design.

13. *Eye-Cue Puzzles*
  (Dale Seymour)
  Geometric Shape Three-Sided Dominoes
  (Judy/Instructo)
  Attribute Dominoes
  Geopiece Set
  Geopiece Math Book
  Triangles
  (Delta)

14. arrange a jumbled list of daily events into correct chronological sequence (e.g., a class schedule).

14. Teacher-prepared material

15. identify and correctly spell deliberately misspelled words included among a list of words from reading vocabulary, spelling words, etc.

15. Teacher-prepared lists

16. fill in the missing factor in mathematical equations (e.g., ___ + 3 = 5, 8 - ___ = 2, etc.).

16. *Math Relationship Cards*
  Horizontal Flash Cards
  (Ideal)
  Cross Math Puzzles
  (Incentives for Learning)

17. cut and place in correct sequence pictures from comic strips, newspapers, comic books, etc.

17. *Sequencing Cards, 4-Scene Cards*
  (Frank Schaffer)
  What Follows Next? Sequence Picture Cards
  (Ideal)

18. arrange pictures of indoor, outdoor, and occupational activities in correct sequence.

18. *Let's Learn Sequence*
  (Judy/Instructo)
  What Follows Next? Sequence Picture Cards

Picture Arrangement

Short-Term Objectives

The learner will be able to

Instructional Level: 3-6

Materials

A Day At School, Logic Sequence Cards
  (Ideal)
Sequential Cards—Levels II and III
Sequential Cards—A Family's Day
  (Incentives for Learning)

19. arrange individual letters in correct sequence to spell specific words.

19. *Avalanche of Letters*
  (Lauri)
Alpha Tiles
Tub O' Letters, Lower Case
Tub O' Letters, Upper Case
  (Educational Insights)
Super Alphabet Pack
  (Judy/Instructo)
Anagrams
  (Selchow & Righter)

20. arrange pictures in correct sequence to produce grammatically correct sentences.

20. *Fokes Sentence Builder*
Fokes Sentence Builder Expansion
  (DLM)
Story Puzzlebooks:
 A Day at the Park
 A Day at the Beach
  (Educational Insights)
Photo Libraries I and II
Photo Packs, Verbs and Verb Tenses
  (Incentives for Learning)
Language Master: Reading Through Pictures
  (Bell & Howell)

Picture Arrangement

Short-Term Objectives

The learner will be able to

1. relate stories viewed in pictures and filmstrips in class.

2. differentiate between different characteristics of objects (e.g., shape, color, size, thickness). (The level of difficulty is controlled by varying the numbers of objects used.)

3. perform gestures illustrating titles of movies, books, etc.

4. complete exercise sheets designed to stimulate thinking and conversation.

Instructional Level: 6-9

Materials

1. *Watership Down*—video
   Mrs. Frisby and the Rats of NIMH—software
   Island of the Blue Dolphins—software
   A Wrinkle in Time—software
      (Sunburst)
   Tricky Picture Stories
      (Educational Insights)
   Tales From the Odyssey—filmstrips
   Famous Tales of Suspense—filmstrips
      (Troll)

2. *Attribute Tiles*
      (Educational Insights)
   Attribute Blocks Class Set
      (Didax)
   Geometric Plastic Forms
      (Ideal)
   Geometric Solids
   Attribute Shapes
      (Delta)

3. *Charades*
      (Selchow and Righter)
   Kids on Stage
      (Troll)
   *Aids to Psycholinguistic Teaching:
   Manual Expression*
      (Charles E. Merrill)

4. *Building Thinking Skills, Books 2 & 3*
      (Midwest)
   Discovering Logic
   Adventures with Logic
      (Fearon)
   *Mind Power II: Thinking Skills in
   Reading and Language Arts*—software
   Thinklab
      (SRA)

Picture Arrangement

Short-Term Objectives

The learner will be able to

Instructional Level: 6-9

Materials

5. locate places on the map where current events are happening.

5. USA map
World map
State map

6. organize material into proper sequence after reading or hearing short stories, plays and open-ended materials.

6. *Scope Plays*
(Scholastic)
American Short Stories
Inductive Thinking Skills: Open-Ended Problems
Organized Thinking
(Midwest)
Classification and Organizational Skills—Developmental
(Curriculum Associates)

7. complete exercise sheets by listening to tapes which are designed to help the student recognize relationships and simple analogies.

7. *Thinkathon I, II, III, IV*
(Educational Impressions)
Basic Thinking Skills: Analogies A, B, C, D
Beginning Thinking Skills, Books 2 & 3
(Midwest)
Thinklab
(Scholastic)
Troll Listening Lab, Grades 5-6, 7-8-9
(Troll)
Connections: Working with Analogies
(Continental Press)
Strategies for Analogies
(DLM)
Cognitive Challenge Cards
(ATP)
MORE Vocabulary To Go
BESST
Semantics for Teens
(LinguiSystems)

PICT.
ARR.

155

Picture Arrangement

Short-Term Objectives

The learner will be able to

Instructional Level: 6-9

Materials

8. determine the best solution to a given problem situation when given more than one possible solution.

8. *Problem Solving for Teens*
   TOPS Kit—Elementary
     (LinguiSystems)
   Six Puzzles—software
   Mind Castles I & II—software
     (Opportunities for Learning)
   A-Way with Problems
     (Educational Impressions)

9. arrange pictures in a sequential order to tell a sensible story.

9. *Sequential Picture Cards*
     (DLM)
   Sequential Cards—Level III
   Sequential Cards—From-To Series
   Sequential Cards—A Family's Day
     (Incentives for Learning)

10. cut apart a cartoon strip, paste on cardboard squares, and arrange the pictures in correct sequence.

10. Newspaper comic strips
    Comic books

11. complete puzzles at the appropriate age level.

11. *Brain Stretchers, Books 1 & 2*
    Mind Benders, Grades 2-6, 6-10
    Mind Benders, Grades 2-6, 6-10—
      software
      (Midwest)
    Comprehension Games:
      Sequence/What Comes First
      Time Capsule—Ten
      (Learning Well)
    I.Q. Games
      (Educational Insights)

12. write in correct sequence basic rules for playing games (e.g., "Dominoes," "Old Maid," etc.).

13. discuss the meanings of fables, proverbs, and idioms.

13. *The World of Reading: The World of Fables*
    Readalong Aesop's Fables
      (Educational Insights)

Picture Arrangement

Short-Term Objectives

The learner will be able to

Instructional Level: 6-9

Materials

Fables, Legends and Folktales
  (Hayes)
Idiom's Delight
  (High Noon Books)

14. make inferences and draw conclusions from reading materials.

14. *Reading Comprehension Series:*
    Making Inferences
    Drawing Conclusions
      (Educational Insights)
    Comprehension Games:
    Drawing Conclusion/Bingo
    Inference/School Days
      (Learning Well)
    Clues for Better Reading Kits 2 and 3
      (Opportunities for Learning)
    Inductive Thinking Skills:
    Inferences A & B
      (Midwest)

15. discuss feelings or emotions appropriate for various situations (e.g., birthdays, weddings, funerals, etc.).

15. *Moods and Emotions Teaching Pictures*
    Children and the Law Teaching
      Pictures
      (Marvel)
    Revised Developing Understanding of
      Self and others—DUSO-R
    Transition
    TAD: Toward Affective Development
      (AGS)
    Thinking About Feelings
      (Opportunities for Learning)
    Living Skills: Every Kid's Guide
      to Feelings
      (Mission)

16. arrange individual words in correct order to produce specific sentences.

16. *Build a Sentence Game*
    Super Sentence Game
      (Creative Teaching Associates)
    Tub O' Words Sentence Tiles
    GrammaRummy
      (Educational Insights)
    What's the Word Game

PICT.
ARR.

Picture Arrangement

Short-Term Objectives

The learner will be able to

Instructional Level: 6-9

Materials

*Word-Picture Program: Everyday
    Words*
The Reading Game Sight Vocabulary
    (Bell & Howell)
Word and Phrase Sentence Building
    (Kenworthy)

17. draw a series of individual pictures depicting a sequence of events or experiences for his classmates to arrange in correct order.

18. arrange in correct sequence individual sentences to make a sensible paragraph.

18. *High Noon Word Card Kits*
    Story Sequence Cards
       (High Noon Books)
    Teacher-prepared sentences

19. draw pictures in correct sequence following taped directions.

19. Teacher-prepared directions

20. report in correct sequence the events that occur in stories.

20. *Comprehension Games: Sequences/
       What Comes Next*
       (Learning Well)
    T.L.C. Reading Center
    Big League Comprehension Kits
       (Educational Insights)
    Scope Visuals 23: Context Clues
    *Scope Visuals 26: Building Critical
       Reading Skills*
       (Scholastic)

21. complete simple experiments designed to illustrate sources and the cycle of water.

21. *Water Cycle Study Cards*
    Water Cycle Poster
    *Water Cycle Simulation Model with
       Study Cards*
       (Hubbard)
    We Care About Our World Chart Pack
    Environmental Awareness Chart Pack
       (American Teaching Aids)

Picture Arrangement

Short-Term Objectives

The learner will be able to

22. discuss the recycling of various waste materials.

Instructional Level: 6-9

Materials

22. *Reduce, Reuse, Recycle!*
    (Trend)
    The Perils of Pollution
    (Creative Teaching Press)
    Recycling Game
    Recycling Filmstrip
    (Hubbard)

PICT.
ARR.

Picture Arrangement

Short-Term Objectives

The learner will be able to

1. arrange in correct sequence four- and five-picture series cartoon strips which have been cut apart to tell a story.

2. prepare a tape stressing rules of conduct within the school setting.

3. complete an open-ended story so that it will have a social lesson.

4. list what is considered to be good sportsmanlike conduct in a particular game (e.g., baseball, volleyball, etc.).

5. perform tasks in game situations with only one try at a time (e.g., matching turned-down cards on a table).

6. verbally describe current events in correct order of occurrence.

Instructional Level: 9-12

Materials

1. Newspaper comic strips
   Comic books

2. School handbook

3. *Transitions*
   (AGS)
   Values
   Decision Making For Success in Life
   (Educational Insights)
   Relationships & Values: What Really Matters?
   (Opportunities for Learning)
   Scope Skills Books: Developing Thinking Skills
   Scope Visuals: Building Critical Reading Skills
   (Scholastic)
   You Are the School Counselor
   (High Noon Books)

5. *Concentration*
   (Milton Bradley)
   Deck of playing cards

6. Pictures and articles cut from newspapers and magazines

Picture Arrangement

Short-Term Objectives

The learner will be able to

Instructional Level: 9-12

Materials

7. discuss vocations and avocations with the class, choose a job to apply for, and role-play an interview with predetermined questions.

7. *Learning About Careers Teaching Pictures*
   (Marvel)
   Working Choices Game
   (Media Materials)
   Getting a Job
   Preparing for Your Career:
   Career Awareness
   Finding a Job
   The Interview
   Get Hired!
   Job Interview Skills
   (Opportunities for Learning)
   Vocational Entry—Skills for Secondary Students
   (ATP)
   You Are the Boss
   (High Noon Books)

8. write in the missing words when given sentences with every fifth word missing. (This activity should begin with the reading material two grades below independent reading level.)

8. *Sentence Tracking*
   Word Tracking: High Frequency Words
   Word Tracking: Proverbs
   Word Tracking: Limericks
   (Ann Arbor)
   Teacher-prepared material

9. state the events of a short story in correct order after hearing it read aloud.

10. complete paper and pencil tracking exercises.

10. *Symbol/Letter Tracking*
    Symbol Discrimination and Sequencing
    Sentence Tracking
    Thought Tracking
    (Ann Arbor)

11. discuss feelings and emotions in various situations (e.g., when parents refuse to give permission, when "stood up" by a date, etc.).

11. *Getting Through the Bad Times: Teen-Age Crises*
    If It Were You—filmstrip
    (Opportunities for Learning)

PICT. ARR.

Picture Arrangement

Short-Term Objectives

The learner will be able to

12. record a tape describing proper behavior in various situations (e.g., parties, games, eating dinner, weddings, etc.).

13. differentiate between attributes of objects, people, etc. (e.g., differences in appearance, size, color, etc.).

14. discuss the changes that occur as a person grows from birth to death.

15. describe in correct sequence the steps required to cook a particular recipe.

16. relate to the class the step-by-step process involved in various craft projects.

17. list the steps involved in doing household chores (e.g., making up the bed, preparing a meal, washing the car).

Instructional Level: 9-12

Materials

12. *If It Were You*—filmstrip (Opportunities for Learning)

15. *A Special Picture Cookbook* (Edmark)
    Bake and Taste (Cambridge Development Laboratory)

16. *The Ultimate Airplane*
    Make Your Own Working Paper Clock (Dale Seymour)
    Container Crafts
    String Art (Judy/Instructo)
    Using Recyclables for Arts & Crafts (Instructional Fair)
    Crafts magazines
    Model kits
    Leather craft kits
    Cross stitch kits

Picture Arrangement

Short-Term Objectives	Instructional Level: 9-12
The learner will be able to	**Materials**

18. discuss the sequence of events that occur in the life cycle of insects.

18. *Some Cycles Study Cards*
    (Hubbard)
    The World of Insects
    (Eye Gate Media)
    Science Activities Center:
    Insects
    (Educational Insights)
    Insect Life Cycles Flannelboard Aid
    (Judy/Instructo)

19. place color slides and prerecorded music and sound effects in specific sequences to develop slide-and-sound stories.

19. *Some Sounds*—filmstrip
    (Hubbard)

20. list on a job application the information required.

20. *Real Life Program:*
    Decision Making
    Employment
    Getting a Job Series: The Job
    Application Form
    Preparing for Your Career Workbooks:
    Applying for a Job
    (Opportunities for Learning)
    Vocational Entry-Skills for Secondary
    Students
    (ATP)
    Applications for jobs from various businesses and industries

PICT.
ARR.

BLOCK DESIGN

Block Design

I. Purpose of the Subtest

To measure the ability to look at an abstract design, analyze it into parts, and reproduce it using appropriately colored blocks.

II. Factors Affecting Subtest and Academic Performance

A. Discrimination
B. Visualization of parts
C. Perceptual organization
D. Spatial orientation
E. Concrete and abstract conceptualization
F. Visual-motor integration and coordination
G. Anxiety
H. Concentration
I. Color consciousness
J. Time element

III. Educational Significance

A. In preparing assignments which must be copied from the chalkboard or from other sources of written or printed material, consideration should be given to the amount of information the student will be able to complete in the given period of time. Begin with a minimum amount of copy work and increase the amount as the child's ability to perform improves.

B. Keep all visually presented material simple in format and uncluttered by excessive stimuli. Words should be written or typed in large letters and well spaced. Restrict the amount of work required on a single page.

C. Assist the student in planning and organizing assigned tasks written on paper by providing visual cues such as color coding, numbering lines, arrows, and boxes in which to work, etc.

D. When giving directions, be specific and use concrete cues. For example, say, "Write this word next to the number one on your paper," rather than "Write this word on your paper."

E. Additional time should be allowed for the student to complete and master a task. Frequent reinforcement exercises will be necessary.

F. Teaching techniques should begin with the identification of individual parts, moving to integrated wholes.

IV. Long-Term Goal

The learner will be able to analyze a meaningful whole into individual parts and reproduce it.

BLOCK
DES.

Block Design

Short-Term Objectives

The learner will be able to

1. sort concrete objects according to color, size, and shape.

2. reproduce a design by using his body as part of a geometric shape. (This could be more easily achieved by utilizing small groups of students and assigning one particular shape to recreate.)

3. reproduce designs drawn on paper or cards using manipulative materials such as colored cubes, pegs, etc.

Instructional Level: K-3

Materials

1. *Sort and Stack*
   Geometric Pegboard
   Shapes and Color Abacus
      (Constructive Playthings)
   Attribute Set: Shapes, Sizes, Colors
   Shapes, Sizes and Shapes, Colors and
      Shapes
      (Judy/Instructo)
   Attribute Block Desk Set
      (Learning Resources)
   Attribute Sorting Set
      (Ideal)
   Shape Sorter and Stacker
      (Media Materials)
   Shape and Color Sorter
      (Lauri)
   Counting and Sorting Tray
      (Summit Learning)

2. *Positions in Space*
      (Constructive Playthings)

3. *Color Tiles Activities*
      (Cuisenaire)
   Large Parquetry Designs
   Large Parquetry
   Colored Inch Cubes and Designs in
      Perspective
      (DLM)
   Classroom Manipulative Organizer Kits
      (Houghton Mifflin)
   Large Colored Beads and Patterns
   Shapes and Form Game
      (Constructive Playthings)
   Find-a-Form Magnet Set
      (Judy/Instructo)

Block Design

Short-Term Objectives

The learner will be able to

Instructional Level: K-3

Materials

The Math Machine:
  Pattern Block Games
  Tangram Puzzles
Pegboard Fun with Patterns
Two-Dimensional Color Block Designs
Cube Pattern Cards
One-Inch Colored Cubes
    (Ideal)
Large Parquetry Design Blocks
Large Parquetry Patterns
Cubical Counting Blocks
Cubical Blocks Pattern Cards
    (Media Materials)
Stickybear Shapes—software
    (EBSCO)
Half 'n Half Design and Color
    (Ann Arbor)

4. select a geometric figure from a group presented on the chalkboard and draw it on paper.

4. *Geoboard Set*
    (Childcraft)

5. make a ball or a pyramid by putting together forms of graduated sizes.

5. *Shape Sorter and Stacker*
    (Playskool)
Stacking Clown
Shape Stack Tower
    (Learning Resources)

6. reproduce in correct perspective patterns using colored blocks. (The level of difficulty can be increased by setting a time limit.)

6. *Colored Inch Cubes and Designs*
   in Perspective
    (DLM)
Design Blocks and Patterns
Cube Pattern Cards
One-Inch Colored Cubes
    (Ideal)
Cubes in Color
Cubes in Color Design Cards
    (Incentives for Learning)
Color Cubes
Cube Patterns
    (Judy/Instructo)

Block Design

Short-Term Objectives
The learner will be able to

Instructional Level: K-3
Materials

Cubical Counting Blocks
Cubical Block Pattern Cards
  (Media Materials)
Colored Counting Cubes
Plain Counting Cubes
Colored Cube Activity Cards
  (Summit Learning)

7. toss bean bags through the holes in a toss board. (This could be a game if you have more than one hole and set different scores for each hole.)

7. *Clown Bean Bag Set*
  (Judy/Instructo)
  Beano Bean Bag Set
  (Ideal)

8. fit correctly holes in squares over a specific number of pegs.

8. *Number Puzzle*
  Shape Sorter
  (Childcraft)
  Number Sorter
  (Constructive Playthings)
  Geometric Color Clown
  (Learning Resources)
  Fit-a-Group
  Number Sorter
  (Lauri)
  Match Pegs
  (Judy/Instructo)

9. "build" an animal or figure using building toys, pipe cleaners, or other materials.

9. *Large DUPLO Basic Set*
  Large LEGO Basic Set
  (LEGO)
  Snap 'N Play
  Magnet Blocks
  (Marvel)
  Tinkertoys
  (Milton Bradley)
  Googolplex
  Rods and Connectors
  (Delta)
  Straws
  Pipe cleaners

Block Design

Short-Term Objectives

The learner will be able to

Instructional Level: K-3

Materials

10. hit a ball which is hanging suspended on a string. (A foam bat or a bat made from a broom handle may be used. The level of difficulty of this activity may be increased by painting different color stripes on the handle of the bat and specifying which color should hit the ball. Another variation of the activity requires the student to hit the ball while blindfolded.)

11. play "Perceptual Bingo" by matching the "called" shapes to the appropriate form on a tablet or card.

11. *Kitty Kat Color and Shape Bingo*
    (Educational Insights)
    Color & Shape Bingo
    Color & Shape Lotto
    (Trend)
    Bearamores Learn Colors and Shapes
    (Media Materials)

BLOCK DES.

12. construct number staircases and number pictures using colored cubes or beads.

12. *Cubicle Counting Blocks*
    (Milton Bradley)
    Counting Towers
    (Constructive Playthings)
    Unifix 1-10 Stair
    Unifix Cubes
    (Didax)
    Multilinks Counting Board
    Magnetic Counting Game and Abacus
    (Delta)
    Cuisenaire Rods
    (Cuisenaire)

13. "make" cookies from play dough which match a shape drawn on paper.

13. *Play-Doh*
    (Playskool)
    Modeling clay
    Cookie cutters

14. create an original design for the class to reproduce using pegs and pegboards.

14. *Jumbo Tactilmat Pegboard*
    Easy Grip Pegs
    Large Pegboard Patterns
    Deluxe Pegboard Set

171

Block Design

Short-Term Objectives

The learner will be able to

Instructional Level: K-3

Materials

Developmental Pegboard Activities
Beaded Pegboard Set
Pegboard Fun with Patterns
    (Ideal)

15. play games with dominoes which require the matching of designs and pictures.

15. *Dominoes*
    (Ideal)
    Animals Dominoes
    Colors and Shapes Dominoes
    (Frank Schaffer)
    Early Concepts Skillbuilder:
      Match It—software
    Tactile Dominoes
    (EBSCO)
    Animal Dominoes
    Shadow Dominoes
    Arrow Dominoes
    (Marvel)

16. complete cutting and folding exercises.

16. *Fables and Tales Papercrafts*
    A Paper Menagerie
    (Fearon)
    Paper Folding with Origami Techniques
    Paper Shapes Projects
    Fold-A-Circus
    Creative Paper Animals
    (Judy/Instructo)

17. complete written activity sheets which stress exercises in figure-ground perception.

17. *Graphing Hidden Pictures (K-1), (2-3)*
    (Carson-Dellosa)
    Hidden Alpha-Pix
    (Zaner-Bloser)
    Teddy Bear Search
    (Media Materials)
    Hidden Pictures K-1, 1-2
    (Frank Schaffer)
    Hidden Pictures and Objects
    (Hayes)
    Perceptual Activities
    (Ann Arbor)

Block Design

Short-Term Objectives

The learner will be able to

Instructional Level: K-3

Materials

18. reproduce designs using triangles, hexangles, and quadrilaterals.

18. *Tangram Treasury*
      (Cuisenaire)
    Paper Shapes Projects
    Find-a-Form Magnet Set
    Geometric Shape Three-Sided Dominoes
    Tangram Puzzles
    Tangram Patterns
      (Judy/Instructo)
    Wooden Pattern Blocks
    The Math Machine: Tangram Puzzles
      (Ideal)

19. match cards with separate objects corresponding in number to a group of objects.

19. *Numbers Lotto Game*
      (Trend)
    Locking Numbers
    Numberite
      (Constructive Playthings)
    Number Plaques
    Number Play
      (Lauri)
    Count and See
      (Learning Resources)
    Peg-It Number Boards
    Dominoes
      (Ideal)
    Number and Picture Matching Cards
      (Didax)
    Number Play
      (Marvel)

20. reproduce spelling words with individual letters.

20. *Beaded Alphabet Cards*
    Foam Letters
    Jumbo Alphabet:
      Upper Case
      Lower Case
      (Ideal)
    Magnetic Capital Letters
    Magnetic Lowercase Letters

BLOCK
DES.

173

Block Design

Short-Term Objectives	Instructional Level: K-3
The learner will be able to	**Materials**

<table>
<tr><td></td><td>

Red Felt Letters/Uppercase
Red Felt Letters/Lowercase
   (Judy/Instructo)
Avalanche of Letters
   (Lauri)
Tub O' Letters
   (Educational Insights)
Spelling Wheels
   (Constructive Playthings)
Link Letters
   (Milton Bradley)

</td></tr>
<tr><td>

21. match a required number of geometric forms within specified time limits.

</td><td>

21. *Fit-a-Shape*
Fit-a-Space
Fit-a-Size
   (Lauri)
Overhead Attribute Blocks
Attribute Blocks Desk Set
   (Learning Resources)
Geometric Shapes Lotto
   (Judy/Instructo)
Colors and Shapes Lotto
   (Trend)

</td></tr>
<tr><td>

22. complete dot-to-dot activities.

</td><td>

22. *Alphabet Dot-to-Dot*
   (Frank Schaffer)
Perceptual Activities Packets:
 Dot-to-Dot
Perceptual Activities
   (Ann Arbor)
Dot-to-Dot Wipe-Off Books
   (Trend)

</td></tr>
</table>

174

Block Design

Short-Term Objectives

The learner will be able to

1. sort objects made of wood or plastic according to shapes within specified time limits.

2. complete worksheets containing incomplete geometric designs or figures.

3. select from a box of tactile materials the appropriate pieces to reproduce a design presented on a card.

4. reproduce forms with match sticks, Tinkertoys, popsicle sticks, etc.

Instructional Level: 3-6

Materials

1. *Counters*
   Counting Sheep
      (Lauri)
   Attribute Sorting Set
      (Ideal)
   Teddy Bear Counters
   Blocks 'N Bears
   Cubical Counting Blocks
   Plastic Counters
      (Media Materials)

2. *Visual-Motor Readiness Set*
      (Continental Press)
   Perceptual Development Cards
      (Ideal)
   Shape Tracer Set
   Attribute Block Templates
      (Learning Resources)
   Perceptual Activities Packets:
    Finish the Picture 1 & 2
   Half 'n Half Design and Color
      (Ann Arbor)

3. *Patterns for Pattern Blocks*
   Puzzle Grams
      (Ideal)
   Bigbeads
   Bigbead Pattern Cards
   Puzzle Tiles
   Puzzle Tile Pattern Cards
      (Educational Insights)
   Perception Puzzles
   Crepe Foam Rubber Picture Puzzles
   Fit-a-Space
      (Lauri)

4. *Tinkertoys*
      (Playskool)
   Rods and Connectors
      (Delta)
   LEGO Basic Set

BLOCK DES.

175

Block Design

Short-Term Objectives

The learner will be able to

Instructional Level: 3-6

Materials

DUPLO Basic Set
(LEGO)

5. reproduce designs using objects such as pegboards, ceiling tiles with golf tees or colored thumbtacks, board with nails or tacks.

5. *Classroom Manipulatives and Organizer Kits*
(Houghton Mifflin)
Deluxe Pegboard Set
Pegboard Fun with Patterns
(Ideal)
Mosaic Shapes and Designs
(LEGO)
Plastic Geoboard
Rubber Bands
(Learning Resources)
Hold-Tight Pegboard Set
Jumbo Hold-Tight Peg Sets
(Marvel)

6. outline specified figures such as a map of the U.S. in colors or with a dark pencil.

6. *Common Shapes Stencils*
Dinosaurs and Prehistoric Stencils
(Trend)
Blank Map Outlines—U.S. and the World
(Instructional Fair)
Pencil Stencils
(Ideal)
Outline Maps of the USA
(Hayes)

7. perform dot-to-dot activities.

7. *Perceptual Activities Packets: Dot-to-Dot, 1 & 2*
Perceptual Activities
(Ann Arbor)
Aids to Psycholinguistic Teaching: Visual Sequential Memory
(Charles E. Merrill)
Vocabulary Connection
"What Shall I Do Now, Teacher?"
(Remedia)

176

Block Design

Short-Term Objectives

The learner will be able to

Instructional Level: 3-6

Materials

8. put together puzzles appropriate for age and grade level.

8. *Block Construction*—software
(Sunburst)
Crepe Foam Rubber Picture Puzzles
Large Pattern Puzzles
Map Skills
Dinorama
(Lauri)

9. identify the hidden object in figure-ground exercises.

9. *Frostig Program for the Development of Visual Perception*
(Follett)
'M' Is for Mirror: Find the Hidden Pictures
(Dale Seymour)
Graphing Hidden Pictures, 4, 5, 6
(Milliken)
Hidden Alpha-Pix
(Zaner-Bloser)
Puzzle Pals
(Scholastic)
Teddy Bear Search
(Media Materials)
TalkAbout Books:
In the City
In the Country
(Educational Insights)

10. arrange individual alphabet letters into words from a reading, vocabulary, spelling, or Dolch word list.

10. *Avalanche of Letters*
(Lauri)
Letter Perfect
Tub O' Letters
(Educational Insights)
Economo Word Builder
Link Letters
(Milton Bradley)
Make-a-Word Spelling Game
(Didax)
Word Builder:
Small Letter Cards
Large Letter Cards
(Kenworthy)

BLOCK DES.

Block Design

Short-Term Objectives

The learner will be able to

Instructional Level: 3-6

Materials

*Michigan Programmed Spelling,
Levels 1, 2, 3*
*Word Express: The First 2,500 Words
of Spoken English—Illustrated*
(ATP)
Spelling Wheels
(Constructive Playthings)

11. arrange individual word cards into sensible sentences.

11. *Easy Sight Words Flash Cards,
Sets 1, 2, 3*
(Frank Schaffer)
GrammaRummy
Sight Words Flash Cards, Levels 1 & 2
(Educational Insights)
Sentence Builder
Economo Sentence Builder
Educational Flash Words
(Milton Bradley)
Word and Phrase Sentence Builder
(Kenworthy)
Super Sentence Game
Build a Sentence Game
(Creative Teaching Associates)
Color Coded Sentence Building Kit
(Didax)
*Switchboard: A Sentence Game for
Word Operators—*software
(Sunburst)
Sentence Cube Game
(Selchow and Righter)

12. circle the words in a list of real and nonsense words.

12. *Word Tracking: High Frequency
Words*
Sentence Tracking
*Sentence Tracking: High Frequency
Words*
(Ann Arbor)
Teacher-prepared list

13. recognize misspelled words from a spelling list and correctly spell them either orally or in writing.

Block Design

Short-Term Objectives

The learner will be able to

Instructional Level: 3-6

Materials

14. arrange various sentences into a sensible story.

14. *Hide 'N Sequence*—software
    (Sunburst)
    What Comes First/Sequence—
    software
    (Troll)

15. put together correctly models, mosaic patterns, bead patterns, etc.

15. *Mosaic Shapes and Designs*
    Mosaic Puzzles:
      Countryside
      Town
      Domestic Animals
      Farm Animals
      Wild Animals
      (LEGO)
    Exploring with Color Tiles
    Color Tiles Activities
    Color Tiles
      (Dale Seymour)
    Plastic Disks for Lacing
    Laces for Stringing
    Building Bead Patterns
    Large Colored Beads & Patterns
      (Ideal)
    Model kits
    Mosaic tile kits

16. match parts of compound words, using a master list for reference.

16. *Language Master:*
      Reading Game
      Sound System—Discoveries
      Compound Words and Simple
      Endings
        (Bell & Howell)
    Compound Word Puzzles
      (Ideal)
    Syllable Systems
    Compound Word Puzzles
      (Incentives for Learning)
    Skill Power Teaching Units:
      Compounds
    SkillKeepers, Levels C, D, E
      (Remedia)
    Teacher-prepared list of words

BLOCK
DES.

Block Design

Short-Term Objectives

The learner will be able to

Instructional Level: 3-6

Materials

17. reproduce designs in correct perspective with colored cubes.

17. *DIME Mathematics:*
      Book 1: DIME Build-Up
      DIME Solids Kit
    Exploring with Squares and Cubes
       (Dale Seymour)
    Cube Pattern Cards
    One-Inch Multicolored Cubes
    Color Pattern Board
    Two-Dimensional Color Block
       Designs
       (Ideal)
    Colored Inch Cubes and Designs in
       Perspective
       (DLM)
    Cubes in Color
    Cubes in Color Design Cards
       (Incentives for Learning)
    Cubical Counting Blocks
    Cubical Block Pattern Cards
       (Media Materials)

18. reproduce small parquetry designs with progressively greater abstraction.

18. *Small Parquetry and Designs I and II*
       (DLM)
    Pocket Parquetry and Patterns
       (Ideal)
    Pattern Blocks
    Pattern Blocks Activities
       (Dale Seymour)

19. reproduce complex designs using multicolored blocks or puzzles.

19. *Tangram Treasury*
       (Cuisenaire)
    Tangram Kit
    Tangrammables
       (Learning Resources)
    ESS Tangram Cards, Sets I-III
       (Dale Seymour)
    Design Blocks and Patterns
    The Math Machine:
       Tangram Puzzles
       Pattern Blocks Puzzles
       (Ideal)

Block Design

Short-Term Objectives

The learner will be able to

Instructional Level: 3-6

Materials

20. fill in outlines of designs with parquetry pieces.

20. *Small Parquetry Designs I-III*
    Tangram and Puzzle Cards
       (DLM)
    Tangram Puzzles
    Tangram Patterns
       (Judy/Instructo)
    Puzzlegrams
    Pocket Parquetry and Patterns
       (Ideal)
    Pattern Blocks
    Pattern Blocks Activities
       (Dale Seymour)

21. match random arrangements of designs with structured arrangements of the same design.

21. *Colored Inch Cubes*
    Colored Inch Cube Designs
       (DLM)
    Geometric Shape Three-Sided
       Dominoes
       (Judy/Instructo)
    Random Pattern Dominoes
       (Marvel)
    Memory: Memory Building Blocks—
       software
    Discrimination, Attributes, and Rules:
       *Tip 'N Flip—*software
       (Sunburst)

BLOCK
DES.

Block Design

Short-Term Objectives

The learner will be able to

1. reproduce figures on paper that have been presented by a tachistoscopic method. (Progress from simple to complex designs.)

2. play games requiring the student to recall what was seen, such as matching playing cards turned face down.

3. complete eye-hand coordination exercises by tapping a suspended ball with a bat to certain rhythm patterns.

4. reproduce an abstract design on paper or with objects from memory.

5. complete dot-to-dot exercises.

6. embroider with a simple cross-stitch designs stamped on fabric.

7. reproduce a design presented on one half of a checkerboard on the other half.

Instructional Level: 6-9

Materials

1. Tachistoscope

2. *Visual Sequential Memory Exercises*
     (DLM)
   Memory Jogger, Gr. 4-6
   Memory Master—software
     (EBSCO)
   Original Memory
     (Milton Bradley)
   Playing cards

4. *Perceptual Activities Packets:*
     Dot-to-Dot 1, 2
   Perceptual Activities
     (Ann Arbor)
   One-Inch Colored Cubes
     (Ideal)
   Attribute Blocks Desk Set
     (Learning Resources)

5. *Vocabulary Connection*
     (Remedia)
   Perceptual Activities
   Perceptual Activities Packets:
     Dot-to-Dot 1, 2
     (Ann Arbor)

7. Checkers and checkerboard

Block Design

Short-Term Objectives

The learner will be able to

Instructional Level: 6-9

Materials

8. copy various designs from the chalkboard on a small chalkboard or slate.

9. cut flash strip sentences into separate words and rebuild the sentences.

9. *Sentence Strips and Rolls* (Bemiss-Jason)

10. perform penmanship exercises using a guide.

10. *Trace 'n' Write* (Educational Insights) *Trace-a-Bet Laminated Cards Peek Thru Overlays* (Zaner-Bloser) *Handwriting: A Fresh Start* (Curriculum Associates) Graph paper Quadrille paper

11. locate and trace overlapping pictures and designs using a grease pencil or marker and acetate overlays.

11. *The Remediation of Learning Disabilities* (Fearon) *Trace 'N Erase* (Bemiss-Jason) *Peek Thru Overlays* (Zaner-Bloser)

12. assemble a science project such as a toy motor kit.

12. *Science Shelf Activities: Simple Machines* (Ideal) *Universal Buggy Manual Control Technic I, Simple Machines* (LEGO) Toy motor kits Science project kits

13. trace another student's silhouette by using a light to cast a shadow of profile on paper mounted on a board or wall.

13. Light source

BLOCK DES.

Block Design

Short-Term Objectives

The learner will be able to

Instructional Level: 6-9

Materials

14. assemble various abstract-shaped pieces into a specific design.

14. *Tangram Treasury*
    (Cuisenaire)
    Tangram and Puzzle Cards
    (DLM)
    Tangoes
    Tangrams
    ESS Tangram Cards, Set III
    (Dale Seymour)
    Tangrammables
    (Learning Resources)
    Pentominoes Pattern Cards
    Design Blocks and Patterns
    Puzzlegrams
    (Ideal)

15. assemble three-dimensional puzzles.

15. *Soma Puzzle Game*
    (Parker Brothers)
    Scrambled Egg
    Torus
    Create-A-Cubes
    (Varis)
    *Spatial Problem Solving with
     Cuisenaire Rods*
    (Cuisenaire)

16. complete puzzle pictures by shading or coloring specific parts as directed.

16. *Contemporary Reading Shade-Ins*
    More Reading Shade-Ins
    Contemporary Math Shade-Ins
    Contemporary Shade-In Posters
    (Prentice-Hall Learning Systems)

17. arrange fractional pieces to complete designs.

17. *Action Fractions Games*
    Fractions Are a Piece of Cake
    (Judy/Instructo)
    Half 'n' Half Design and Color
    (Ann Arbor)
    Pizza Party
    *Fraction Flash Cards, Basic and
     Advanced*
    (Ideal)

Block Design

Short-Term Objectives

The learner will be able to

Instructional Level: 6-9

Materials

Eye-Cue Puzzles
Geometric Fraction Shapes
  (Dale Seymour)
Delta Fraction Burger
Fractional Wood Fruit Plate
  (Delta)
Fraction Squares
Fraction Circles
  (Didax)

18. identify root words, prefixes, and suffixes.

18. *Pursuit*
Escape
Triad
  (Creative Teaching Associates)
Skill Power Teaching Units:
  Prefixes
  Suffixes
  (Remedia)
Structured Skills Quizmo
  (Milton Bradley)
Syllable Systems
Prefix-Suffix Puzzles
  (Incentives for Learning)

19. recognize syllables in words.

19. *Syllabo: Vocabulary Builder*—software
  (Curriculum Associates)
Syllable Systems
Syllable Puzzles
  (Incentives for Learning)
Hayes Spelling Skills and Drills,
  Gr. 6, 7, 8
  (Hayes)

20. classify words in sentences according to parts of speech.

20. *Parts of Speech*
Sentence Shuffle
  (DLM)
GrammaRummy
Basic Language Skills
  (Educational Insights)
Cues and Comprehension (Reading)
  (Ann Arbor)

BLOCK
DES.

185

Block Design

Short-Term Objectives

The learner will be able to

Instructional Level: 6-9

Materials

Word and Phrase Sentence Builder
  (Kenworthy)
Name That Word
Build a Sentence Game
Super Sentence Game
  (Creative Teaching Associates)
Wally Word Works—software
  (Sunburst)
Sentence Builder
  (Milton Bradley)
Mastering Basic Parts of Speech
All About Nouns
All About Verbs
All About Adjectives and Adverbs
  (Incentives for Learning)

21. recognize the parts of sentences (e.g., subject, predicate, and modifiers).

21. *Build a Sentence Game*
    Super Sentence Game
      (Creative Teaching Associates)
    Word and Phrase Sentence Builder
      (Kenworthy)
    Language Arts and Grammar, Jr. High
      (Instructional Fair)
    Basic Language Skills
    GrammaRummy
      (Educational Insights)

22. diagram simple sentences using color and shape cues.

22. *Color Coded Sentence Building Kit*
      (Didax)
    Basic Language Skills
      (Educational Insights)

Block Design

Short-Term Objectives

The learner will be able to

Instructional Level: 9-12

Materials

1. construct circuits, bells, lights, and simple machines.

1. *Minigroup Science*
   (ATP)
   Science Shelf Activities:
    Electricity
    Simple Machines
   Build-A-Battery
    (Ideal)
   Science Inquiry Labs:
    Lab II Machines and Energy
     (Weber Costello)
   Manual Control
   Technic I, Simple Machines
   Technic II, Motorized Transmission
   Universal Buggy
   Technic Activity Center
    (LEGO)

2. complete puzzles appropriate for age and grade level.

2. *GeoSafari: Puzzles and Thinking Games*
    (Educational Insights)
   Design Blocks and Patterns
   The Math Machine:
    Tangram Puzzles
    Pattern Blocks
    Pentominoes Puzzles
    Pattern Blocks Puzzles
     (Ideal)
   Pattern Blocks Activities
   Pattern Blocks
   Tangoes
   The Eighth Book of Tan
   Tangrams
   Tangrams: 330 Puzzles
    (Dale Seymour)
   Jigsaw puzzles of all sizes

3. draw a plan of the school campus or a floor plan of the school building.

3. *Where I Am*
    (DLM)
   Put 'Er There 1, 2
    (Remedia)

BLOCK DES.

Block Design

Short-Term Objectives

The learner will be able to

4. separate real words from nonsense words on a list prepared by the teacher by circling the real words.

5. construct sentences from jumbled words according to a master list or meaning.

6. reproduce complex designs using geometric shapes. (Timing may be added to increase level of difficulty.)

Instructional Level: 9-12

Materials

4. *Word Tracking: High Frequency Words*
   Sentence Tracking: High Frequency Words
   Sentence Tracking
      (Ann Arbor)
   Teacher-prepared worksheets

5. *GrammaRummy*
   Tub O' Words
      (Educational Insights)
   Sentence Builder
      (Milton Bradley)
   Word and Phrase Sentence Builder
      (Kenworthy)
   Sentence Shuffle
      (DLM)

6. *The Math Machine:*
      Tangram Puzzles
      Pattern Blocks Games
      Pattern Blocks Puzzles
      Pentominoes Puzzles
   Design Blocks and Patterns
      (Ideal)
   Geometric Shape Three-Sided
      Dominoes
      (Judy/Instructo)
   Triangles
   Scope Puzzles
      (Delta)
   Tangoes
   Tangrams
   Tangrams: 330 Puzzles
   The Eighth Book of Tan
      (Dale Seymour)

Block Design

Short-Term Objectives

The learner will be able to

7. copy designs of varying complexity using pegboards and pegs.

Instructional Level: 9-12

Materials

7. *Pegs, Pegboard, and Pegboard Designs*
   Lite-Brite
      (DLM)
   Centimeter Geoboard
      (Didax)
   Pegboard Activities Book
   Wooden Pegs
   Wooden Pegboard
   Plastic Pegboard
   Geoboard Activity Sheets
   Wooden Geoboard
   Plastic Geoboard
   Transparent Geoboard
      (Delta)
   100-Pin Geoboard Activity Set
      (Educational Insights)

BLOCK
DES.

8. design items such as a table top, wooden tray, etc., using mosaic tiles to form color patterns.

8. Mosaic kits

9. use interlocking cubes to reproduce patterns and pictures.

9. *Unifix Pattern Building Underlay Cards*
   Unifix Cubes
      (Didax)
   Multilink Activity Cards
   Multilink Cubes
      (Delta)
   Construction Combination Interlocking Cubes
      (Childcraft)
   Spatial Problem Solving with Cuisenaire Rods
   Student Activity Cards for Cuisenaire Rods
   Roddles—Cuisenaire Rod Games
      (Cuisenaire)

Block Design

Short-Term Objectives	Instructional Level: 9-12

The learner will be able to

Materials

10. reproduce block designs in correct perspective using blocks and patterns.

10. *Colored Inch Cube Designs*
    Colored Inch Cubes
       (DLM)
    Cube Pattern Cards
    One-Inch Multicolored Cubes
       (Ideal)
    Cubes in Color
    Cubes in Color Design Cards
       (Incentives for Learning)

11. reproduce a three-dimensional object using clay, papier mache, or a similar modeling material while looking at a model.

12. complete kits for model cars, boats, planes, etc.

13. reproduce the floor plan of the classroom using desks, chairs, tables, etc., which have been cut out of different colored pieces of paper. (These objects could be cut to scale so that they would "fit" on the piece of paper representing the classroom.)

14. design a different arrangement of furniture, etc., for the classroom, using different colored pieces of paper cut to scale.

15. complete jigsaw puzzles forming pictures and/or words.

15. *Jabble*
       (Varis)

16. assemble three-dimensional designs.

16. *Soma Puzzle Game*
    Instant Insanity
       (Parker Brothers)
    Mystic Wedge
    Scrambled Egg
    Creat-A-Cube
       (Varis)

190

Block Design

Short-Term Objectives

The learner will be able to

Instructional Level: 9-12

Materials

*Spatial Problem Solving with
Cuisenaire Rods*
(Cuisenaire)

17. spell correctly words that do not follow the rules of spelling.

17. *Spell It Plus!*—software
(Davidson)
Spelling Bee, Level III
Spelling Four Square
(Creative Teaching Associates)
Michigan Programmed Spelling
(ATP)
Spellbusters
(Opportunities for Learning)
Funtastic Spelling
Spelling Gremlins
(Remedia)
Jungle Rescue/Spelling—
software
Spellicopter—software
Customized "Flash" Spelling—
software
(Troll)
Spello
(Ideal)
Demon Spelling Words
(Educational Activities)

18. put together a map of the United States using state puzzle pieces.

18. *United States Map Puzzle*
(Playskool)
United States Woodboard Map
Mini U.S. Map Puzzle
United States Map Floor Puzzle
(Judy/Instructo)
U.S./World Map Puzzle
(Milton Bradley)
Fit-a-State
(Lauri)

BLOCK
DES.

191

Block Design

Short-Term Objectives	Instructional Level: 9-12
The learner will be able to	**Materials**

19. classify words in sentences according to parts of speech.

19. *Parts of Speech*
    (DLM)
    Gaming It
    (Opportunities for Learning)
    Grammar Gremlins—software
    (Davidson)
    What's the Word Game
    Mastering Basic Parts of Speech
    All About Nouns
    All About Verbs
    All About Adjectives and Adverbs
    (Incentives for Learning)
    Basic Language Skills
    Binders Keepers: Parts of Speech
    (Educational Insights)
    Cues and Comprehension (Reading)
    (Ann Arbor)
    Super Sentence Game
    (Creative Teaching Associates)
    Wally's Word Works—software
    (Sunburst)

20. identify the subject, predicate, and their modifiers in a sentence.

20. *Basic Skills in Using Our Language: Subjects and Verbs*
    Writing
    (Opportunities for Learning)
    Grammar Gremlins—software
    (Davidson)
    Language Arts and Grammar, Jr. High
    (Instructional Fair)
    Basic Language Skills: Parts of Sentences
    (Educational Insights)
    Super Sentence Game
    (Creative Teaching Associates)

21. diagram sentences successfully.

21. *Color Coded Sentence Building Kit*
    (Didax)
    Basic Language Skills: Diagramming Sentences
    (Educational Insights)
    English textbooks and workbooks

OBJECT ASSEMBLY

Object Assembly

I. **Purpose of the Subtest**

To measure the ability to assemble individual concrete parts to make a recognizable whole.

II. **Factors Affecting Subtest and Academic Performance**

   A. Visual-motor coordination and integration
   B. Spatial relationships and orientation
   C. Visual and perceptual organization
   D. Gestalt awareness
   E. Goal orientation
   F. Time
   G. Body imagery
   H. Problem-solving techniques
   I. Concentration

III. **Educational Significance**

   A. All sensory modalities should be incorporated in class activities stressing kinesthetic and manipulative aspects.
   B. Emphasis should be placed upon the final goal of the task rather than on the individual steps necessary to attain the desired result. Assist the student in organizing work so that involvement with minor detail is avoided.
   C. The student must understand the "whole" of the concept before analyzation of "parts" becomes meaningful in academic learning.
   D. Additional time should be allowed to complete academic assignments.
   E. In lesson planning, avoid teaching techniques that employ the "parts" approach to learning (e.g., individual letter sounds, syllabication of words, missing addends in math, etc.). Instead, employ "whole" methodology such as sight words and blended phonic analysis for reading and spelling and math facts in their entirety.

IV. **Long-Term Goal**

The learner will be able to assemble individual parts into meaningful wholes.

OBJECT ASSEM.

Object Assembly

Short-Term Objectives

The learner will be able to

1. put together puzzle pieces to form the human body.

2. put together puzzle pieces to form various animals.

Instructional Level: K-3

Materials

1. *Early Learning Curriculum Units:*
   Body Parts & Senses Unit
   My Face and Body
   Body Parts Puzzle, 6 pcs.
   Body Parts Puzzle, 12 pcs.
   Girl Puzzle
   Boy Puzzle
      (Judy/Instructo)
   Body Awareness—software
      (Troll)
   Body Parts Set
   Body Parts Floor Puzzle
      (Frank Schaffer)
   Body Parts Puzzle
      (Lauri)
   I Can Dress Myself
      (Milton Bradley)
   Peabody Language Development Kit—
      Revised: Level P
      (AGS)
   Body and Self-Awareness Big Box
      (DLM)

2. *Animal Puzzles with Knobs*
      (Childcraft)
   Trachodon
   Tyrannosaurus
   Triceratops
   Brontosaurus
   Kittens
   Cow
   Rabbit
   Giraffe
   Elephant
   Animal Parents and Babies:
      Panda and Cub
      Pig and Piglets
      Sheep and Lambs
      Horse and Foal
      Monkey and Baby
      (Judy/Instructo)

Object Assembly

Short-Term Objectives

The learner will be able to

3. complete drawings of the human body which have various parts missing.

4. draw a human body with parts in the appropriate positions.

5. trace the outlines of familiar objects such as shapes, toys, animals, household objects, etc.

Instructional Level: K-3

Materials

3. *My Face and Body*
   Body Parts Puzzle, 6 pcs.
   Body Parts Puzzle, 12 pcs.
   Girl Puzzle
   Boy Puzzle
   Face Parts Puzzle
      (Judy/Instructo)
   Readiness: Strategies and Practice
      (Curriculum Associates)
   Body Parts Set
      (Frank Schaffer)
   Body and Self-Awareness Big Box
      (DLM)
   Teacher-prepared drawings

4. *Body Awareness*—software
      (Troll)
   Body and Self-Awareness Big Box
      (DLM)

5. *Common Shapes Stencils*
   Dinosaurs and Prehistorics
      (Trend)
   Pencil Stencils:
    Shapes
    Farm Animals
    People
    Wild Animals
    Circus
      (Ideal)
   Attribute Block Desk Set
   Shape Tracer Set
      (Learning Resources)
   Paper Shapes Projects
      (Judy/Instructo)
   Stencils
      (Highlights for Children)

OBJECT
ASSEM.

Object Assembly

Short-Term Objectives	Instructional Level: K-3
The learner will be able to	**Materials**

6. complete incomplete drawings of forms and objects.

6. *Finish the Picture*
   (Trend)
   Perceptual Activities Packets:
   Finish-the-Picture, 1, 2
   Perceptual Activities
   Half 'n' Half Design and Color
   (Ann Arbor)
   Tell What Part Is Missing
   What's Missing Lotto
   (Milton Bradley)
   Finish Me Pages
   (Communication Skill Builders)

7. complete simple jigsaw puzzles.

7. *Peanuts Picture Puzzles*—software
   (Troll)
   Seasons/Weather Puzzles
   Early Learner Puzzles
   Fairy Tales and Nursery Rhymes
   Puzzles
   Occupation Puzzles
   Holidays and Celebrations Puzzles
   (Judy/Instructo)
   Fruit and Vegetable Puzzles
   First Puzzles Set
   (Childcraft)

8. put together correctly basic forms that have been cut into two or three parts.

8. *Attribute Block Desk Set*
   Fraction Activity Cards
   (Learning Resources)
   Action Fraction Games
   (Judy/Instructo)
   Half 'n' Half Design and Color
   (Ann Arbor)
   Triangles, squares, and circles cut into two and three parts

9. reproduce pegboard designs.

9. *Pegboard; Pegs; Pegboards Designs*
   (DLM)

O
A

198

Object Assembly

Short-Term Objectives

The learner will be able to

Instructional Level: K-3

Materials

Large Pegboard Patterns
Deluxe Pegboard Set
Beaded Pegs—Class Set
Developmental Peg Board Activities
  (Ideal)
Pegboard Kit
  (Incentives for Learning)

10. match simple words that have been cut in half lengthwise, repeating the word after the teacher.

10. Teacher-prepared words

11. copy a design, verbally describing each step required in its reproduction.

11. *Traceables*
  (Lauri)
Attribute Block Desk Set
Attribute Block Templates
Shape Tracer Set
  (Learning Resources)
Sequencing Beads and Design Cards
  (Incentives for Learning)
Clear Stencils
Colored Inch Cubes
Colored Inch Cubes Designs
Large Parquetry Blocks
Large Parquetry Designs
  (DLM)
Large Colored Beads & Patterns
Building Bead Patterns
  (Ideal)

12. differentiate between the concepts right and left, top and bottom, front and back by responding appropriately on worksheets and/or with concrete objects.

12. *Half 'n' Half Design and Color*
  (Ann Arbor)
Stamp-It! Activity Sheets for Concept Development
  (Communication Skill Builders)
Primary Concepts I
  (Troll)
Front/Back Lotto
  (Milton Bradley)

OBJECT ASSEM.

199

Object Assembly

Short-Term Objectives

The learner will be able to

Instructional Level: K-3

Materials

13. illustrate prepositions—*in, on, under, behind, in front of, over*, etc.—by using a chair and an object and placing it appropriately.

13. *Spatial Relationship Cards*
    (DLM)
    Location Lotto
    (Trend)
    Primary Concepts I
    (Troll)
    Where Is It? Spatial Relationship Cards
    Spatial Relationship Puzzles
    (Ideal)
    Spatial Relationships Flannelboard Aid
    (Judy/Instructo)
    Stamp-It! Activity Sheets for Concept Development
    The Flipbook for Individualizing Prepositions and Pronoun Practice
    (Communication Skill Builders)

14. find hidden objects and shapes in pictures.

14. *Fun and Do Pack*
    (Highlights for Children)
    Freddy's Puzzling Adventures—software
    Spellagram—software
    (Troll)
    Hidden Pictures, K-1, 1-2
    (Frank Schaffer)
    Hidden Pictures and Objects
    (Hayes)
    Spatial Specials
    (Love)
    Paper Shapes Projects
    (Judy/Instructo)

15. perform matching, cutting, pasting, and coloring tasks.

15. *Half 'n' Half Design and Color*
    (Ann Arbor)
    Color and Cut: Think and Paste
    Holiday Posters and Decorations
    Easy to Make Art Activities
    (Hayes)

Object Assembly

Short-Term Objectives

The learner will be able to

Instructional Level: K-3

Materials

Visual Perception Series
  (Media Materials)
Paper Shapes Projects
  (Judy/Instructo)
Cut, Match and Paste
  (DLM)
Learn to Cut
Pre-Scissor Skills
    (Communication and Therapy Skill
    Builders)
Learn to Cut
    (Communication Skill Builders)
Community Helpers Lotto
Color and Shape Lotto
Color and Shape Bingo
    (Trend)

16. look at a simple design or object for a few seconds, cover it, and then draw it.

17. complete dot-to-dot designs, pictures, etc.

17. *Perceptual Activities Packets:*
    Dot-to-Dot 1, 2
    Perceptual Activities
      (Ann Arbor)
    Dot-to-Dot 1-100
    Dot-to-Dot 2's, 5's, 10's
    Math Dot-to-Dot
    Teddy Bear Alphabet Dot-to-Dot
    Alphabet Dot-to-Dot
      (Frank Schaffer)

18. use sewing cards to outline designs, figures, and objects.

18. *Teaching Tiles*
    Lacing Shapes
    Lacing Bears
    Puppets
      (Lauri)
    Sewing Cards
      (Milton Bradley)

OBJECT
ASSEM.

201

Object Assembly

Short-Term Objectives

The learner will be able to

Instructional Level: K-3

Materials

19. match appropriate parts to pictures of objects, animals, etc., with the parts missing.

19. *Half 'n' Half Design and Color*
    (Ann Arbor)
    Missing Parts Lotto
    Tell What Part Is Missing
    (Milton Bradley)
    Finish Me Pages
    Stamp It! Activity Sheets for Concept Development
    (Communication Skill Builders)

20. reproduce rhythm patterns with pencils, sticks, or rhythm instruments.

20. *Rhythm Sticks*
    Sand Blocks
    Triangle Set
    Chromatic Bell Set
    (Judy/Instructo)
    Xylophone
    (Playskool)

21. put together simple words that have been cut up into individual letters.

21. Teacher-prepared words in large print

22. match individual parts with pictures of objects consisting of those parts.

22. *Peanut Butter and Jelly Game*
    (Parker Brothers)

Object Assembly

Short-Term Objectives

The learner will be able to

1. put together puzzles, moving from simple to complex.

2. make a collage using various shapes of different colors traced, cut out, and pasted on a large sheet of paper or poster board.

3. arrange a series of specific shapes such as circles, squares, etc., from small to large.

4. select the figure among four possible answers that matches a specific key figure.

Instructional Level: 3-6

Materials

1. *Lauriland 3-D Puzzle Playsets*
   Large Pattern Puzzles
   Crepe Foam Rubber Picture Puzzles
   Fit-a-State
   Fit-a-World
   Perception Puzzles
      (Lauri)
   Visual Thinking, Set A
   Eye-Cue Puzzles, Sets A & B
      (Dale Seymour)

3. *Patchworks: Size Perception*
      (Milton Bradley)
   Size Puzzles:
     Animals
     Clothes
   Fit-a-Size
      (Lauri)
   Sequential Cards—By Color, Shape, and Size
      (Incentives for Learning)
   Attribute Blocks Desk Set
      (Learning Resources)

4. *Color and Shape Lotto*
   Color and Shape Bingo
   Alphabet Lotto
   Alphabet Bingo
   Community Helpers Lotto
   Dinosaurs and Prehistorics Lotto
   Location Lotto
   Numbers Lotto
   Number Bingo
   Rhyming Bingo
      (Trend)

OBJECT
ASSEM.

Object Assembly

Short-Term Objectives

The learner will be able to

Instructional Level: 3-6

Materials

5. reproduce designs varying in shapes, sizes, and colors using blocks, beads, pegs, etc.

5. *Large Colored Beads and Patterns*
   Building Bead Patterns
   Easy Grip Pegs and Pegboards
   Pegboard Fun with Patterns
      (Ideal)
   Pattern Blocks
   Pattern Blocks Activities
      (Dale Seymour)
   Tangram and Pattern Cards
      (Milton Bradley)
   Parquetry Blocks
   Parquetry Pattern Cards
      (Learning Resources)
   Multivariant Sequencing Beads and
      Bead Patterns
   Pegs, Pegboards, and Designs
      (DLM)

6. reproduce individual words within sentences using both auditory and visual aids simultaneously and then separately. (Provide a master list.)

6. *Putting Words in Order/*
      Sentence Structure
      (Troll)
   Word Builders
   Word and Phrase Sentence Builder
      (Kenworthy)
   Sentence Builder
      (Milton Bradley)
   Switchboard—software
      (Sunburst)

7. develop a code to be used in matching shapes with figures and numbers.

7. *Kids Book of Secret Codes, Signals,*
      and Ciphers
      (Dale Seymour)
   Challenging Codes:
   Riddles & Jokes
   Quips & Quotes
      (Midwest)

8. use map legends to find cities, etc.

8. State maps

Object Assembly

Short-Term Objectives

The learner will be able to

Instructional Level: 3-6

Materials

9. arrange in correct sequence a group of objects that have been disarranged after viewing them.

9. Objects such as toys, blocks, pencils, etc.

10. identify an object after listening to a description of color, shape, size, texture, etc.

11. identify geometric shapes or common objects in a bag or box by feeling them.

11. *Geometric Plastic Forms*
    (Ideal)
    Small toys and other objects

12. reproduce a design made of building toys from a model. (This activity may be timed to increase the level of difficulty.)

12. *American Plastic Blocks*
    Bristle Blocks
    Tinkertoys
    (Playskool)
    DUPLO Basic Set-On Wheels
    LEGO Basic Set
    (LEGO)

13. arrange his body in a certain position and let the other children imitate by arranging themselves similarly (e.g., with arms crossed right over left, legs crossed, one hand on knee and other hand on elbow, etc.).

14. use pictures in a sequence to develop and tell a story.

14. *Sequence Cards, Groups I, II, III*
    (Educational Insights)
    Sequential Cards—Levels I, II, III
    Sequential Cards—A Family's Day
    (Incentives for Learning)
    3 Scene Sequence Cards
    4 Scene Sequence Cards
    (Milton Bradley)

15. arrange in correct sequence directions for a specific task which have been individually written on several pieces of paper.

15. Teacher-prepared directions

OBJECT ASSEM.

Object Assembly

Short-Term Objectives

The learner will be able to

Instructional Level: 3-6

Materials

16. complete puzzles of shapes, animals, people, parts of the body, etc.

16. *Paper Shapes Projects*
    Mini U.S. Map Puzzle
    World Map Floor Puzzle
    United States Map Floor Puzzle
       (Judy/Instructo)
    Soma Puzzle Game
    Peanut Butter and Jelly Puzzle
       (Parker Brothers)

17. arrange individual letters or blends to form words.

17. *Scrabble*
    Scrabble Junior
       (Selchow and Righter)
    Boggle Word Puzzle
    Boggle Junior
       (Parker Brothers)
    Word Yahtzee
    Economo Word Builder
    Link Letters
    Letter Cards
    Magnetic Plastic Letters
    Cardboard Letters and Numbers
       (Milton Bradley)
    Letter Fun
       (Ideal)
    Letter Perfect
    Tub O' Letters
       (Educational Insights)
    Avalanche of Letters
    Jumbo Fit-a-Letter
       (Lauri)
    Word Builder
       (Kenworthy)
    Super Alphabet Pack
       (Judy/Instructo)

Object Assembly

Short-Term Objectives

The learner will be able to

Instructional Level: 3-6

Materials

18. put together geometrically shaped pieces to make specific designs.

18. *Puzzle Grams*
(Ideal)
Tangram and Puzzle Cards
Small Parquetry and Designs I, II
(DLM)
Pattern Blocks Activities
Pattern Blocks
(Dale Seymour)
Parquetry Blocks
Parquetry Pattern Cards
Tangram and Pattern Cards
Parquetry Inlay Mosaics
(Learning Resources)

19. match the printed word to the appropriate picture.

19. *Noun Puzzles*
Verb Puzzles
(DLM)
Picture Flash Cards
Educational Flash Cards
(Milton Bradley)
Peel & Put
Stamp-It!
(Communication Skill Builders)
CVC Picture-Word Program
(Incentives for Learning)

20. arrange individual words to produce a simple sentence of four words or more.

20. *Word and Phrase Sentence Builder*
(Kenworthy)
Switchboard—software
(Sunburst)
Sentence Builder
Economo Sentence Builder
(Milton Bradley)
Build a Sentence
Super Sentence
(Creative Teaching Associates)
Teacher-prepared words

OBJECT ASSEM.

207

Object Assembly

Short-Term Objectives

The learner will be able to

1. complete jigsaw puzzles of varying complexity (e.g., geometric forms and map puzzles).

2. match pictures of baseball and football players which have been cut in half or thirds.

3. arrange word and phrase cards to make a logical sentence. (Pictures may be used for stimulation.)

4. put together model cars, airplanes, boats, etc.

5. identify pictures of objects when a portion of the pictures is hidden.

6. complete incomplete drawings.

Instructional Level: 6-9

Materials

1. *Picture Puzzles with Cuisenaire Rods*
   Tangram Treasury
   Cuisenaire Geo-Board
     (Cuisenaire)
   Tic Tac Toe—software
   Gertrude's Puzzles—software
     (Troll)
   Tangram and Puzzle Cards
     (DLM)
   Pentominoes Puzzles
   Pentominoes
   Pattern Blocks Puzzles
     (Ideal)

2. Baseball and football cards

3. *Word and Phrase Sentence Builder*
     (Kenworthy)
   Sentence Builder
   Economo Sentence Builder
     (Milton Bradley)
   GrammaRummy
     (Educational Insights)
   Switchboard—software
     (Sunburst)

6. *Half 'n' Half Design and Color*
   Perceptual Activities Packets:
     Finish the Picture 1, 2
   Perceptual Activities
     (Ann Arbor)
   See It—Do It
     (DLM)

Object Assembly

Short-Term Objectives

The learner will be able to

7. put together word cards cut in two or more pieces to make words.

8. select from several choices the design which has been verbally described.

9. make objects from papier mache, wire, clay, etc.

10. identify various objects by feeling them while blindfolded.

11. identify by feeling sandpaper or rubber textured letters or numbers while blindfolded.

12. reproduce designs on a foam board according to cue cards. (Progress to higher levels of difficulty as ability increases.)

13. reproduce a design while looking at the model and then reproduce the design *without* looking at the model.

Instructional Level: 6-9

Materials

7. Student-prepared word cards

8. *Visual Memory Cards*
   (DLM)

9. Papier mache, modeling clay, popsicle sticks, pipe cleaners

10. Toys and other small objects

11. *Beaded Alphabet Cards*
    Foam Letters
    Foam Numbers
    Jumbo Alphabet
    A-Z Panels
    1-10 Panels
    Avalanche of Letters
    (Lauri)

12. *Stencils*
    (Highlights for Children)
    Clear Stencils
    (DLM)
    Tangram and Pattern Cards
    (Milton Bradley)
    Tangram Puzzles
    Tangram Patterns
    (Judy/Instructo)
    Wooden Pattern Blocks
    Patterns for Pattern Blocks
    (Ideal)

13. *Tangram and Pattern Cards*
    (Milton Bradley)
    Parquetry and Parquetry Designs
    (DLM)
    Classroom Manipulatives and
    Organizer Kits
    (Houghton Mifflin)

OBJECT
ASSEM.

Object Assembly

Short-Term Objectives	Instructional Level: 6-9

The learner will be able to

Materials

Tangram Puzzles
Tangram Patterns
 (Judy/Instructo)

14. reproduce models using building toys.

14. *Lincoln Logs*
 Tinker Toys
  (Playskool)
 DUPLO Basic Set-On Wheels
 LEGO Basic Set
  (LEGO)

15. find the key idea in paragraphs or stories.

15. *Specific Skill Series: Getting the Main Idea*
  (Barnell/SRA)
 Sentences and Paragraphs
 Paragraphs Skills
  (Eye Gate Media)
 Comprehension Games:
  Time Capsule/Reading
  The Main Idea/Space Trek
 Getting the Main Idea/
  Around-the-World
  (Learning Well)
 Basic Reading Units:
  Multi-Skills I & II
  (Continental Press)
 Reading Comprehension Series:
  Getting the Main Idea
  (Educational Insights)

16. complete exercises dealing with making circles, ovals, and lines for good penmanship habits.

17. put together puzzles and play games emphasizing careers and occupations.

17. *Nonsexist Career Puzzles*
  (Childcraft)
 Career Capers
  (Opportunities for Learning)
 Working Choices
 Employ Bingo
 Steady Job Game
  (Milton Bradley)

Object Assembly

Short-Term Objectives

The learner will be able to

Instructional Level: 6-9

Materials

18. create an advertisement similar to those in newspapers.

18. *Survival Guide: Using the Want Ads*
(Opportunities for Learning)
NewsSchool
Newspaper Math
(Dale Seymour)
Using the Newspaper to Improve Reading Skills
(Hayes)

19. arrange words and phrases to form sentences of five or more words.

19. *Switchboard*—software
(Sunburst)
Build a Sentence
Super Sentence
(Creative Teaching Associates)
GrammaRummy
(Educational Insights)
Word and Phrase Sentence Builder
(Kenworthy)
Sentence Builder
(Milton Bradley)

20. put together syllables to form words.

20. *Syllable Flip Cards*
(Kenworthy)
Activities for Dictionary Practice
Syllabo Vocabulary Builder—software
(Curriculum Associates)
Syllable Systems
Syllable Puzzles
(Incentives for Learning)

OBJECT ASSEM.

Object Assembly

Short-Term Objectives

The learner will be able to

1. describe various objects for others to identify.

2. describe another student for others to identify.

3. develop a code to use in matching geometric figures and numbers.

4. work picture-form puzzles with pieces that represent recognizable parts of objects or people.

5. design a mural of a large fish or animal and construct a paper mosaic with the group working together as a class project.

6. create a jigsaw puzzle by gluing pictures on poster board and cutting them up and then putting them together.

7. cut phrases from a magazine or newspaper to form a story.

8. complete simple outlining of a selected story or article.

Instructional Level: 9-12

Materials

3. *Kid's Book of Secret Codes, Signals, and Ciphers*
   (Dale Seymour)
   Challenging Codes:
   Riddles and Jokes
   Quips and Quotes
   (Midwest)
   Code Quest—software
   (Sunburst)

5. *The Remediation of Learning Disabilities*
   (Fearon)
   Small pieces of different colored paper

8. *Study Skills: Strategies and Practice*
   The Outlining Kit
   Thirty Lessons in Outlining
   (Curriculum Associates)

Object Assembly

Short-Term Objectives

The learner will be able to

Instructional Level: 9-12

Materials

9. find the key idea in paragraphs or stories.

9. *Reading Comprehension 2-5—* software
Return-to-Reading Library (Troll)
Reading Comprehension Series: Getting the Main Idea (Educational Insights)
Building Comprehension, Grades 7, 8, 9 (Milliken)
Getting the Main Idea/Around-the-World
The Main Idea/Space Trek (Learning Well)

10. relate orally and/or in writing a story, movie, or TV program.

11. create stories or poetry.

11. *Writing for Fun* (Eye Gate Media)
*Magical Myths—*software
*Adventures of Sinbad—*software
Tales from the Arabian Nights— software (Troll)
Create-a-Story Series
Using Guided Visualization for Better Writing: A Handbook for Teachers
Laughing Matters (Educational Impressions)
The Writing Workshop, Vol. 1 and 2 (Dale Seymour)
Story Sparkers
Cliffhangers (Educational Insights)
Creative Writing Skills, 6, 7, 8 (Instructional Fair)
Creative Writing 6-8 (Milliken)

OBJECT ASSEM.

213

Object Assembly

Short-Term Objectives The learner will be able to	Instructional Level: 9-12 Materials
12. form words from a group of letters.	12. *Economo Word Builder* *Word Yahtzee* (Milton Bradley) *Tub O' Letters* *Letter Perfect* (Educational Insights) *Boggle Word Game* (Parker Brothers) *Scrabble* *Scoring Anagrams* (Selchow and Righter)
13. arrange words from a master list to make a logical sentence.	13. *GrammaRummy* (Educational Insights) *Switchboard*—software (Sunburst) *Sentence Builder* (Milton Bradley) *Word and Phrase Sentence Builder* (Kenworthy) *Super Sentence* (Creative Teaching Associates) *Sentence Cube Game* (Selchow and Righter)
14. construct sensible sentences from randomly selected words.	14. *Switchboard*—software (Sunburst)
15. arrange pictures which reflect a number of events into a logical sequence to develop a story.	15. *Sequential Cards—From-To Series* *Sequential Cards, Levels I, II, III* (Incentives for Learning) *Sequencing Cards—6 Scene Cards* (Frank Schaffer) *8 Scene Sequence Cards* (Milton Bradley) *Sequential Picture Cards, Level 3* (DLM)

Object Assembly

Short-Term Objectives	Instructional Level: 9-12
The learner will be able to	**Materials**

16. put together three-dimensional puzzles.

16. *Soma Puzzle Game*
    (Parker Brothers)
    Scrambled Egg
    Torus
    Create-A-Cube
    (Varis)
    Creature Cube—software
    The Super Factory—software
    (Sunburst)

17. write a want ad for a job, to buy a car, etc.

17. *Survival Guide: Using the Want Ads*
    (Opportunities for Learning)
    NewsSchool
    Newspaper Math
    (Dale Seymour)
    Using the Newspaper to Improve Reading Skills
    (Hayes)

18. write an ad to sell an item (e.g., car, boat, appliance, etc.).

18. *Survival Guide: Using the Want Ads*
    (Opportunities for Learning)

19. complete designs by putting together fractional parts.

19. *Fraction Games*
    (Lauri)
    Fraction Activity Cards
    Circular Fraction Set
    Square Fraction Set
    (Learning Resources)
    Understanding Fraction Games:
    Circles
    Squares
    Geometric Shape Three-Sided Dominoes
    Fractions Are a Piece of Cake
    Introduction to Fractions
    (Judy/Instructo)
    Fractions Are as Easy as Pie
    (Milton Bradley)
    Pizza Party
    (Ideal)

OBJECT ASSEM.

Object Assembly

Short-Term Objectives

The learner will be able to

20. create an artistic project in a selected medium (e.g., painting, sculpture, weaving, pottery, etc.).

Instructional Level: 9-12

Materials

20. *Color 'N' Canvas*—software
    (Sunburst)
    Dazzle Draw—software
    (Troll)
    I Can Make a Rainbow
    Puddles & Wings & Grapevine Swings
    The Tabletop Arts & Crafts Library
    (Kids' Stuff)

FACTOR III—FREEDOM FROM DISTRACTIBILITY

FREEDOM FROM DISTRACTIBILITY

ARITHMETIC

ARITH.

Arithmetic

I. **Purpose of the Subtest**

To measure the ability to solve arithmetic problems received auditorily through mental computation.

II. **Factors Affecting Subtest and Academic Performance**
   A. Numerical fluency
   B. Concentration
   C. Memory
   D. Educational background
   E. Attention
   F. Anxiety
   G. Mental alertness
   H. Abstract conceptualization
   I. Visualization

III. **Educational Significance**
   A. The vocabulary basic to mathematics should be continually reviewed and reinforced.
   B. Concrete and manipulative materials to introduce and/or reinforce concepts and operations of arithmetic should be utilized, such as counting sticks, abacus, cash registers, etc.
   C. Adequate time allowances are necessary to insure that the student has mastered the concept or operation taught. Variations in attention span should determine lengths of instructional periods.
   D. The classroom environment should be structured to minimize auditory and visual distractions in order to enhance concentration ability.
   E. Teaching methodology should include rote memory when necessary.

IV. **Long-Term Goal**

The learner will be able to solve arithmetic computations involving the major operations of addition, subtraction, multiplication, and division.

ARITH.

Arithmetic

Short-Term Objectives

The learner will be able to

Instructional Level: K-3

Materials

1. sort objects according to sizes.

1. *Big and Little Pegboard*
   Square Pegs 'N Board
      (Marvel)
   Fit-A-Size
      (Lauri)
   *Sequential Cards—By Color, Shape
   and Size*
      (Incentives for Learning)
   Attribute Sorting Set
      (Ideal)
   Various objects and toys of differing
   sizes

2. repeat the words for numbers one
   through ten with the examiner and
   classmates.

3. repeat number words up to ten while
   counting fingers, toys, etc. (Expand
   to 50 when appropriate.)

3. *Count-My-Fingers*
      (Lauri)
   Counting Hands Puzzle
   Counting Feet Puzzle
      (Judy/Instructo)
   Toys and other objects

4. sort colored shapes into a group of all
   one shape such as all circles, all
   squares, etc.

4. *Count and Sort Set*
   Attribute Blocks Desk Set
      (Learning Resources)
   Attribute Sorting Set
      (Ideal)

5. place correct shapes in appropriate
   openings in a shape box or sorter.

5. *Form Fitter*
      (Playskool)
   Shape and Color Sorter
      (Lauri)
   Color/Shape Sorting Box Program
   Primary Shape Sorter
      (Childcraft)
   Shape Drop Box
   Shape Sequence Box
      (Marvel)

Arithmetic

Short-Term Objectives
The learner will be able to

Instructional Level: K-3
Materials

Sort and See Bucket
  (Lakeshore)
Tupperware Ball
  (Tupperware)

6. sort various kinds of objects in groups according to likeness (e.g., all the circles, forks, square nuts, oval buttons, etc.).

6. *Sorting Box Combination for Counting and Color*
  (Marvel)
Lauri's Build-a-Skill
  (Lauri)
Attribute Sorting Set
Shellsorts
Fasteners
  (Ideal)
Color Bear Sorting Kit
  (Milton Bradley)
Lakeshore Sorting and Order Kit
  (Lakeshore)

7. compare objects by arranging them according to size.

7. *Size Seriation Circus*
  (Judy/Instructo)
Peg Grading Board
Big and Little Peg Board
Square Pegs 'N Board
  (Marvel)

ARITH.

8. arrange a row of pegs in a pegboard to match a prearranged design of ten pegs.

8. *Deluxe Pegboard Sets*
Large Pegboard Patterns
  (Ideal)
Pegboard Kit
Jumbo Tactilmat Pegboard
Easy Grip Pegs
  (Incentives for Learning)
Peg Play Set
  (Lauri)
Square Pegs 'N Board
Big and Little Pegboard
Jumbo Hold-Tight Peg Set
  (Marvel)

Arithmetic

Short-Term Objectives

The learner will be able to

Instructional Level: K-3

Materials

Wooden Pegboard
Plastic Pegboard
2-inch Wooden Pegs
180 Wooden Pegs for Plastic
  Pegboard
Pegboard Activities Cards
Pegboard Activities Book
  (Delta)

9. "take" or "give" up to ten objects on request. (Increase in number as student's abilities improve.)

9. *Plastic Counters*
Teddy Bears in a Tub
Blocks 'n Bears
  (Milton Bradley)
Attribute Sorting Set
  (Ideal)

10. match simple domino patterns.

10. *Jumbo Dominoes*
Deluxe Dominoes
  (Ideal)
Animal Dominoes
Color Dominoes
  (Marvel)
Hainstock Blocks
  (Lakeshore)

11. copy a circle using a stencil. (Progress to square as skills develop.)

11. *Pencil Stencil Shapes*
  (Ideal)
Montessori Shapes and Stencils
  (Learning Resources)
Tracing Stencils: Common Shapes
  (Trend)

12. fill a plastic milk bottle with a specified number of objects (e.g., dried beans, bottle caps, paper clips, etc.).

Arithmetic

Short-Term Objectives

The learner will be able to

Instructional Level: K-3

Materials

13. recognize numerals one through ten.

13. *Math Readiness: Numbers*
    Learning Numbers
       (Milliken)
    Math Pegs
    Numeral Inlays
    Numberite
    Stepping Stones Numerals
       (Judy/Instructo)
    Jumbo Fit-A-Numeral
    Count My Fingers
    Number Sorter
    Numberite
    Peg-It Number Boards
    Magnetic Plastic Numerals
    Giant Number Cards
    Foam Numbers
       (Lauri)
    Numbers and Numerals
       (Ann Arbor)
    Charlie: Math Readiness
       (Educational Insights)
    Giant Sponge Number/Numeral Dice
       (Lakeshore)

14. imitate a ten cube pyramid.

14. *Cubes in Color*
    Cubes in Color Design Cards
       (Incentives for Learning)
    Cubical Counting Blocks
    Cubical Block Pattern Cards
       (Milton Bradley)
    Plain Wooden Cubes
    Colored Counting Cubes
    Colored Cube Task Cards
       (Learning Resources)

15. put two halves together to make a rectangle.

15. *Square Fraction Set*
       (Learning Resources)
    Action Fractions
       (Judy/Instructo)
    Fraction Squares
       (Didax)

ARITH.

225

Arithmetic

Short-Term Objectives

The learner will be able to

16. copy the basic geometric shapes (circle, square, triangle, and rectangle) using a stencil.

17. identify objects as being members of a set (1-5; 1-12).

18. match the basic shapes of circle, square, triangle, rectangle, diamond, and cross.

19. recite numbers from one through twenty. (Progress from twenty higher as skill improves.)

20. print a set of numbers up to ten on paper, cardboard, slate, etc.

21. tap out combinations of numbers on a table or board in imitation of a pattern given by the teacher.

Instructional Level: K-3

Materials

16. *Pencil Stencil Shapes*
(Ideal)
Tracing Stencils: Common Shapes
(Trend)

17. *Experiences for Early Childhood: Early Mathematics Kit*
(Cuisenaire)
One Dozen Count and Match Eggs
(Lakeshore)
Attribute Sorting Set
(Ideal)

18. *Lauri's Build-A-Skill*
Fit-A-Shape
Fit-A-Space
(Lauri)
Geometric Three-Sided Dominoes
(Judy/Instructo)
Colors & Shapes Bingo
Colors & Shapes Lotto
(Trend)
Disney's Let's Learn Shapes
(Walt Disney Educational Media)
Shapes Game
(BLIP)
Muppetville—software
(Sunburst)

Arithmetic

Short-Term Objectives

The learner will be able to

Instructional Level: K-3

Materials

22. string a specified number of beads upon request.

22. *Beads/Strings/Pattern Cards*
    (Childcraft)
    Large Beads and Laces
    Jumbo Beads
    Bead Laces
    Beads and Laces
        (Media Materials)
    Jumbo Wooden Beads
    Easy-Lace Beads
        (Lakeshore)

23. walk on a number line with painted numerals of one through ten placed on the floor.

23. *Walk-On Number Line (0-10)*
    Stepping Stones: Number Patterns
    Stepping Stones: Numerals
        (Judy/Instructo)

24. match the numeral 1 with an object saying the word "one" aloud. (Expand to ten when appropriate.)

24. *Wipe-Off Cards*
        (Trend)
    Bead Abacus
    Number Plaques
        (Lauri)
    Let's Count
    Slide Abacus
        (Learning Resources)
    Getting Ready to Read and Add—
      software
        (Sunburst)
    Math Rabbit: Early Math Skills—
      software
    I Can Count
        (Troll)

ARITH.

25. park a toy car with a painted numeral on its side in the "parking place" with the same numeral on a "parking lot" which has been drawn on a poster board.

Arithmetic

Short-Term Objectives	Instructional Level: K-3
The learner will be able to	**Materials**

26. fill cups that have different numerals on them with a matching number of items (e.g., five beans in the cup with a five on its side).

27. pour sand, water, or beans into the correct number of containers to match a specified number (e.g., three glasses of sand).

27. *It's the Thought That Counts* (Dale Seymour)

28. match colored objects in pairs (e.g., red apples, green balls, blue dots).

28. *Lauri's Build-A-Skill* (Lauri) *Attribute Sorting Set* (Ideal)

29. tell which items are "below" and "above" a flat surface such as a table.

29. *Boehm Resource Guide for Basic Concept Teaching* (Psychological Corporation) *Primary Concepts 1* (Troll) *Spatial Relationship Puzzles* (Ideal)

30. distinguish between before, after, smaller, larger, greater, and lesser, etc.

30. *Primary Concepts 1 Knowing Numbers*—software (Troll) *Building Blocks of Readiness: More, Fewer, As Many As* (Judy/Instructo) *Boehm Resource Guide for Basic Concept Teaching* (Psychological Corporation)

31. count the objects in a set one by one up to five. (Expand to 10 as student's ability increases.)

31. *Lauri's Build-A-Skill* (Lauri) *Attribute Sorting Set* (Ideal) *Cuisenaire Rods* (Cuisenaire)

Arithmetic

Short-Term Objectives	Instructional Level: K-3

The learner will be able to

Materials

32. demonstrate comprehension of the concept zero.

32. *Unifix Dual Number Board*
    (Didax)

33. identify and arrange coins with respect to value: penny, nickel, dime, and quarter.

33. *Money Counts 1*
    Big Bag of Change
        (Incentives for Learning)
    Enlarged U.S. Coins
        (Judy/Instructo)
    Toy Coins, Jumbo Assortment
    Dollars and Cents Kit
        (Ideal)

34. identify the missing number when given a series of numbers with one omitted.

34. *Numberite*
    Number Worm Puzzle
    Walk-On Number Line (0-10)
        (Judy/Instructo)

35. place an object first, next, or last as specified.

35. *Attribute Sorting Set*
        (Ideal)
    Cardinal/Ordinal Puzzles
        (Incentives for Learning)
    Sequencer
    Lauri's Build-A-Skill
        (Lauri)
    Colored Sticks
        (Ideal)
    Unifix Pre-School Kit
        (Didax)

36. recite from one to one hundred.

37. cut a whole picture into halves to make a puzzle.

38. complete halves to whole puzzles.

38. *Fraction Discs*
        (Media Materials)
    Half 'n' Half Design and Color
        (Ann Arbor)

ARITH.

229

Arithmetic

Short-Term Objectives	Instructional Level: K-3
The learner will be able to	**Materials**

39. compare three to five objects with respect to length: longest to shortest, shortest to longest.

39. *Cuisenaire Rods*
    (Cuisenaire)
    Unifix Foundation Kit
    (Didax)
    Rulers
    Yardsticks
    Measuring tapes

40. compare three to five objects with respect to weight: heaviest to lightest, lightest to heaviest.

40. *Super Beamer Balance*
    (Didax)
    Simple Scales
    (Learning Resources)

41. compare three to five objects with respect to volume: most to least, least to most.

41. *Liter Volume Set*
    (Learning Resources)
    It's the Thought that Counts
    (Dale Seymour)

42. play games involving number recognition.

42. *Cross the Brook*
    (Ideal)
    Ice Cream Cone Darts
    Tens
    Ladybug
    Sneaky Snake
    (Mattel)

43. write numerals zero through twenty.

43. *Wipe-Off Books: Let's Write Numbers*
    (Trend)
    Odd 'N Even Duck
    (Constructive Playthings)

44. sort picture cards in groups according to likeness (e.g., transportation, people).

44. *Classifying*
    (Judy/Instructo)
    Classification Picture Card Library
    (Lakeshore)

Arithmetic

Short-Term Objectives

The learner will be able to

Instructional Level: K-3

Materials

45. play games that involve counting objects from 1-100.

45. *One Hundred Chart*
    Hundred Number Board:
      100 Activities for the Hundred
      Number Board
      (Ideal)
    TOPS Beginning Problem Solving:
      Frederika and the Big Bad Biting Bee
      (LinguiSystems)

46. identify the numbers 1-100.

46. *Number Flash Cards*
    One Hundred Chart
      (Ideal)

47. demonstrate an awareness of basic numerals 1-100 in a sequential order using a counting board.

47. *1-100 Chart*
    Counting 1 to 100, Turn to Learn
      (Judy/Instructo)
    100 Activities for the Hundred
      Number Board
    One Hundred Chart
      (Ideal)
    Unifix 1-100 Number Tiles
      (Didax)

48. demonstrate awareness of the concepts first, last, second, middle, and next to last.

48. *Cardinal/Ordinal Puzzles*
      (Incentives for Learning)

49. match sets of pictures and/or objects according to number and classification (e.g., sets of animals: dogs, cows, horses).

49. *Duplo Playville Farm*
      (LEGO Systems)
    Lauri's Build-A-Skill
      (Lauri)
    Attribute Sorting Set
      (Ideal)

50. count by groups of 10 to 100 using objects and drill sheets.

50. *Beginning Base 10 Set*
      (Ideal)
    Base Ten Blocks
      (Learning Resources)

ARITH.

Arithmetic

Short-Term Objectives
The learner will be able to

Instructional Level: K-3
Materials

Unifix 100 Tracks
Unifix Building to 100 Board
Unifix Operational Grid and Tray
Unifix Cubes
    (Didax)
Numbers and Numerals
    (Ann Arbor)

51. match the numerals 1-10 to their printed or written number names.

51. *Game Bag 1*
    (Ideal)
    Cardinal/Ordinal Puzzles
        (Incentives for Learning)
    Number Value Desk Tape
        (Judy/Instructo)

52. name the number of the empty set (zero).

53. demonstrate comprehension of "one-ness," "twoness," etc., using objects (e.g., toothpicks, blocks).

53. *Unifix Dual Number Board*
    Developing Number Concepts Using Unifix Cubes
        (Didax)
    Number Concepts, Pt. 1 & 2
        (Milliken)

54. name and identify days, dates, and months on a calendar.

54. *Judy Calendar*
        (Judy/Instructo)
    Calendar
        (Childcraft)

55. count the objects in a set from 0-12.

55. *Math Chips*
        (Creative Teaching Associates)

56. construct sets of objects from 0-12.

57. compare two numbers from 0-12 identifying which number is greater or lesser ($>$, $<$).

57. *Less Than, Greater Than Flash Cards*
        (Ideal)

Arithmetic

Short-Term Objectives

The learner will be able to

Instructional Level: K-3

Materials

58. use the words first, last, second, third, fourth, fifth to describe the position of objects in a series.

58. *Cardinal/Ordinal Puzzles*
    (Incentives for Learning)
    Number Concepts Pt. 1 & 2
    (Milliken)

59. identify the missing number in a given pattern of numbers (ex. 1, 2, 3, 1, 2, 3, 1, __ , __).

59. *Winker's World of Patterns*—software
    Winker's World of Numbers—software
    (Sunburst)

60. name two-digit numerals that represent sets of ten objects and single objects.

60. *Counting Frame*
    (Childcraft)
    Base Ten Blocks
    (Learning Resources)
    Beginning Base 10 Set
    (Ideal)

61. identify "one-fourth," "one-third," and "one-half" by moving to the appropriate place on a walking board or number line.

61. *Harmon Walking Rail*
    (Ideal)
    Walk-On Number Line
    (Judy/Instructo)

62. separate a set into two sets using sets with no more than twelve objects total.

62. Egg cartons
    Cubes

63. demonstrate the meaning of the equals sign by using a card with the sign and sets of objects drawn on it to show an equation (a true number sentence) with one set of the same number of objects as the set on the other side of the card. (Expand to unequal number in the sets arrange to discriminate equal from unequal.)

63. *Speak and Math*
    (Texas Instruments)
    Teacher-made materials

64. perform the operation of addition using a card with the plus sign drawn on it and proceeding in the manner described in Activity 21 to demonstrate a true number sentence or equation.

64. Teacher-made materials

ARITH.

Arithmetic

Short-Term Objectives

The learner will be able to

Instructional Level: K-3

Materials

65. identify different addition facts that give the same sum (e.g., 5 is 1 + 4, 2 + 3, 5 + 0).

66. demonstrate an awareness that the sums of two reverse addition facts are the same (e.g., 1 + 4 = 5 and 4 + 1 = 5).

67. demonstrate skills in addition by "building a ten" to find sums, regrouping when necessary.

67. *Cuisenaire Rods*
    (Cuisenaire)
    Developing Number Concepts Using Unifix Cubes
    (Didax)

68. demonstrate knowledge of basic addition facts using games, cards, shapes, flashcards, and drill sheets.

68. *Stickeybear Math*—software
    (Cambridge Development Laboratory)
    Sum Clown
    (DLM)
    Speak and Math
    (Texas Instruments)
    Cross Math Puzzles
    (Incentives for Learning)
    Basic Facts Flashcards: Addition
    Mathfacts Games: Addition/ Subtraction
    Arithmetic Quiz
    (Media Materials)
    Basic Math Games: Book 1
    (Dale Seymour)
    Basic Math Games
    (BLIP)
    All Facts Flash Cards
    (Ideal)
    TOPS Beginning Problem Solving: Sam and the Storm at Willow Pond
    (Dale Seymour)
    Balancing Bear—software
    (Sunburst)

Arithmetic

Short-Term Objectives

The learner will be able to

69. perform the operation of subtraction using a card with the minus sign drawn on it with sets of objects to demonstrate a true number sentence.

70. demonstrate knowledge of subtraction facts, regrouping when necessary.

71. perform tasks in subtraction using games, cards, shapes, flashcards, and drill sheets.

Instructional Level: K-3

Materials

69. Teacher-made materials

70. *All Fact Flash Cards: Subtraction*
    (Ideal)
    Basic Facts Flash Cards: Subtraction
    Arithmetic Quiz:
    Addition/Subtraction
    Mathfacts Games;
    Addition/Subtraction
    (Media Materials)
    Touch 'N Tell Me—Math:
    Addition/Subtraction
    Tortoise and the Hare
    (Creative Teaching Association)

71. *Stickybear Math*—software
    (Cambridge Development
    Laboratory)
    Charlie the Drill Instructor:
    Subtraction
    (Educational Insights)
    I Can Add and Subtract—software
    (Troll)
    Primary Math Coloring Book
    (Cuisenaire)
    TOPS Beginning Problem Solving:
    Maggie, the Mischievous Mouse
    (LinguiSystems)
    Basic Math Games—Book 1
    (Dale Seymour)
    Basic Math Games
    (BLIP)
    Subtract with Balancing Bear—
    software
    (Sunburst)

ARITH.

Arithmetic

Short-Term Objectives	Instructional Level: K-3
The learner will be able to	**Materials**

72. add the value of a set of coins up to twenty-five cents. (Expand to $1.00 as student's ability increases.)

72. *Money Big Box*
    (DLM)
    Coin Set
    (Learning Resources)
    Toy Coins, Economy Set
    (Ideal)

73. demonstrate the meaning of the cent sign (¢) by writing sums of money up to 99 cents.

73. *Money Counts 1*
    (Incentives for Learning)
    Buy and Sell
    (DLM)

74. tell time to the hour, half-hour, quarter-hour.

74. *Flip and Learn: Time*
    Laminated Teaching Clocks
    (DLM)
    Tell Time Quizmo
    (Milton Bradley)
    Time Flash Cards
    (Ideal)
    Clock Class Pack I
    (Judy/Instructo)

75. compare and order three liquids with respect to temperatures: hottest to coldest, coldest to hottest.

75. *Student Thermometer*
    Jumbo Fahrenheit-Celsius
    Thermometer
    (Ideal)
    Demonstration Thermometer
    (Learning Resources)

76. identify time concepts of hours, morning, noon, night, afternoon, and o'clock.

76. *All About Time Box*
    (Incentives for Learning)
    Judy Primary Clock
    (Judy/Instructo)
    Learning to Tell Time—software
    (Troll)
    Telling Time Games
    (BLIP)
    Learning About Time
    (Frank Schaffer)
    Teddy Bear Time
    (Hayes)

Arithmetic

Short-Term Objectives

The learner will be able to

Instructional Level: K-3

Materials

77. measure lengths of objects in the classroom to the nearest whole inch, and to the nearest whole yard.

77. Ruler
Yardstick

78. measure the weight of objects to the nearest whole pound.

78. *Platform Scale*
(Learning Resources)

79. measure quantities to the nearest cup and to the nearest quart.

79. *Liquid Measure Set*
(Ideal)
Graduated Beakers
(Learning Resources)
Store-bought measuring utensils

80. identify and name cube, sphere, and cylinder.

80. *Geometric Plastic Forms*
(Ideal)

81. perform addition and subtraction exercises using fingermath techniques.

81. *The Complete Book of Fingermath*
(Webster)
Complete Book of Chisenbop
(Fingermath)

82. solve word problems by building true number sentences, using single digits, plus, minus, and equal signs.

82. *How to Solve Story Problems: Grade 1*
(Instructional Fair)
Getting Started with Story Problems
(DLM)

83. complete self-correcting challenge activities designed to develop classification skills.

83. *Beginning Classification*
(Lauri)
Counting: Ourselves and Our Families
Sorting: Groups and Graphs
(Dale Seymour)

84. use ordinal numbers while placing classmates or objects in the classroom in first, last, second, third, fourth, fifth, sixth, seventh, eighth, ninth, and tenth positions.

84. *Cardinal/Ordinal Puzzles*
(Incentives for Learning)
Game Boy I
(Ideal)
Number Concepts Pt. 1 & 2
(Milliken)

ARITH.

Arithmetic

Short-Term Objectives

The learner will be able to

Instructional Level: K-3

Materials

85. divide and cut pieces of construction paper into "one-fourth," "one-third," "one-half," to identify a given model.

85. *Introduction to Fractions*
    (Educational Insights)
    Fraction Bars
    (Cuisenaire)
    Introduction to Fractions
    Fractional Parts Circles
    (Judy/Instructo)
    Fractions
    (Ann Arbor)
    Fraction Circles
    Fraction Squares
    (Ideal)

86. place objects into given groups of sets to show ones, tens, and hundreds.

86. *Place Value Board*
    Fundamath
    Place Value Building Set
    (Ideal)
    Place Value Materials
    (Cuisenaire)
    Understanding Place Value
    (Creative Publications)
    Unfix Hundreds, Tens and Ones
    Place Value Tray
    (Didax)

87. count by groups of 2's to 100 using a number line, objects, and/or drill sheets. (Extend to 5's and 10's when appropriate.)

87. *Counting by 5's and 10's Turn to Learn*
    (Judy/Instructo)
    Math Concepts I & II—software
    (Troll)

88. demonstrate knowledge of the principles of fractional parts after viewing filmstrips and through the manipulation of objects and materials.

88. *Fractions Are Easy As Pie*
    Fraction Discs
    (Media Materials)
    Fraction Stax Teacher's Set
    (Ideal)
    Fit-A-Fraction—Circles
    (Lauri)

Arithmetic

Short-Term Objectives

The learner will be able to

Instructional Level: K-3

Materials

Fraction Pattern Blocks
Fractional Pattern Block Thinkcards
    (Creative Teaching Associates)
Galaxy Math Facts Game:
    Fractions—software
    (Troll)

89. utilize objects to demonstrate comprehension of fractional parts: halves, thirds, fourths.

89. *Action Fraction Games 1*
Fraction Stax Teacher's Set
    (Ideal)
Fractions Are As Easy As Pie
    (Media Materials)
Fractions Kit
    (Didax)

90. measure objects in the room to the nearest whole inch, whole foot, and whole yard.

90. *Measurement*
    (Frank Schaffer)
Ruler
Yardstick

91. measure the weight of an apple, orange, etc., to the nearest whole ounce and nearest whole pound.

91. *Bucket Balance*
Rocker Scales
    (Ideal)

92. read picture and bar graphs.

92. *Visual Math, Grades 2-3*
    (Instructional Fair)
Graphing Primer
    (Dale Seymour)

93. make bar graphs using heights of classmates.

93. *Graphs and Charts Skills Box*
    (Troll)

94. measure quantities of sand, rice, or beans to the nearest cup, nearest pint, and the nearest quart.

94. *Liquid Measure Set*
    (Ideal)
Measuring cup
Pint bottle or jar
Quart bottle or jar

ARITH.

Arithmetic

Short-Term Objectives
The learner will be able to

Instructional Level: K-3
Materials

95. tell time to hour, half-hour, quarter-hour, and to the nearest five minutes.

95. *Time Flash Cards*
    (Ideal)
    Big Clock
    (Didax)
    Time Puzzles
    Two-Faced Clock Dial
    (Incentives for Learning)
    Learning To Tell Time—software
    How To Tell Time
    (Troll)

96. demonstrate comprehension of the vocabulary words relating to time: quarter till, quarter after, half past.

96. *All About Time Box*
    (Incentives for Learning)

97. draw a clock face and time notation to read and write time to the nearest five minutes including the use of a.m. and p.m.

97. *Time Stamps*
    (Incentives for Learning)

98. measure lengths of yarn to the nearest whole centimeter and to the nearest whole meter.

98. *Metric Stick*
    (Ideal)
    Vinyl Tapes
    (Cuisenaire)

99. measure weight of an object to the nearest kilogram.

99. *Invicta Simple Balance*
    (Cuisenaire)
    Platform Scale
    (Ideal)

100. measure quantities to the nearest liter.

100. *Liter Measuring Pitcher*
     (Cuisenaire)
     Metric Bottle Set
     (Ideal)

101. read a Fahrenheit thermometer to the nearest ten degrees.

101. *Jumbo Wall Thermometer*
     (Ideal)

102. read a Fahrenheit thermometer and use the words cold, cool, warm, and hot appropriately.

102. *Student Thermometer*
     (Ideal)

Arithmetic

Short-Term Objectives	Instructional Level: K-3

The learner will be able to

Materials

103. solve simple word problems.

103. *Story Problems Resource Pak*
(Opportunities for Learning)
How to Solve Story Problems
Getting Started With Story Problems
(DLM)
Understanding and Solving Story Problems
(Nasco)
Wizard Math: Word Problems Zany Zoo (Grades 1-3)
(Opportunities for Learning)
Math Word Problems
(Frank Schaffer)

104. complete a true number sentence (equation) of basic facts by supplying missing addends.

104. *Equations*
(Educational Teaching Aids)
Basic Math Drills
(Milliken)
Ship's Ahoy—software
(Troll)

105. build an equation (a true number sentence) involving one operation from a group of three numbers and two signs:

(ex: [3 1 2 + =] $\longrightarrow$ [1 + 2 = 3]).

106. complete classifying activities.

106. *Classifying*
(Milliken)
Sort & Fit Shapes
Classroom Sorting Material
(Lakeshore)
Sorting: Groups and Graphs
(Dale Seymour)

ARITH.

Arithmetic

Short-Term Objectives

The learner will be able to

1. read and write numbers containing tenths, hundredths. (Extend to thousandths when appropriate.)

2. count to 50 by twos, fives, and tens using manipulatives.

3. count by 5's backward from 50 to 0.

4. group sets of tens and sets of one to show standard numerals such as 18. (Extend to 100 when appropriate.)

5. place counting items in four open paper bags representing ones, tens, hundreds, thousands to illustrate up to four-digit numbers. (Extend up to ten thousands, hundred thousands, and million when appropriate.)

6. make an individual place value chart using construction paper and stapling individual pockets for ones, tens, hundreds, thousands, and ten thousands.

Instructional Level: 3-6

Materials

1. *The 1 to 100 Chart*
    (Didax)
   Everything You Always Wanted to Know About Arithmetic
    (Ann Arbor)

2. *Plastic Counters*
    (Media Materials)
   Math Concepts I & II—software
    (Troll)
   Counting By 5's and 10's Turn To Learn
    (Judy/Instructo)
   Number Line
   Quiet Counters
    (Ideal)

4. *Cuisenaire Rods*
    (Cuisenaire)
   Developing Number Concepts Using Unifix Cubes
    (Didax)

6. *Place Value Tray*
   Unifix One Step At A Time: Operations and Place Value
    (Didax)

Arithmetic

Short-Term Objectives

The learner will be able to

7. illustrate on a place value chart, numerals containing tenths and hundredths. (Extend to thousandths, etc. when appropriate.)

PLACE VALUE CHART									
BILLIONS	HUNDRED MILLIONS	TEN MILLIONS	MILLIONS	HUNDRED THOUSANDS	TEN THOUSANDS	THOUSANDS	HUNDREDS	TENS	ONES

8. separate a set of objects into two sets to illustrate a true number sequence (equation).

9. divide three sets of objects like pencils, crayons, and erasers into two sets and one set to show how different groups may reach the same sum (e.g., $2 + 9 = 11$ and $8 + 3 = 11$).

10. demonstrate knowledge of basic addition and subtraction facts, using shapes, games, flashcards, and drill sheets.

11. circle the largest number no higher than 9999 written on the chalkboard.

Instructional Level: 3-6

Materials

7. *The Place Value Connection*
   (Didax)
   Place Value I, II
   Face Value—Place Value
   (Creative Teaching Associates)

8. *Cuisenaire Rods*
   (Cuisenaire)
   Attribute Sorting Kit
   (Ideal)

9. *Attribute Sorting Set*
   (Ideal)

10. *Facts Arcade Games*—software
    (Gamco)
    Missing Facts Flash Cards
    The Game Bag Series
    (Ideal)
    Digitor Drillmaster
    (Educational Insights)
    The Little Professor
    (Texas Instruments)
    Everything You Always Wanted To Know About Arithmetic (but didn't want to count on your fingers)
    (Ann Arbor)
    TOPS Beginning Problem Solving: When Barney Stopped Laughing
    (Dale Seymour)

ARITH.

Arithmetic

Short-Term Objectives

The learner will be able to

Instructional Level: 3-6

Materials

12. read and write numerals given orally to 9999. (Extend to seven digits when appropriate.)

13. indicate even numbers on a number line by skipping every other number. (Extend to odd numbers when appropriate.)

13. *Table Top Number Lines*
(Didax)
Number Lines
(Judy/Instructo)

14. identify the odd numbers that come next in a repeated number pattern (ex. 5, 4, 7, 4, 9, 4, __ , __).

14. *Winker's World of Number*—software
(Sunburst)

15. order numbers from greatest to least and from least to greatest. (Extend to seven digits when appropriate.)

15. *Less Than, Greater Than Flash Cards*
(Ideal)

16. demonstrate the properties of equality and inequality using balance scales.

16. *Bucket Balance*
Rocker Scales
(Ideal)
Clothes hanger
Paper plates
String

17. identify, name, and write fractions for parts of whole regions or parts of sets of objects using halves, thirds, fourths. (Extend to sixths, eighths, and tenths when appropriate.)

17. *Overhead Fraction Circles*
Fraction Activity Flash Cards
(Learning Resources)
Pizza Party Fraction Game
(Ideal)
Fraction Discs
Fractions Are As Easy As Pie
(Media Materials)

18. rewrite problems written either vertically or horizontally and find the sum and/or difference of two numbers, each having one to four digits. (Extend to seven digits when appropriate.)

19. relate multiplication to addition by use of a number line and arrays.

19. *One Hundred Chart*
Student Number Line
(Ideal)

Arithmetic

Short-Term Objectives

The learner will be able to

Instructional Level: 3-6

Materials

20. demonstrate the equation of multiplication by using a card with the times sign and numbers drawn on it to illustrate a true number sentence (equation).

21. recognize the multiplication sign using a tactile approach differentiating among the signs of addition, subtraction, and equals (e.g., tracing over sandpaper signs).

21. Sandpaper signs

22. illustrate the product of a multiplication problem with a factor of zero (e.g., $5 \times 0 = 0$) by use of empty plastic bags.

22. Plastic bags

23. demonstrate using stacks of sticks, rods, etc., to show that the product of a whole number and one is that number.

23. *Cuisenaire Rods*
    (Cuisenaire)
    *Developing Number Concepts
    Using Unifix Cubes*
    (Didax)

24. demonstrate knowledge of basic multiplication facts using games, flashcards, objects, practice exercises.

24. *Little Professor and Speak Math*
    (Texas Instruments)

ARITH.

25. name the missing factor when the product and one of the factors is given in a true number sentence (equation).

25. *Math Relationship Cards
    Missing Facts Flashcards*
    (Ideal)

26. create a way to show that division by zero is meaningless.

27. find the product of numbers up to four digits.

28. name the product by any whole number and 10, 100, 1,000, or 10,000 by use of manipulative material.

Arithmetic

Short-Term Objectives
The learner will be able to

Instructional Level: 3-6
Materials

29. separate a set of objects into equivalent sets and express the operation as multiplication and its inverse—division (e.g., 8 sets of 3 is $24 \div 3 = 8$ because $24 = 8 \times 3$).

30. demonstrate the use of the divide symbol by showing how a set can be divided into subsets to make a true number sentence (equation).

30. *Cuisenaire Rods*
    (Cuisenaire)

31. demonstrate knowledge of division facts using drill activity sheets, games, and flashcards.

31. *Speak & Math*
    (Texas Instruments)
    Facts Arcade Games: Division Shooting Gallery—software
    (Gamco)

32. find the quotient and check by multiplication when given up to a four-digit dividend and a two-digit divisor.

32. *Math Relationship Cards*
    (Ideal)

33. illustrate the meaning of multiplication when given up to a four-digit dividend and a two digit divisor.

34. name the product in its lowest terms when one or both of the factors contain fractions.

35. review mathematical vocabulary relating to multiplication and division.

35. *Mathematics Dictionary*
    Crescent Dictionary of Mathematics
    Webster's New World Mathematics Dictionary
    (Dale Seymour)

Arithmetic

Short-Term Objectives

The learner will be able to

Instructional Level: 3-6

Materials

36. circle designated parts of pictures or flash cards to show equivalent fractions using halves, thirds, fourths, fifths, sixths, eighths and tenths.

36. *Fraction Flash Cards: Basic and Advanced*
     (Ideal)
    Fractions Kit
    Equivalent Fractions Matching Cards
     (Didax)
    Fraction Activity Flashcards
     (Learning Resources)
    Fraction Recognition/Mixed Number Recognition—software
    Fraction Factory—software
     (Troll)

37. make a fraction kit containing cards illustrating the fractions 1/2, 2/3, 3/8, 1/4, 5/6, 3/5, 9/10, and place one of each in an envelope labeled appropriately.

37. *Basic Fraction Game*
     (BLIP)

38. play games such as Concentration using fraction kits.

38. *Pizza Party*
     (Ideal)
    Fractions Are As Easy As Pie
     (Media Materials)
    Fraction Flash Cards
     (Kenworthy)
    Tic Tac Frac
    Tic Tac Fraction Slices
    Fraction Dominoes and Match Wits Games
     (Creative Teaching Associates)

39. figure out the rule so that a fraction number pattern can be completed (ex: 1/2, 1/3, 1/4, 1/5, etc.).

40. demonstrate the relationship of 100 percent to a whole through the manipulation of fractional parts of objects.

40. *Fractions Are As Easy As Pie*
    Fraction discs
     (Media Materials)
    Pizza Party
     (Ideal)
    Visual Fraction Discs
     (Didax)

ARITH.

Arithmetic

Short-Term Objectives
The learner will be able to

41. indicate fractional parts of 1/10, 1/4, 1/2, and 3/4 on hundreds board and relate the fractional part to a decimal value (e.g., shade one square which is 1/10 and the same as .1 or .10.)

42. explain the relationship between fractions, decimals, and percentage equivalents for 1, 1/2, 1/4, 1/8, 1/16, 1/3, 1/6, 1/12, 1/5, and 1/10.

43. compare two whole numbers of three digits using the symbols >, < or = . (Extend to seven digits when appropriate.)

44. define mathematical vocabulary terms.

45. round off numbers of no more than seven digits to the nearest 10; 100; 1000; 10,000; and 100,000 by use of a number line on which is written multiples of ten.

46. state the rule for rounding off numbers. (If the number is halfway or more, round to the larger multiple. If the number is less than halfway, round to the smaller multiple.)

Instructional Level: 3-6
Materials

41. *Building Competency Skills in Math* (Troll)
One Hundred Chart (Ideal)

42. *Percent*—software (Gamco)
Game Bag 4 (Ideal)
Decimals and Percentages (Ann Arbor)
Galaxy Math Facts Game—software
Grand Prix—software (Troll)
Moving Up in Percent (DLM)

43. *Less Than, Greater Than, Flash Cards* (Ideal)

44. *Mathematics Dictionary* (Dale Seymour)

45. *Rounding*—software (Gamco)
Guess, Box I (Dale Seymour)

Arithmetic

Short-Term Objectives

The learner will be able to

Instructional Level: 3-6

Materials

47. round numbers by use of a place value grid (e.g., rounding numbers to the nearest 10 the answer is 370).

H	T	O
3	7	1

48. relate fractions to decimal values graphically through the use of a hundred board or graph paper.

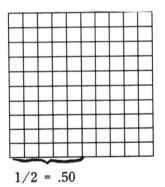

1/2 = .50

48. *Hundred Chart*
   (Judy/Instructo)
   Everything You Always Wanted To Know About Arithmetic (but didn't want to count on your fingers)
   (Ann Arbor)

ARITH.

49. compare the decimal fractions, having not more than three decimal places by using > , < or = .

50. write fractions to identify given points on a number line.

50. *Number Line*
   (Ideal)

51. plot two fractions with the like denominators on a number line.

51. *Number Line*
   (Judy/Instructo)

52. rename a fraction in lowest terms (e.g., 2/4 renamed 1/2).

52. *Fractions*
   (Cuisenaire)
   Fraction Fuel-Up—software
   (Troll)

Arithmetic

Short-Term Objectives

The learner will be able to

Instructional Level: 3-6

Materials

53. change a mixed numeral to an improper fraction and an improper fraction to mixed number.

53. *Fractions*
    (Ann Arbor)
    Fraction Recognition/Mixed Number Recognition—software
    (Troll)

54. express a fraction as a division problem.

54. *Fraction Tiles*
    (Cuisenaire)

55. rewrite numerals on graph paper expressing dollars and cents in horizontal format into numerals vertically, keeping the decimal points aligned.

56. add and subtract numbers containing tenths or hundredths. (Extend to thousandths when appropriate.)

57. add and subtract numbers up to four digits including zeros with and without regrouping. (Extend to larger digit number when appropriate.)

57. *System 80—Developing Math Skills Computation Kits HH and II*
    (Borg-Warner)

58. solve a problem involving addition or subtraction of fractions with like denominators, and express the solution in lowest terms.

58. *Fraction Chart*
    (Ideal)
    Fractions—Book 2
    (Ann Arbor)

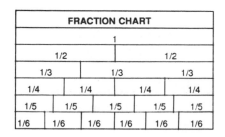

FRACTION CHART					
1					
1/2			1/2		
1/3		1/3		1/3	
1/4		1/4		1/4	1/4
1/5	1/5	1/5		1/5	1/5
1/6	1/6	1/6	1/6	1/6	1/6

Arithmetic

Short-Term Objectives

The learner will be able to

Instructional Level: 3-6

Materials

59. build an equation (a true number sentence) using three fractional numbers and two signs:
    (ex: [1/4 1/4 1/2 + =] $\longrightarrow$ [1/4 + 1/4 = 1/2]).

60. interpret information from a picture or bar graph.

60. *TOPS Problem-Solving Skill Sheets*
    Developing Skills with Tables and Graphs
       (Dale Seymour)
    Graphs and Charts Skills Box
    Bumble Plot—software
       (Troll)

61. record daily the name of the day, the date of the month, and the year in a math notebook.

62. read and interpret line and circle graphs.

62. *Developing Skills with Tables and Graphs*
       (Dale Seymour)
    Bumble Plot—software
       (Troll)

63. construct bar, picture, and line graphs from a given set of data (e.g., weather, game scores, number of library books read).

63. *Developing Skills with Tables and Graphs*
       (Dale Seymour)
    Graphs and Charts Skill Box
       (Troll)

64. estimate sums and differences of two and three digit numbers using a calculator and other manipulative aids.

64. *Calculator Explorations*
    T1-Math Explorer Teacher Kit
    The Little Professor
       (Texas Instruments)
    Guess
       (Dale Seymour)
    Calculator Companions
       (Learning Resources)

65. estimate products of two digit factors by matching correct answers with each of six problems shown on the chalk board or overhead projector.

65. *Guess*
       (Dale Seymour)
    Calc-U-Vue Teacher's Kit
       (Learning Resources)

ARITH.

251

Arithmetic

Short-Term Objectives

The learner will be able to

66. solve word problems from information obtained from a chart or table.

67. relate the six steps for solving word problems: interpret the problem; illustrate the problem; decide the operation(s) for solving the problem; estimate the solution; write the number sentences; and solve the number sentence and label the result.

68. name the operation to be used when given a word problem involving any one operation on whole numbers: write the appropriate number sentence; find the solution; and label the answer.

69. solve problems using measures of length, weight, volume, time, or temperature.

70. use a legend to tell the distance from one point to another on a map.

71. identify missing facts needed to solve word problems to make a true number sentence (equation).

72. find the average of a set of whole numbers by stacking blocks into even stacks.

Instructional Level: 3-6

Materials

67. *Problem Solving Focus: Solving Story Problems*
   (Dale Seymour)

70. *Where I Am: Independent Map and Orientation Activities*
   (DLM)
   Basic Map Skills
   (Educational Insights)
   Prime Time Maps
   (Good Apple)
   Building Primary Maps
   (Judy/Instructo)
   State maps

71. *Missing Facts Flashcards*
   Math Relationship Cards
   (Ideal)

72. *Unifix Cubes*
   (Didax)

Arithmetic

Short-Term Objectives

The learner will be able to

Instructional Level: 3-6

Materials

73. solve a word problem which requires two operations.

73. *TOPS Development Workbooks, Level B & C*
(Dale Seymour)

74. build an equation (a true number sentence) involving two operations from a group of four numbers and three signs:
(ex: $[1 \quad 2 \quad 4 \quad 8 \quad \times \quad \div \quad =]$
$[8 \quad \div \quad 2 \quad \times \quad 1 \quad = \quad 4])$.

75. measure lengths of objects in the classroom to the nearest whole inch, nearest whole yard, and nearest whole foot. (Extend to nearest half-inch when appropriate.)

75. Ruler
Paper clips
Pencils
Tables
Chalkboard
Crayons
Desk tops
Yardstick
Measuring tape

76. measure the weight of objects in metric units, or customary units, using a simple scale balance.

76. *Plastic Stacking Objects*
Simple Scales
(Didax)
Combination English and Metric
Platform Scale
(Learning Resources)
Spring scale

77. compute the difference between birth weight and present weight using pounds and ounces.

78. measure a quantity of liquid such as water to the nearest cup, the nearest pint, and the nearest gallon. (Expand to teaspoons and tablespoons when appropriate.)

78. *Liquid Measure Set*
(Ideal)
Measuring cups
Quart
Pint
Gallon

ARITH.

Arithmetic

Short-Term Objectives

The learner will be able to

Instructional Level: 3-6

Materials

79. tell time on a paper plate clock to the hour, half-hour, quarter-hour, and to the nearest five minutes including the use of a.m. and p.m.

79. *Time Stamps*
   (Incentives for Learning)
   Time Flash Cards
   (Ideal)
   Clock Dial
   (Media Materials)

80. measure lengths of objects to the nearest whole centimeter, the nearest whole meter, and the nearest centimeter.

80. *Vinyl Tapes*
   Basic Metric Activities Kit
   (Cuisenaire)
   Demonstration Metric Stick
   (Ideal)

81. state the value of a set of coins beginning with $1.00 and expanding to $5.00.

81. *Big Bag of Change*
   Big Bag of Bills
   (Incentives for Learning)
   Count Your Change
   (Milton Bradley)
   Toy Money
   (Media Materials)
   School Money Kit: Class Set
   Money Matters
   (Educational Insights)

82. practice exchanging money in a sellers-buyers situation by use of money kit made with brown construction paper for pennies, grey paper for nickels, manilla paper for dimes, white paper for quarters, and green paper for half-dollars.

82. *Buy and Sell*
   (DLM)

83. determine whether the value (up to $5.00) of U.S. currency is equal to, less than, or greater than a given amount of money.

83. *Buy and Sell*
   (DLM)
   Count Your Change
   (Milton Bradley)
   Money Matters
   Dollars & Cents Kit
   (Ideal)

Arithmetic

Short-Term Objectives

The learner will be able to

Instructional Level: 3-6

Materials

84. state the amount of additional money needed to purchase an item (or the amount of change one should get) when given a set of U.S. currency coins and the price of an item is not the same as the value of the set.

84. *What's Your Change Drill Cards* (DLM)

85. name and utilize the appropriate unit for measuring an object.

86. tell weather temperatures.

86. *Student Thermometer Fahrenheit/Celsius Thermometer* (Ideal)

87. answer the questions involving degrees, boiling point, freezing point, and zero by using a Celsius or Fahrenheit weather thermometer.

87. *Demonstration Thermometer* (Ideal) *The Metric System Measuring: Temperature* (Gamco)

88. measure quantities of colored water to the nearest liter or milliliter.

88. *Volume Set* (Ideal) *Liter Measuring Pitcher* (Cuisenaire)

89. convert from one unit of metric measure to another when the units are centimeters, meters, kilometers. (Extend to include grams, kilograms, liters, millimeters.)

89. *Metric Skill Box* (Troll)

90. locate and define the small word(s) in the term perimeter.

90. *From Here to There with Cuisenaire Rods—Area, Perimeter, and Volume* (Cuisenaire)

91. measure the perimeter of a polygon.

92. compute the area of a polygon (e.g., covering the surface of a math book).

92. *Perimeter, Area & Volume* (Gamco)

ARITH.

Arithmetic

Short-Term Objectives
The learner will be able to

Instructional Level: 3-6
Materials

93. build a mobile from paper, string, and wire to show a circle, triangle, square, oval, rectangle, square. (Extend to pentagon, hexagon, and octagon when appropriate.)

93. Construction paper
String
Wire

94. identify a cube, sphere, cylinder, cone, pyramid. (Extend to triangle and rectangular prisms when appropriate.)

94. *Geometric Plastic Forms*
(Ideal)
Geometric Wooden Models
(Learning Resources)

95. identify, name, and draw to represent a point, line, line segment, ray, and angle.

95. *Elementary Geometry Charts*
(Ideal)

96. identify parallel, horizontal, vertical, intersecting and perpendicular lines.

96. *Concepts of Geometry: Geometric Constructions*
(Gamco)

97. find the appropriate volume of a container by counting unit cubes.

98. measure angles with a protractor.

98. *Angle Study Dominoes*
(Didax)
Concepts of Geometry: Basic Figures of Geometry
(Gamco)

99. identify and name a quadrilateral, trapezoid, parallelogram, rhombus, rectangle, and square.

99. *Concepts of Geometry: Basic Figures of Geometry*
Geometry for Grades K-6
(Dale Seymour)

100. identify and name the radius, the center, and/or diameter of a circle.

100. *Geometry Dominoes*
(Didax)

101. identify and name an angle as acute, right, or obtuse.

101. *Everything You Always Wanted to Know About Arithmetic (but didn't want to count on your fingers)*
(Ann Arbor)

Arithmetic

Short-Term Objectives

The learner will be able to

102. identify a triangle as isosceles, equilateral, or right.

103. construct a line segment congruent to a given line segment AB and name it with letters.

104. use a protractor to construct an angle of a given number of degrees.

105. construct a circle with a given radius.

Instructional Level: 3-6

Materials

102. *Concepts of Geometry: Basic Figures of Geometry* (Gamco)
Geometry for Grades K-6 (Dale Seymour)

ARITH.

Arithmetic

Short-Term Objectives

The learner will be able to

1. compare two whole numbers with no more than ten digits using the symbols > , < , or = .

2. name the place value and period for each digit of a numeral up to ten digits.

3. read and write numerals containing tenths, hundredths, thousandths, and ten thousandths.

4. write a numeral in expanded form.

5. write, in exponential notation, a four-digit numeral written in standard or expanded form.

6. round off numbers to the nearest 10; 100; 1,000; 10,000; 100,000; 1,000,000.

7. demonstrate written numerals utilizing a place value chart, abacus, or other manipulative device.

8. identify and demonstrate fractional parts of objects or sets of objects, using halves, thirds, fourths, sixths, eighths, fifths, tenths.

Instructional Level: 6-9

Materials

2. *Place Value Building Set*
   (Ideal)
   Digits By Chance—software
   Decimals By Chance—software
   (Wings for Learning)

4. *Charlie the Drill Instructor: Place Value*
   (Educational Insights)
   Expanded Notation—software
   (Troll)

8. *Recognizing Fractional Numbers and Their Relationships*
   (Creative Teaching Resources)
   Teacher or student made fraction kit
   1 large envelope
   5 whole circles
   3 circles cut in half
   3 circles cut in thirds
   3 circles cut in fourths

Arithmetic

Short-Term Objectives	Instructional Level: 6-9
The learner will be able to	**Materials**

3 circles cut in sixths
3 circles cut in eighths
3 circles cut in fifths
3 circles cut in tenths

9. express common fractions as decimals.

9. *Picture Grids for Fractions and Decimals*
   (Delta)
   Decimals and Percentages
   (Ann Arbor)

10. figure out the rule guiding a sequential number pattern in order to complete the pattern or supply the missing numbers.

10. *Gnee or Not Gnee*—software
    Tip 'n Flip—software
    High Wire Logic—software
    (Sunburst)

11. compare two decimal fractions having not more than three decimal places by using > , < , or = .

12. compare two fractions with like denominators using the correct sign > , < , or = . (Extend to include unlike denominators when appropriate.)

13. rename a fraction in lowest terms.

13. *Game Bag 5*
    (Ideal)

14. build a true number sentence (equation) using a group or two whole numbers and a fraction and two signs.
    (ex: [1/2 4 8 × =] → [1/2 × 8 = 4]).

14. *Integers/Equations*—software
    (Hartley)

15. illustrate by a drawing how to change a mixed numeral to an improper fraction and an improper fraction to a mixed numeral.

15. *Fraction Recognition/Mixed Number Recognition*—software
    (Troll)

Arithmetic

Short-Term Objectives	Instructional Level: 6-9

The learner will be able to | **Materials**

16. express a fraction as a division problem.

17. round a decimal numeral to tenths, hundredths, or thousandths.

17. *Basic Skills in Mathematics: Decimals* (Nasco)

18. write a common fraction or a decimal fraction as a percent.

18. *Decimals and Percentages* (Ann Arbor)

19. name the least common multiple of numbers, using power notation.

20. identify numbers as prime or composite.

21. write the set of all factors of a number.

22. name the greatest common factor of two factors of two numbers.

23. locate Roman numerals for Arabic numerals.

24. locate positive and negative integers on a number line.

24. *Integers/Equations*—software (Hartley)

25. perform review exercises using the four basic operations in timed situations using flashcards, games, and drill activities.

25. *Little Professor* (Texas Instruments) *Games in Math Skill Building* (Incentives for Learning) *The King's Rule*—software *Targets*—software (Wings for Learning)

26. demonstrate an understanding of the basic principles involved with the use of money through pre-vocational experiences.

26. *Using Dollars and Sense Math for Everyday Living* (Ideal) *Consumer Math Success Kit* (Incentives for Learning)

Arithmetic

Short-Term Objectives

The learner will be able to

Instructional Level: 6-9

Materials

Math for Everyday Living—software
(Educational Activities)

27. write the product or quotient of a problem when one factor is expressed in money notation and the other factor is a standard number.

28. write checks appropriately through the use of practice pads.

28. Sample checks

29. perform the four basic computational operations with fractions.

29. *Fractions—Book 2*
(Ann Arbor)
Partial Fractions—software
(Sunburst)
Mathfacts Games—Addition and Subtraction, Multiplication and Division
(Media Materials)

30. demonstrate understanding of the concept of expanded notation and place value including thousands and millions through practice activities.

30. *System 80—Developing Math Skills: Decimals Kit L*
(Borg-Warner)
Expanded Notation—software
(Troll)

ARITH.

31. name the product or quotient in its lowest terms when one factor is a whole number and the other is a fraction.

32. complete drill activities to reinforce and review decimal computation.

32. *Math Drill Books, Grades 5, 6, 7, 8*
(Judy/Instructo)
Get to the Point—software
(Sunburst)
System 80—Developing Math Skills: Decimals Kit L, M
(Borg-Warner)

Arithmetic

Short-Term Objectives

The learner will be able to

33. interpret data recorded on picture and bar graphs. (Extend to line and circle graphs when appropriate.)

34. compute distance using a map or globe.

35. construct an appropriate graph utilizing information received from a class activity or assignment (e.g., grades, topics related to social studies or science).

36. measure quantities to the nearest cup, nearest quart, nearest pint, nearest gallon. (Extend to teaspoons, tablespoons, pecks, and bushels when appropriate.)

37. measure weight of objects to the nearest whole pound and whole ounce.

38. demonstrate height and weight relationships through the use of measuring sticks and scales.

39. perform metric measurements using games and drill activities.

40. convert from one unit of metric measure to another when the units are centimeter, meters, kilometers, grams, kilograms, liters, milliliters.

41. find the circumference of a circle using a formula.

42. find the area of a rectangle, a square, and a triangle by using a formula.

Instructional Level: 6-9

Materials

33. *Developing Skills with Tables and Graphs* (Dale Seymour)

34. *Basic Map Skills* (Educational Insights)

36. *Liquid Measure Set* (Ideal) Measuring cup Pint Gallon Measuring spoons

37. *Bathroom Scale* (Enrich/Ohaus)

39. *Metric Skill Box* (Troll)

42. *Geoboards* (Creative Publications)

Arithmetic

Short-Term Objectives

The learner will be able to

Instructional Level: 6-9

Materials

43. identify and name cube, sphere, cylinder, cone, pyramid, triangular, and rectangular prisms.

43. *Geometric Plastic Forms*
    (Ideal)
    Wooden Geometric Solids
    (Creative Publications)

44. identify from a set of four-sided polygons, a quadrilateral, trapezoid, parallelogram, rhombus, rectangle, and a square.

44. *Geometry: Quadrilaterals*
    (Gamco)

45. identify and name the radius, the center, and the diameter of a circle.

45. *Geometry: The Circle*
    (Gamco)

46. identify an angle as acute, right, or obtuse.

46. *Geometry: Parallel Lines*
    (Gamco)

47. identify a triangle as isoceles, equilateral, or right.

47. *Geometry: Congruent Triangle*
    (Gamco)

48. construct a line segment congruent to a given line segment AB and name it with letters.

48. *Geometry: The Basics*
    (Gamco)

49. solve story problems.

49. *Math Story Problems Grades 5-7*
    (Educational Insights)
    Problem Solving Focus: Solving Story Problems
    Problem Solving Focus: Time and Money
    Solving Problems Kids Care About
    Make It Simpler
    (Dale Seymour)
    Cooperative Problem Solving
    (Creative Publications)

ARITH.

50. build an equation (a true number sentence) by rearranging a group of five numbers and four signs:
    (ex: [8 5 3 1 2 - × ÷ =]
    [8 × 2 - 1 ÷ 3 = 5]).

Arithmetic

Short-Term Objectives

The learner will be able to

Instructional Level: 6-9

Materials

51. build a true number sentence (equation) by rearranging a group of four fractions of unlike denominators and three signs:
(ex: [1/3 2/3 1/2 5/6 + - =] →
[5/6 + 1/3 - 1/2 = 2/3]).

51. *Fraction Stax Teacher's Set* (Ideal)

264

Arithmetic

Short-Term Objectives

The learner will be able to

1. complete exercises designed to review the meanings of mathematical vocabulary terms.

2. demonstrate an understanding of place value.

3. read and write numerals containing thousands, ten thousands, hundred thousands, and millions.

4. read and write numerals up to ten digits in expanded notation.

5. compute exponents by multiplying a number times itself, once, twice, etc., to demonstrate that a number times itself is the same as that number squared; that a number to the first power is that number unchanged; that the number times itself two times is that number to the third power, etc.

6. demonstrate comprehension of exponents by completing drill exercises and playing games.

7. demonstrate an understanding of the concept of rounding numbers.

Instructional Level: 9-12

Materials

1. *Silver Burdett Mathematical Dictionary*
   Mathematics Dictionary
   (Dale Seymour)

2. *Math Marvel*
   (Texas Instruments)

5. *Basic Algebra Exponents*
   (Gamco)

ARITH.

Arithmetic

Short-Term Objectives

The learner will be able to

8. complete activities centering around the four computational operations.

Instructional Level: 9-12

Materials

8. *No Frill Math Drill*
   (Judy/Instructo)
   Mixed Math Drill
   (Educational Insights)
   Facts Arcade Games—software
   (Gamco)
   Mathfacts Games
   (Media Materials)
   Math Marvel
   (Texas Instruments)
   Moving Up in Numbers
   (DLM)
   Everything You Always Wanted To Know About Arithmetic (but didn't want to count on your fingers)
   Michigan Prescriptive Program in Math
   (Ann Arbor)

9. change common fractions to decimals.

9. *Game Bag 6*
   (Ideal)

10. compare two decimal fractions and use the symbols $>$, $<$, or $=$.

11. contrast two fractions with like and unlike denominators and use the correct sign $>$, $<$, or $=$.

11. *Game Bag 4*
    Fraction Flashcards
    Game Bag 5 & 6
    (Ideal)

12. rename fractions to the lowest terms.

13. change mixed numerals to an improper fraction and an improper fraction to a mixed numeral.

13. *Partial Fractions*—software
    (Sunburst)

14. express a fraction as a division problem.

Arithmetic

Short-Term Objectives

The learner will be able to

Instructional Level: 9-12

Materials

15. build a true number sentence (equation) by rearranging a series of three whole numbers, a fraction, and four signs including parentheses.
(ex: [1/2 1 3 5 - × ( ) =] →
[(5 - 3) × 1/2 = 1]).

16. write a common fraction or a decimal fraction as a percent.

17. demonstrate comprehension of percentage forms by using drill exercises utilizing manipulative objects, puzzles, worksheets, and story problems.

17. *Moving Up in Percent*
    (DLM)
    Know the Essentials of: Decimals and Percents
    (Hayes)
    Big Deal
    (Creative Teaching Associates)
    Percents—software
    Percentage Panic—software
    (Troll)
    Focus on Percent
    Percentage Dominoes
    (Delta)

18. perform computations needed in real life situations involving percentages, simple and compound interest, and ratio and proportion (e.g., salary, tasks).

18. *50 Easy Mathagrams in General Math*
    (Incentives for Learning)
    Survival Math Skills
    Consumer Math Success Kit
    (Educational Insights)
    Ratios and Proportions—software
    (Troll)
    Managing Lifestyles—software
    (Sunburst)

19. demonstrate an understanding of the four basic computational operations with fractions.

19. *Moving Up in Fractions*
    (DLM)
    Fraction Action—software
    (Troll)

ARITH.

Arithmetic

Short-Term Objectives

The learner will be able to

20. name the least common multiple (LCM) of numbers using power notations.

21. identify prime numbers.

22. convert Roman numerals into Arabic numbers.

23. locate positive and negative integers on number line and name the coordinate of a given point.

24. compute in money notation mathematical functions utilizing the four basic operations.

25. calculate the amount of earnings needed to meet household expenditures (e.g., rent or house payments, utilities, insurance).

26. compute in money notation the student's own weekly expenses based on allowance or earnings.

27. complete application forms for employment purposes.

28. write the product or quotient of a problem when one factor is expressed in money notation and the other factor is in standard form.

29. write checks appropriately.

Instructional Level: 9-12

Materials

22. *Math Amusements in Developing Skills, Volume 2*
    (Activity Resources)

23. *PreAlgebra with Pizzazz*
    (Creative Publications)

25. *Consumer Math Success Kit*
    Math for Everyday Living
    (Incentives for Learning)
    Budget
    (Creative Teaching Associates)

26. *Grocery Cart (CART)*
    (Creative Teaching Associates)
    Newspapers

29. *Bank Account*
    (Creative Teaching Associates)

Arithmetic

Short-Term Objectives

The learner will be able to

Instructional Level: 9-12

Materials

30. maintain a checking account based on teacher prepared data.

30. *Money Matters: Bank On It, Checking Account*
    (DLM)

31. complete vocational study units involving math.

31. *Photomath*
    Choosing A Job You'll Like
    Steps to Independent Living
    How To Get Along On the Job
    (Incentives for Learning)

32. interpret data recorded on picture, bar, line, and circle graphs.

32. *Developing Skills with Tables and Graphs*
    (Dale Seymour)

33. construct an appropriate graph from given information (e.g., favorite television characters, game scores, grades).

34. demonstrate an awareness of measurement terms for liquid and dry quantities.

34. *Liquid Measure Set*
    (Ideal)
    Bathroom Scale
    (Enrich/Ohaus)

35. demonstrate an awareness of metric measurement concepts using games and practice activities.

36. convert from one unit of metric measurement to another.

37. demonstrate awareness of geometric formulas involving area, circumference, and perimeter.

37. *Know the Essentials of Geometry: Problems, Drills, Tests*
    (Hayes)

38. identify and name cube, sphere, cylinder, cone, pyramid, triangular and rectangular prism.

38. *Geometric Wooden Models*
    (Learning Resources)
    Geometric Plastic Forms
    (Ideal)

39. identify and name four-sided polygons.

39. *Geometry: Similar Polygons*
    (Gamco)

ARITH.

Arithmetic

Short-Term Objectives

The learner will be able to

40. identify and name a triangle as isoceles, equilateral, or right and give a characteristic of each.

41. construct congruent line segments and name them.

42. solve equations including missing elements to make true number sentences.

43. compare the population of the largest five cities in the world, ranking them in order.

44. build a true number sentence (equation) by rearranging a series of four numbers and four signs.
    (ex: [2 5 8 9 - × ( ) =] ➔ [(9 - 5) × 2 = 8]).

45. figure out the rule guiding a number pattern in order to complete the pattern, or to supply the missing number.

46. follow a map on an imaginary tour of the United States.

47. draw a tree diagram to show possible outcomes of probabilities when tossing a coin, rolling dice, or spinning a 3- or 4-colored spinner.

48. graph the results of linear equations on a coordinate plane.

49. define and determine mean, median, and mode.

Instructional Level: 9-12

Materials

40. *Geometry: Congruent Triangles*
    (Gamco)
    Wooden Geometric Solids
    (Creative Publications)

41. *Geometry: The Basics*
    (Gamco)

43. World Almanac

46. *The Math Map Trip*
    (Incentives for Learning)

47. *What Are My Chances? Probability Kits*
    (Creative Publications)

48. Graph paper

Arithmetic

Short-Term Objectives

The learner will be able to

50. solve word problems using algebraic activities.

Instructional Level: 9-12

Materials

50. *Trivia Math: Pre-Algebra*
    Trivia Math: Algebra
    Pre-Algebra with Pizzazz
    Algebra with Pizzazz
        (Creative Publications)

ARITH.

DIGIT SPAN

Digit Span

I. **Purpose of the Subtest**

To measure the ability to retain and repeat in correct sequence both forward and backward information received auditorily.

II. **Factors Affecting Subtest and Academic Performance**
   A. Attention
   B. Concentration
   C. Anxiety
   D. Organization and reorganization
   E. Memory
   F. Conceptualization

III. **Educational Significance**
   A. Instructions to the student should be specific, simple, and given slowly, one at a time. The number of instructions should be increased as the student is able to respond appropriately.
   B. Support and aid may be given to the student by standing physically nearby to insure the understanding of the instruction and the beginning of the task.
   C. Structure the student's environment to decrease or eliminate noises, sounds, and other auditory distractions. This may include the use of earphones, carrels, or isolated seating arrangements.
   D. Frequent breaks may be necessary to insure attention to tasks. Variations in lengths of instructional time should be considered according to student needs.
   E. Teaching techniques may employ the visual modality to reinforce the development of auditory-memory skills.

IV. **Long-Term Goal**

The learner will be able to retain, recall, and repeat auditorily received information in correct sequence and detail.

DIGIT SPAN

Digit Span

Short-Term Objectives

The learner will be able to

1. repeat simple letter and number sequences beginning with a combination of two letters or numerals.

2. color a sheet of simple abstract designs following oral directions (e.g., "Color the circle," etc.).

3. color a sheet of simple abstract designs a specified color (e.g., "Color the circle red," etc.).

4. follow one or more simple directions (e.g., "Put the pencil on the table," etc.).

Instructional Level: K-3

Materials

1. *Goal: Levels I and II*
   (Milton Bradley)
   Audiofunics: Developmental Program in Basic Listening Skills
   (Opportunities for Learning)
   Auditory Processes
   (ATP)

2. *Learning Shapes*
   (Milliken)
   Preschool Concepts: I Know My Colors and Shapes
   (Hayes)
   Teacher-prepared worksheets

3. *I Know My Colors and Shapes*
   (Hayes)
   Shapes
   Colors
   Colors and Shapes
   (Instructional Fair)
   Teacher-prepared worksheets

4. *Learning to Follow Directions, K-1*
   Following Directions, K-1, 1-2, 2-3
   (Milliken)
   Following Directions Activity Cards, K-2, 1-3
   (Frank Schaffer)
   I Can Follow Directions: Grades K-1, 1-2, 2-3
   (Educational Insights)
   Following Directions: Primary
   (Curriculum Associates)
   Following Directions Bulletin Board Aid
   (Judy/Instructo)

Digit Span

Short-Term Objectives
The learner will be able to

Instructional Level: K-3
Materials

5. repeat a sequence of two or more nonsense syllables.

5. *Aids to Psycholinguistic Teaching: Auditory Sequential Memory* (Charles E. Merrill)
Auditory Processes (ATP)
Audiofunics: Developmental Program in Basic Listening Skills
Developing Auditory Awareness & Insight—Level 1 (Opportunities for Learning)

6. repeat a sequence of two or more unrelated words.

6. *Aids to Psycholinguistic Teaching: Auditory Sequential Memory* (Charles E. Merrill)
Teacher-prepared word list

7. repeat a sequence of numerals in reverse order.

7. *Audiofunics: Developmental Program in Basic Listening Skills* (Opportunities for Learning)

8. repeat a sequence of names of objects and arrange pictures of the objects in the same order.

8. *Peabody Language Development Kit (Revised)—Level P* (AGS)
Listen and Jump (Ideal)
Auditory Perception Program: Auditory Memory (Incentives for Learning)
Aids to Psycholinguistic Teaching: Auditory Sequential Memory (Charles E. Merrill)

9. arrange word cards in a specific sequence after hearing the words.

9. *Easy Vowels Flash Cards*
Easy Consonants Flash Cards (Frank Schaffer)

10. arrange number cards in a stated sequence.

10. *Large Number Cards* (Ideal)
Number Flash Cards, 0-25 (Trend)

DIGIT SPAN

Digit Span

Short-Term Objectives

The learner will be able to

11. clap a series of rhythmic patterns.

12. tap a rhythmic sequence twice in succession.

13. repeat short poems and rhymes from memory.

14. remember and perform instructions in games (e.g., "Simon Says," "May I?" etc.).

15. repeat his/her telephone number.

16. identify the voices of the children in class while blindfolded.

17. identify sounds that may be heard indoors, outdoors, in the classroom, and from various instruments.

Instructional Level: K-3

Materials

11. *Rhythm and Rhyme*
    (Melody House)
    Fun Activities Perceptual Motor Skills
    Clap, Snap, and Tap
    (Kimbo)

12. Xylophone and other rhythm instruments

13. *Gypsies in Tuxedos, Funnies in Eponyms*
    (Houghton Mifflin)
    Whole Language Program
    Story Pictures Plus
    (Curriculum Associates)

14. *Memory*—software
    (Apple)

16. Tape
    Tape recorder/player
    Scarf for blindfolding

17. *Sound Matching*
    (Incentives for Learning)
    What Do You Hear?
    Listening to the World
    (AGS)
    New Goals in Listening
    (Troll)
    Developing Auditory Awareness & Insight—Level 1
    (Opportunities for Learning)
    Auditory Processes
    (ATP)

278

Digit Span

Short-Term Objectives
The learner will be able to

18. repeat a series of digits in correct order after an interval of 30 to 60 seconds.

19. repeat a series of words in correct sequence after an interval of 30 to 60 seconds.

20. repeat a series of unrelated words in correct order.

21. repeat verbal information from memory.

Instructional Level: K-3
Materials

18. *Developing Auditory Awareness & Insight—Level 1*
    (Opportunities for Learning)
    Cues and Signals in Math
    (Ann Arbor)

19. *Auditory Processes*
    (ATP)
    Auditory Comprehension Series
    (Opportunities for Learning)
    Auditory Perception Program: Auditory Memory
    (Incentives for Learning)

20. *Auditory Perceptual Program: Auditory Memory*
    (Incentives for Learning)

21. *Auditory Comprehension Series*
    (Opportunities for Learning)
    I'm All Ears
    (Media Materials)
    Developing Auditory Awareness & Insight—Level 1
    (Opportunities for Learning)

DIGIT
SPAN

Digit Span

Short-Term Objectives

The learner will be able to

1. relate the days of the week in correct sequence.

2. relate the months of the year in correct sequence.

3. orally repeat sentences of varying length.

4. repeat a list of a series of events and correctly place in sequence pictures illustrating the events.

5. tell the sequence of directions for making something.

6. retell a simple story in correct sequence.

Instructional Level: 3-6

Materials

1. *Days of the Week Bulletin Board Set*
   (Carson-Dellosa)
   Today's the Day
   (Milton Bradley)

2. *Judy Calendar*
   (Judy/Instructo)
   Calendar Studies
   (Troll)

3. *Auditory Perception Program:*
   Auditory Memory
   (Incentives for Learning)

4. *Listen and Jump*
   (Ideal)
   3 Scene Sequence Poster Cards
   4 Scene Sequence Poster Cards
   8 Scene Sequence Poster Cards
   (Milton Bradley)
   Sequential Cards—Level I
   Sequential Cards—Level II
   Sequential Cards—Level III
   Sequential Cards—A Family's Day
   (Incentives for Learning)

6. *Flannelboard Stories, Combos A, B, C*
   (Judy/Instructo)
   Storybooks Plus
   Story Pictures Plus
   (Curriculum Associates)
   Listen, My Children—Book 1
   (Pro-Ed)

Digit Span

Short-Term Objectives

The learner will be able to

Instructional Level: 3-6

Materials

7. repeat a sequence of pairs of rhyming words.

7. *Aids to Psycholinguistic Teaching:*
    Auditory Sequential Memory
      (Charles E. Merrill)
    Pictures That Rhyme
      (Media Materials)
    Rhyming Pictures
      (Judy/Instructo)
    Trend Bingo: Rhyming
      (Trend)

8. play the game "I am going on a trip and I am going to take . . . ," repeat the list and add to the list.

9. develop a shopping list of things to buy at the grocery store, department store, etc.

9. Catalogues
   Newspaper ads

10. act out a story in correct sequence.

10. *Fairy Tale Plays for Oral Reading*
    Fable Plays for Oral Reading
      (Curriculum Associates)
    Roxy the Robin
      (Ann Arbor)
    Magnetic Wooden Stand-Up Figures:
      The Little Red Hen
      The Three Billy Goats Gruff
      The Three Little Pigs
    Puppet Playmates
    Hand-Held Puppet Masks
      (Judy/Instructo)

11. repeat tongue twisters correctly and rapidly.

11. *Aids to Psycholinguistic Teaching:*
    Auditory Sequential Memory
      (Charles E. Merrill)

12. remember and repeat other students' telephone numbers.

DIGIT
SPAN

Digit Span

Short-Term Objectives

The learner will be able to

Instructional Level: 3-6

Materials

13. participate in spelling bees and games.

13. *Stickybear Spellgrabber*—software (EBSCO)
    M-ss-ng L-nks—software (Sunburst)

14. synthesize a sequence of spaced sounds into a word and pronounce it correctly.

14. *First Time Phonics* (Steck-Vaughn)
    Blend Dominoes (Incentives for Learning)
    Sort and Sound Word-Making Puzzles
    Sort and Sound Vowel Digraph Puzzles
    Make-a-Word Spelling Games (Didax)
    Auditory Processes (ATP)

15. indicate whether sounds are the same or different after listening to two or more sounds, in beginning, medial, or final positions.

15. *Sound It!* (Imperial International)
    Consonant Puzzles (Incentives for Learning)
    Working with Vowels & Consonants (Opportunities for Learning)
    Phonics for Reading: First and Second Levels (Curriculum Associates)

16. repeat combinations of numbers, sounds, and letters.

16. *Language Master* (Bell & Howell)
    SOS Auditory Perception: Level II (Follett)

17. follow directions for paper folding tasks.

17. *Paper Folding with Origami Techniques* (Judy/Instructo)
    Origami Paper (Bemiss-Jason)
    Origami Paper
    Origami, Sets A & B

Digit Span

Short-Term Objectives

The learner will be able to

Instructional Level: 3-6

Materials

Complete Origami
Wings and Things: Origami that Flies
Paper Pandas and Jumping Frogs
(Dale Seymour)

18. repeat a tapped rhythmic sequence twice in succession.

19. name in correct sequence the objects making a series of noises or sounds.

20. identify missing alphabet letters in a series of letters presented orally by the teacher.

20. *Aids to Psycholinguistic Teaching:*
    Auditory Sequential Memory
    (Charles E. Merrill)

DIGIT
SPAN

Digit Span

Short-Term Objectives

The learner will be able to

1. differentiate among orally presented phrases or sentences that may or may not differ in grammar (e.g., word endings, word order, verb tense, etc.).

2. tell whether phrases or sentences presented orally are the same or different in intonation or inflection.

3. broadcast a sequence of events in a sports or news item in correct order.

4. list items in a particular recipe in the order of recipe preparation.

5. explain how to play a particular game.

6. memorize and recite poems or choral reading passages.

7. relate in sequence events heard in a story.

8. retain a statement for a specified length of time and then repeat the statement correctly.

Instructional Level: 6-12

Materials

3. Sports or news articles from the newspaper

6. *Studying Poetry*
    (Curriculum Associates)
    Stage: Creative Dramatics
    (Opportunities for Learning)
    Together We Speak
    (Scholastic)

7. *Read-Aloud Anthology*
    (Scholastic)
    Cassette Bookshelves
    Classics on Cassettes
    (Opportunities for Learning)
    Listen, My Children—Books 2, 3
    (Pro-Ed)

Digit Span

Short-Term Objectives
The learner will be able to

Instructional Level: 6-12
Materials

9. complete exercises designed to focus attention and to develop concentration skills.

9. *Auditory Perception Program*
   (Incentives for Learning)
   Developing Auditory Awareness & Insight: Levels 2, 3
   (Opportunities for Learning)

10. recognize absurd sentences in a group of sentences.

10. *Aids to Psycholinguistic Teaching Auditory Sequential Memory*
    (Charles E. Merrill)
    Teacher-prepared sentences

11. play "Gossip" by whispering in a classmate's ear a statement whispered into his ear by another child.

12. prepare a list of the many sounds heard throughout the day at home and at school.

13. describe what is heard on tapes of familiar sounds.

13. *Sounds in My World*
    (Ideal)
    Auditory Familiar Sounds
    (DLM)

14. repeat and record on tape words, phrases or sentences previously recorded by the teacher.

14. *Language Master: Set 3—Language Reinforcement and Auditory Retention*
    (Bell & Howell)

DIGIT
SPAN

15. recognize and identify a specific word in a list of words after hearing it pronounced.

15. Teacher-prepared list of words

16. memorize and perform a part in a class play.

16. *Stage: Creative Dramatics Drama-Pak #1, #2*
    (Opportunities for Learning)
    The Reader's Theater of Classic Plays
    The Reader's Theater of American Plays
    (Curriculum Associates)
    The Elementary School Play
    (High Noon Books)

Digit Span

Short-Term Objectives

The learner will be able to

17. with eyes closed, identify classmates who speak specific words.

18. repeat tongue twisters.

19. recognize and identify absurdities in sentences.

20. tap out a rhythmic sequence twice in succession.

21. repeat or list descriptive words heard in a paragraph or short story read to the class.

22. tell in correct sequence a story sentence presented orally in jumbled order.

23. repeat in order of presentation the nouns in varied lists of words.

24. repeat a mixed series of numbers and words in reverse order.

25. repeat a mixed series of numbers and words after a delay of 60 seconds.

26. relate specific directions to and from particular locations (e.g., from home to school, from one classroom through the school to another, etc.).

27. describe or list directions for making a particular project.

Instructional Level: 6-12

Materials

18. *Creative Dramatics*
    (Scholastic)

21. *Aids to Psycholinguistic Teaching: Auditory Sequential Memory*
    (Charles E. Merrill)

26. *Where I Am: Independent Map and Orientation Activities*
    (DLM)

Digit Span

Short-Term Objectives

The learner will be able to

28. act out a series of stage movements in the sequence described by the teacher.

29. identify the musical instruments heard in classical and semi-classical recordings.

30. repeat jokes told by classmates.

Instructional Level: 6-12

Materials

28. *Stage: Creative Dramatics*
   (Opportunities for Learning)

DIGIT
SPAN

FACTOR IV—PROCESSING SPEED

CODING

Coding

I. **Purpose of the Subtest**

To measure the ability to reproduce symbols through pencil manipulation as a part of a set code.

II. **Factors Affecting Subtest and Academic Performance**
   A. Visual-motor dexterity
   B. Speed
   C. Accuracy
   D. Flexibility in learning
   E. Associative thinking
   F. Anxiety
   G. Spatial orientation
   H. Visualization
   I. Memory
   J. Time
   K. Motivation and goal orientation

III. **Educational Significance**
   A. Assist the student on a one-to-one basis when presenting new materials to be learned.
   B. Time allowances will need to be extended for all copied and written assignments, particularly those from the chalkboard. Do not allow the student to rush through pencil-and-paper tasks.
   C. Rote exercises and drill to focus visual attention and increase motor speed will be beneficial to the student in new learning situations.
   D. Classroom and homework assignments should be explained to the child in a step-by-step fashion to insure understanding.
   E. Arithmetic symbols may present difficulties and recall of the correct operational method should be checked for accuracy.
   F. The student may require markers or pointers to maintain place and position of writing or math problems.

CODING

IV. **Long-Term Goal**

The learner will be able to reproduce symbols as part of a set code through pencil manipulation.

Coding

Short-Term Objectives

The learner will be able to

1. copy pegboard designs from those presented by the teacher.

2. copy symbols from a prepared series for practice in timed and competitive situations.

3. trace vertical lines and circles.

4. separate assorted nails, bolts, nuts, and screws into proper boxes within a specified amount of time.

5. copy a pattern of square, round, and cylindrical beads on a lace in a given amount of time.

Instructional Level: K-3

Materials

1. *Pegboard*
   Pegboard Designs
      (DLM)
   Plastic Pegs and Pegboard
      (Media Materials)
   Pegboard Fun with Patterns
      (Ideal)
   Deluxe Pegboard Set
   Large Pegboard Patterns
   Pegboard Kit
      (Incentives for Learning)

2. *See It, Make It Wipe-Off Cards*
      (Trend)
   Colorama (PreK—Grade 2)
      (AGS)
   PREPARE: An Interdisciplinary
      Approach to Perceptual-Motor
      Readiness
      (Communication Skill Builders)

3. *Before I Print! Wipe-Off Book*
      (Trend)
   Starting to Print
      (Educational Insights)
   Zaner-Bloser Handwriting: Basic
      Skills and Application
      (Zaner-Bloser)

4. Nails, bolts, nuts, screws
   Small boxes

5. *Multivariant Sequencing Beads and*
      Multivariant Sequencing Bead Patterns
      (DLM)
   Large Beads and Laces
   Large Beads/Laces Pattern Cards
   Beads and Laces
      (Media Materials)

Coding

Short-Term Objectives

The learner will be able to

Instructional Level: K-3

Materials

Stringing Beads
Stringing Beads Patterns
   (Judy/Instructo)
Wooden Beads
Large Colored Beads & Patterns
Building Bead Patterns
   (Ideal)

6. outline with colored laces on sewing cards or fabric figures and designs in a timed situation.

6. *Lacing Boards*
   (DLM)
   Lace-a-Saurus
   Lacing Shapes
   Lace-a-Pet Puppets
   (Lauri)
   Sewing Cards—Class Set
   (Ideal)

7. match symbols or specific colors to pictures of animals in a given length of time.

7. *Match-Ups*
   (Playskool)
   Animal Shapes
   (Novo)
   Colored Cubes
   (Ideal)

8. separate objects according to name, color, or shape in a given time period (e.g., boxes of buttons, marbles, beads, etc.).

8. *Sorting Box Combination*
   (Marvel)
   Sorting and Order Kit
   (Novo)
   Attribute Sorting Kit
   (Ideal)
   Attribute Block Desk Set
   (Learning Resources)
   Sorting Box & Accessories
   (DLM)

CODING

9. insert toothpicks in salt shaker top within a given period of time.

9. Toothpicks
   Salt shaker top

10. remove cylinders or boxes graduated in size from a tray and replace them in the tray in a given period of time.

10. *Shape Sorter and Stacker*
    (Playskool)
    Stacking Clown
    (Learning Resources)

Coding

Short-Term Objectives
The learner will be able to

Instructional Level: K-3
Materials

11. trace geometric shapes in specified length of time.

11. *Shape Tracer Set*
    Shape Tracer Extension Set
      (Ideal)
    Clear Stencils
    Shapes Templates
    Shapes Stamps
    Eye-Hand Integration Exercises
      (DLM)
    Common Shapes Tracing Stencils
      (Trend)
    Tracing Paper
      (Bemiss-Jason)

12. complete geometric shapes puzzles in timed situations.

12. *Geometric Shapes*
      (Media Materials)
    Fit-a-Shape
    Shape Squares
    Junior Fit-a-Space
      (Lauri)
    Montessori Shapes
      (Novo)
    Shape Form Board
      (Learning Resources)

13. complete dot-to-dot patterns in varying complexity, gradually working into timed situations.

13. *The I'm Ready to Learn Series:*
      Dot-to-Dot
      (Kid's Stuff)
    Dot-to-Dot
      (Frank Schaffer)
    Perceptual Activities Packets:
      Dot-to-Dot 1 & 2
    Perceptual Activities
      (Ann Arbor)

14. participate in activities that require moving a marker in a specified manner.

14. *Honey Bear, Funny Bear*
    Magic Rainbow
    Gameboards, K-1
      (Frank Schaffer)
    Candy Land Game
    Chutes and Ladders
      (Milton Bradley)

Coding

Short-Term Objectives

The learner will be able to

Instructional Level: K-3

Materials

Kat Tracks
(Educational Insights)

15. place colored clothespins (on a line or a piece of cardboard) randomly at first, and then to match given patterns in a timed situation.

15. Colored clothespins
Clothesline

16. complete visual tracking exercises.

16. *Symbol/Letter Tracking*
Letter Tracking
Perceptual Activities
Symbol Discrimination and
  Sequencing
  (Ann Arbor)
Visual Tracking Cards
  (Ideal)
Beginning Kindergarten Skills
  (Frank Schaffer)
Visual Tracking
  (Communication Skill Builders)
Visual Tracking—software
  (Hartley)

17. insert geometric shapes through appropriately shaped openings in the sides of a box or ball.

17. *Shape Sorter and Stacker*
Form Fitter
  (Playskool)
Shape Sequence Box
Shape Drop Box
  (Marvel)

18. reproduce mosaic design patterns.

18. *Shape Sorting Box*
  (DLM)
Wooden Pattern Blocks
Patterns for Pattern Blocks
Large Parquetry & Patterns
  (Ideal)
Mosaics
  (Lego)

CODING

Coding

Short-Term Objectives

The learner will be able to

19. match shapes of words to shape or configuration designs.

20. copy series of symbols, letters, and numbers from the chalkboard, stressing accuracy first, then speed.

21. write things from rote memory in a timed situation (e.g., numbers and the alphabet).

22. type spelling words.

Instructional Level: K-3

Materials

22. *Typing Keys*—software
(ATP)
Stickybear Typing—software
(Cambridge Development
Laboratory)

Coding

Short-Term Objectives

The learner will be able to

1. string various sizes of beads or colored macaroni pieces in a specified order, making simple pieces of jewelry.

2. complete simple paint-by-number pictures.

3. complete penmanship exercises by tracing ovals, circles, letters, etc.

4. match Roman numerals to Arabic numbers in a specified length of time.

5. locate cities, counties, rivers, highways, etc., on a map by using the map legend.

Instructional Level: 3-6

Materials

1. *Multivariant Sequencing Beads and Multivariant Sequencing Bead Patterns*
(DLM)
Do-it-yourself jewelry kits
Macaroni
Food dye

2. Paint-by-number kits

3. *Trace 'N' Write*
(Educational Insights)
Kin-Tac Alphabet Cards
Desk-Top Practice Mats
(Zaner-Bloser)
Handwriting Practice
(Carson-Dellosa)
Harvey Hippo Handwriting
(Frank Schaffer)
Eye-Hand Integration Exercises I
(DLM)

4. Teacher-prepared worksheet
Student-prepared Roman numeral flash cards

5. *Where I Am—Individual Map and Orientation Activities*
(DLM)
Map Skills
Maps, Charts, and Graphs
(Frank Schaffer)
Developing Map Skills: Book 1
(Hayes)
Basic Map Skills
(Educational Insights)
Various state maps

CODINC

Coding

Short-Term Objectives

The learner will be able to

6. complete simple anagrams using a number-letter or a geometric form-letter code system in a specified period of time.

7. memorize short poems, song lyrics, and proverbs or adages.

8. mark on a page of printed faces those reflecting a specified mood.

9. use sewing cards and laces to reproduce designs in a given length of time.

10. reproduce a design drawn on paper by using an *Etch-A-Sketch*.

11. play games following specific rules (e.g., jacks, pick-up sticks, marbles, etc.).

Instructional Level: 3-6

Materials

6. *Anagrams*
    (Selchow and Righter)
   Coding Game
    (Love)
   Kids Book of Secret Codes, Signals, and Ciphers
    (Dale Seymour)
   Castles, Codes, and Calligraphy
    (Learning Works)

7. *The Magic of Music, Movement, and Make Believe*
    (DLM)
   Studying Poetry
   Whole Language Program
    (Curriculum Associates)

8. *Face Matching Plaques*
    (Marvel)
   Teacher-prepared activity sheet

9. *Sewing Cards*
    (Ideal)
   Sewing Cards
    (Media Materials)
   Lacing Boards
    (DLM)

10. *Etch-A-Sketch*
     (Ohio Art)

11. Jacks and ball
    Pick-up sticks
    Marbles
    Chinese Checkers

Coding

Short-Term Objectives

The learner will be able to

Instructional Level: 3-6

Materials

12. put geometric shapes through appropriately shaped openings in the sides of a box or ball in a given length of time.

12. *Shape Sorting Box*
     (DLM)
     Shape Sorter and Stacker
     Form Fitter
       (Playskool)
     Shape Drop Box
     Shape Sequence Box
       (Marvel)

13. complete various puzzles and keep a record of time performances.

13. *United States Floor Mat Puzzle*
     Mini U.S. Map Puzzle
       (Judy/Instructo)
     Frank Schaffer Floor Puzzles:
       Circus Time
       Farm
       Dinosaur Sets 1 & 2
       (Frank Schaffer)

14. spin jacks, trying to keep as many spinning at one time as possible.

15. hang painted or colored plastic clothespins on a string in a specific order in a given period of time.

15. Painted clothespins
    Plastic colored clothespins

16. write and read simple rebus stories.

16. *First Reading Laboratory Story Cards*
       (SRA)
     Clark Early Language Program
     Rebus Reading: Beginning Sentence
       Building
       (DLM)
     Standard Rebus Glossary
     Rebus Stick-Ons
       (AGS)
     Catchword
       (High Noon Books)

CODING

301

Coding

Short-Term Objectives	Instructional Level: 3-6
The learner will be able to	**Materials**

17. complete visual tracking exercises in a given period of time.

    17. *Symbol/Letter Tracking*
       Cues and Signals (Reading)
       Symbol Discrimination Series
       Classroom Visual Activities
       Letter Tracking
       Word Tracking: High Frequency Words
       Symbol Discrimination and Sequencing
         (Ann Arbor)
       Visual Tracking
         (Communication Skill Builders)

18. reproduce a series of designs or symbols from memory.

    18. *Visual Memory Cards*
       (DLM)

19. complete crossword puzzles.

    19. *Crossword Puzzles—USA*
       (Frank Schaffer)
       Holiday Cross-Riddles: Grades 3-4
         (Instructional Fair)
       Store-purchased crossword puzzle books

20. write words in sand within a given period of time.

    20. Box of sand

21. type spelling or vocabulary lists in complete sentences.

    21. *Typing Keys*—software
       (ATP)
       Typewriter

Coding

Short-Term Objectives

The learner will be able to

1. complete paper-folding or Origami exercises in a specific period of time.

2. identify a letter traced on the palm of the hand while eyes are closed.

3. list the abbreviations for the days of the week and the months of the year.

4. put together nuts and bolts, keys and locks, electrical connectors of variously colored wire, jars and lids, etc., in a timed situation.

5. complete activities involving manipulation of screw drivers, wrenches, hand-operated can openers, etc.

6. tie knots according to specific directions.

7. make macrame objects according to given directions (e.g., belts, hanging pot holders, etc.).

8. perform written tasks on the typewriter.

9. make use of mnemonics to learn names of great lakes (such as the acronym HOMES), states, cities, etc.

Instructional Level: 6-12

Materials

1. *Paper Folding with Origami Techniques*
   (Judy/Instructo)
   Origami Paper
   (Bemiss-Jason)
   Complete Origami
   Wings and Things: Origami that Flies
   Paper Pandas and Jumping Frogs Origami
   Origami Paper
   (Dale Seymour)

4. Various sizes of nuts and bolts
   Keys and locks
   Jars and lids
   Electrical clips and eyes, etc.

5. Various tools and kitchen aids

6. Boy Scout Manual
   Macrame instructions

7. Macrame kits and instructions

8. *Typing Keys*—software
   (ATP)

9. *Demonic Mnemonics*
   (Dale Seymour)
   Memory Foundations for Reading
   (ATP)

CODING

Coding

Short-Term Objectives	Instructional Level: 6-12
The learner will be able to	**Materials**

10. complete crossword puzzles and games appropriate for age level.

    10. *Scrabble Crossword Dominoes*
         Scrabble Crossword Cubes
         Scrabble
         Scrabble for Juniors
         RSVP
           (Selchow and Righter)
         Crossword Cubes
         Ad-Lib Crossword Cubes
           (Milton Bradley)
         Crossword Magic—software
           (Cambridge Development
           Laboratory)
         Crossword Puzzles—USA
           (Frank Schaffer)

11. decipher jumbled word or sentence exercises.

    11. *GrammaRummy*
           (Educational Insights)
         Word and Phrase Sentence Builder
           (Kenworthy)

12. complete mosaic-type projects using mosaic kits or bits of colored paper to copy a design.

    12. Mosaic kits
         Pieces of colored paper

13. reproduce from memory, using paper and pencil, a series of symbols flashed in front of him.

    13. *Visual Memory Cards*
         Visual Sequential Memory Exercises
           (DLM)

14. describe what was seen in correct sequence after looking at a series of action pictures flashed before him.

    14. *Photopacks: Verbs*
           (Incentives for Learning)

15. identify specified objects hidden in pictures.

    15. *Figure-Ground Activity Cards*
           (DLM)

16. assemble abstract designs using tangram puzzle pieces.

    16. *Puzzlegrams*
         Tangrams
         Tangram Puzzles
           (Ideal)
         Tangram Puzzles
         Tangram Patterns
           (Judy/Instructo)

Coding

Short-Term Objectives
The learner will be able to

Instructional Level: 6-12
Materials

Tangram Treasury
  (Cuisenaire)
Tangrams and Puzzles Cards
  (DLM)

17. decipher messages written in code.

17. *Codebusters! Sets 1, 2, 3*
  (Educational Insights)
  *Kids Book of Secret Codes, Signals
  and Ciphers*
  (Dale Seymour)

18. act out familiar stories and song
titles.

18. *Folk Tale Drama Kits 1, 2, 3*
  Playkit—The Velveteen Rabbit
  (Opportunities for Learning)
  The Reader's Theatre Series of Plays
  (Curriculum Associates)

19. use a map legend to find roads, rivers,
cities, etc.

19. *Basic Map Skills*
  (Educational Insights)
  Developing Map Skills, Book 2
  Practicing Map Skills
  (Hayes)
  Various state maps

20. trace guides to improve handwriting
skills.

20. *Handwriting*
  (Milliken)
  Practice Writing Series, Books 1-4
  (Hayes)
  Handwriting: A Fresh Start
  (Curriculum Associates)
  Trace 'N' Write
  (Educational Insights)

CODING

21. write the initials of all classmates.

22. write in cursive the words presented
in manuscript.

23. reproduce given patterns within a
specific period of time.

23. *Etch-A-Sketch*
  (Ohio Art)
  Lite Brite

Coding

Short-Term Objectives

The learner will be able to

Instructional Level: 6-12

Materials

Small Parquetry and Small Parquetry Design I, II, III
(DLM)
Pocket Parquetry Plus Patterns
(Ideal)

24. match the appropriate words to given functional signs.

24. *Functional Signs*
Functional Signs Match-Ups
(DLM)
Signs & Symbols Flash Cards
(Frank Schaffer)

25. write the appropriate word for given functional signs.

25. *Functional Signs*
Functional Signs Match-Ups
(DLM)
Signs & Symbols Flash Cards
(Frank Schaffer)

26. use mnemonics to spell words.

26. *Demonic Mnemonics*
(Dale Seymour)
Memory Foundations for Reading
(ATP)

27. reproduce a series of code units on a telegraph key.

28. use mnemonics to learn the lines and spaces on the musical staff.

28. *Music Books 1, 2, 3*
Let's Learn Music, Books 1, 2, 3
(Hayes)

29. produce a melody using a musical instrument following simple musical symbols.

29. Eight-note diatonic step bell
Chromaharp
Resonator bells
Xylophone

30. recite and discuss song lyrics, poems, proverbs and/or adages, and stories.

30. *Word Tracking: Proverbs*
Word Tracking: Limericks
(Ann Arbor)
Tales for Thinking: Levels 2 and 3
(Curriculum Associates)

SYMBOL SEARCH

Symbol Search

I. Purpose of the Subtest

To measure the speed at which the learner can determine the presence or absence of a given symbol in a line of symbols.

II. Factors Affecting Subtest and Academic Performance

A. Concentration and attention
B. Speed
C. Accuracy
D. Anxiety
E. Spatial orientation
F. Visual perception
G. Visualization
H. Memory
I. Time
J. Motivation and goal orientation

III. Educational Significance

A. Exercises and drill designed to focus visual attention to tasks will be beneficial to the student in new learning situations.

B. Activities for the development of visual perceptual, scanning, and tracking skills will assist in reading, spelling and mathematical performance.

C. To increase processing speed, require the student to complete various assignments within a specified length of time.

D. Verbal classroom instructions (rate of speech) should be presented at student's speed of understanding. As the student's ability to process information improves, rate of speech for instructions and other verbal information may be increased.

E. Keep written or visual instructions short and simple. More complex instructions may be utilized as the student's ability to process them improves.

IV. Long-Term Goal

The learner will be able to determine the presence or absence of a specific symbol in a line of symbols within a given time limit.

SYMB.
SEARCH

Symbol Search

Short-Term Objectives

The learner will be able to

1. match seven of ten geometric forms.

2. match pictures with familiar objects in three out of three trials.

3. complete puzzles requiring recognition of shape, size, and spatial orientation.

4. put together a puzzle of a person.

5. identify an object by touch.

Instructional Level: K-3

Materials

1. *Visual Perception Big Box*
   (DLM)
   Classic Color and Shape Board
   (Lakeshore)
   Large Geometric Plastic Forms
   Shape Tracer Set
   (Ideal)
   Fit-A-Shape
   Fit-A-Space
   (Lauri)

2. *Early Concepts: Match It*—software
   (Edmark)
   Pictures, toys and other small objects

3. *Shapes and Colors "Pinch Puzzles"*
   (Chaselle)
   Bigbeads and Puzzle Tiles
   (Educational Insights)
   Attribute Block Desk Set
   Attribute Block Template
   (Learning Resources)
   Montessori Shapes
   (Didax)

4. *Body Parts Puzzle, 6 pcs.*
   Body Parts Puzzle, 12 pcs.
   Girl Puzzle
   Boy Puzzle
   Face Parts Puzzle
   (Judy/Instructo)
   Body Parts Floor Puzzle
   (Frank Schaffer)

5. *Feel and Match Textures*
   (Lauri)
   Small sack containing small toys and other small objects

Symbol Search

Short-Term Objectives	Instructional Level: K-3

The learner will be able to

Materials

6. choose the correct shape from among five choices.

6. *Shape Discrimination and Memory—*
   software
   (Edmark)
   Visual Discrimination Books
   (Educational Teaching Aids)
   Attribute Block Desk Set
   (Learning Resources)

7. separate assorted nails, bolts, nuts, and screws into the proper boxes or containers within a specified amount of time.

7. *Fasteners*
   (Ideal)

8. reproduce designs drawn on paper or cards using manipulative materials such as colored cubes, etc.

8. *Colored Inch Cubes and Designs in Perspective*
   (DLM)
   Patterns for Pattern Blocks
   Wooden Pattern Blocks
   Plastic Pattern Blocks
   Large Parquetry and Patterns
   (Ideal)

9. screw together threaded objects.

9. *Nuts and Bolts*
   Nuts and Bolts Builder
   Big Bold Board
   (Lakeshore)

10. copy pegboard designs from those presented by the teacher.

10. *Mini Pegboard*
    Mini Pegboard Patterns
    (Judy/Instructo)
    Pegboards, Pegs, and Pegboard Designs
    (DLM)
    Pegboard Fun with Patterns
    Easy Grip Pegs and Pegboard
    Easy Grip Pegs and Pegboard Plus Patterns
    Large Pegboard Patterns
    (Ideal)

SYMB. SEARCH

311

Symbol Search

Short-Term Objectives
The learner will be able to

Instructional Level: K-3
Materials

11. play "Pick-Up Sticks" game.

12. match the sequence or pattern of blocks or beads.

12. *Large Colored Beads and Patterns*
    Patterns for Multicolored Beads
    Building Bead Patterns
        (Ideal)
    Beads and Laces Pattern Cards
    Colored Beads and Laces
        (Milton Bradley)

13. match large parquetry pattern pieces to a design card.

13. *Parquetry Blocks*
    Parquetry Pattern Cards
        (Learning Resources)
    Large Parquetry Design Blocks
    Large Parquetry Pattern Cards
        (Milton Bradley)
    Large Parquetry and Patterns
    Patterns for Pattern Blocks
    Plastic Pattern Blocks
    Wooden Pattern Blocks
        (Ideal)

14. pantomime the use of simple objects such as the telephone, typewriter, computer, hammer, etc.

14. *Functions*
        (DLM)

15. sort concrete objects according to a selected attribute (e.g., size, color, shape, weight, etc.).

15. *Shellsorts*
    Attribute Sorting Kit
    Fasteners
        (Ideal)

16. put cylinders or pegs in size order according to height.

16. *Sort and Stack*
    Peg Grading Board
    Square Pegs 'N Board
        (Marvel)

17. reproduce a bead design of all one color.

17. *Building Bead Patterns*
        (Ideal)

Symbol Search

Short-Term Objectives	Instructional Level: K-3

The learner will be able to

Materials

18. cut out basic designs.

18. *Basic Shapes*
   (Frank Schaffer)
   Attribute Block Template
   (Learning Resources)
   Shape Play Books: Stencils
   (Didax)
   Trend's Tracing Stencils: Common Shapes
   (Trend)

19. draw simple recognizable pictures (e.g., person, tree, etc.).

19. *Kid Pix*—software
   (Edmark)
   Magnetic Drawing Board
   (Lakeshore)
   Etch-A-Sketch
   (Ohio Art)

20. reproduce a pattern without assistance after tracing the pattern from a solid-line pattern and then a dotted-line pattern.

20. *Perceptual Development Cards*
   (Ideal)
   Perceptual Activities Packets Dot-to-Dot 1, 2
   (Ann Arbor)

21. reproduce small parquetry designs.

21. *Pocket Parquetry and Patterns*
   (Ideal)

22. copy symbols from a prepared series in timed situations.

23. complete left-to-right directionality exercises.

23. *See-Quees Storyboards*
   (Judy/Instructo)
   Bozon's Quest—software
   (Edmark)
   Visual Tracking Cards
   (Ideal)
   Symbol Discrimination Series
   Symbol Discrimination and Sequencing
   (Ann Arbor)

SYMB. SEARCH

313

Symbol Search

Short-Term Objectives

The learner will be able to

Instructional Level: K-3

Materials

24. trace vertical lines and circles.

24. *Before I Print*
    (Trend)

25. repeat the alphabet after hearing it (e.g., singing the ABC song).

26. build a recognizable object using manipulative materials (e.g., house, tower, etc.).

26. *DUPLO Basic Bucket*
    Giant DUPLO Basic Set
    Large LEGO Basic Set
    Medium LEGO Basic Set
       (LEGO)
    Log Builders
    People Builder-Starter Set
    Magnashapes
       (Lakeshore)

27. match lower case letters in manuscript to lower case letters in cursive.

27. *Alphabet Wall Cards:*
       Manuscript
       Cursive
        (Milton Bradley)
    Animal Alphabet Photography Portfolio:
       Manuscript
       Cursive
        (Instructional Fair)
    Teacher-made letter cards in both manuscript and cursive

28. match upper case letters in manuscript to upper case letters in cursive.

28. *Alphabet Wall Cards:*
       Manuscript
       Cursive
    Animal Alphabet Photography Portfolio:
       Manuscript
       Cursive
        (Instructional Fair)

Symbol Search

Short-Term Objectives

The learner will be able to

Instructional Level: K-3

Materials

29. match numerals zero to 100.

29. *Number Cubes*
     (Cuisenaire)
    Number Tiles
     (Activity Resources)
    Number Flash Cards
     (Ideal)

30. match upper case letters with lower case letters.

30. *Alpha-Match Board*
     (Lakeshore)
    Letters and Words—software
     (Troll)
    Tub O' Letters:
      Upper Case
      Lower Case
    Letter Perfect
     (Educational Insights)

31. trace a "hidden" picture.

31. *Figure-Ground Activity Cards*
     (DLM)
    'M' Is for Mirror: Find the
      Hidden Picture
      (Dale Seymour)
    Perceptual Activities
     (Ann Arbor)

32. complete dot-to-dot activity sheets.

32. *Teddy Bear Alphabet*
    Alphabet Dot-to-Dot
      (Frank Schaffer)
    Dot-to-Dot Pattern Sheets
      (DLM)
    Perceptual Activities
    Perceptual Activities Packets:
      Dot-to-Dot 1, 2
      (Ann Arbor)

33. draw geometric shapes when requested by the teacher either free-hand or with stencils.

33. *Trend's Tracing Stencils:*
      Common Shapes
      (Trend)
    Color and Shape Resource Chart
      (Lakeshore)

SYMB.
SEARCH

Symbol Search

Short-Term Objectives

The learner will be able to

Instructional Level: K-3

Materials

34. interpret the concept of likeness by using matching and sorting exercises (e.g., red beads, white buttons, etc.).

34. *Sorting Boxes*
    (Judy/Instructo)
    Links
    (Cuisenaire)
    Alike Because
    (DLM)
    Attribute Sorting Set
    (Ideal)

35. complete simple mazes.

35. *Perceptual Skills I*—software
    (Edmark)
    ABC Mazes
    The Maze Book
    (Ann Arbor)
    Algernon—software
    (Sunburst)

36. print or write in cursive his/her name and the names of classmates.

36. *If You're Trying to Teach Kids How to Write, You Gotta Have This Book*
    (Kid's Stuff)
    Printing with Peter Possum
    Handwriting with Harvey Hippo
    (Frank Schaffer)
    Book 1, Let's Write Manuscript
    Book 2, Let's Write Cursive
    (Hayes)

37. demonstrate the differences among first, middle, and last by standing in the appropriate place in a line of students.

38. interpret the concept of "different" using picture cards which reflect differences (e.g., taller, shorter, etc.).

38. *Opposites*
    (DLM)
    Peabody Picture Collection: Opposites
    (AGS)
    Same or Different Wipe-Off Cards
    (Trend)
    Stickybear Opposites—software
    (Ebsco)

Symbol Search

Short-Term Objectives

The learner will be able to

Instructional Level: K-3

Materials

Primary Concepts II
Milk Bottles—software
  (Troll)
Alike and Not Alike
Size Proportion Cards
  (Ideal)

39. determine the presence or absence of a specified symbol in a line of five or more symbols.

40. complete jig-saw puzzles.

41. recognize likenesses and differences among categories of animals, foods, clothing, etc.

    41. *Touch 'N Match*—software
      (Edmark)
    Categories
    Association Picture Cards: Sets I-IV
      (DLM)
    The Classification Game
    Classification Picture Cards
      (Judy/Instructo)

42. describe differences within a single category such as "dogs" by looking at pictures (e.g., size, color, type, etc.).

    42. *Association Picture Cards: Sets 1-IV*
      (DLM)
    Classification Picture Cards
    Sorting Boxes with a Reading
      Curriculum Focus: Same & Different
      (Judy/Instructo)
    Lauri's Build-a-Skill:
      Beginning Classification and Sorting
      Advanced Classification, Sorting and
      Sequencing
      (Lauri)
    Early Concepts: What's the Difference
      (Edmark)

43. recognize and circle the same letter or symbol which appears on a given line of a worksheet.

    43. *Shapes to Learn*
      (Media Materials)
    Symbol Discrimination Series
    Symbol/Letter Tracking
    Symbol Discrimination and
      Sequencing
      (Ann Arbor)

SYMB.
SEARCH

Symbol Search

Short-Term Objectives	Instructional Level: K-3
The learner will be able to	**Materials**

44. circle or match correctly color, objects, shapes, etc., in Bingo and Lotto games.

44. *Lotto Games:*
    Rooms (in the house)
    Colors
    Seasons
    Familiar Settings
    Geometric Shapes
    (Judy/Instructo)
    Object Matching Light & Learn
    Bingo
    Candy Land Bingo
    Candy Land Lotto
    Play Scenes Lotto
    (Milton Bradley)

45. match correctly numbers of dots, designs, and pictures in domino games.

45. *Jumbo Dominoes*
    (Chaselle)
    Geometric Shape Three-Sided
    Dominoes
    (Judy/Instructo)
    Dominoes
    (Frank Schaffer)
    Shadow Dominoes
    Animal Dominoes
    Color Dominoes
    Arrow Dominoes
    (Marvel)

46. put individual parts together to make a whole.

46. *Parts-Whole Puzzle Forms*
    (Lakeshore)

47. reproduce abstract designs.

47. *Visual Discrimination Activity*
    Booklets
    (Didax)

48. complete tangram puzzles.

48. *Tangram Puzzles*
    (Judy/Instructo)
    Tangram Treasury
    (Cuisenaire)

Symbol Search

Short-Term Objectives

The learner will be able to

Instructional Level: K-3

Materials

49. complete paper folding activities.

49. *Pholdit*
    Spatial Problem Solving with Paper Folding
      (Activity Resources)
    Paper Folding with Origami Techniques
      (Judy/Instructo)
    Origami, Set A
      (Dale Seymour)

50. perform typing activities.

50. *Type to Learn*—software
      (Sunburst)
    Typing Keys—software
    Typing Keys
      (ATP)
    Kindercomp
      (Troll)

51. copy maps.

51. *Developing Map Skills, Book I*
      (Hayes)
    Maps, Charts, and Graphs
      (Frank Schaffer)
    Learning About Maps
      (Milliken)

52. copy a picture from a model using a sketch pad and colored chalk.

53. reproduce two and three dimensional patterns.

53. *Kaleidoscope Puzzles*
    Two-Dimensional Color Block Design
      (Ideal)
    Multilinks Spatial Awareness Activity Cards
    Multilinks Explorations
      (Cuisenaire)

SYMB. SEARCH

319

Symbol Search

Short-Term Objectives

The learner will be able to

54. complete weaving activities.

55. fill in the missing elements in a given design.

Instructional Level: K-3

Materials

54. *Weaving Mats*
    (Ideal)
    Weave 'N Stitch Project Pack
    (Bemiss-Jason)

55. *Half 'n' Half Design and Color*
    (Ann Arbor)
    Missing Parts Lotto
    (Milton Bradley)

Symbol Search

Short-Term Objectives

The learner will be able to

1. write things from rote memory in timed activities (e.g., numbers, alphabet, etc.).

2. complete visual tracking exercises.

3. identify missing elements that will complete various pictures.

4. complete tangram puzzles in timed activities.

5. match pictures with the correct printed word in timed activities.

Instructional Level: 3-6

Materials

2. *Symbol/Letter Tracking*
   Word Tracking: High Frequency Words
   Sentence Tracking
   Word Tracking: Proverbs
   Word Tracking: Limericks
      (Ann Arbor)

3. *What Follows, Set II*
   Missing Parts Lotto
      (Milton Bradley)
   Perceptual Activities Packets:
   Finish the Pictures 1, 2
      (Ann Arbor)

4. *Tangram and Puzzle Cards*
      (DLM)
   Tangram Sets
      (Activity Resources)
   Learning with Tangrams
   Tangram Treasury, Books A, B
   Tangrams ABC
   The Math Machine Tangram Puzzles
      (Cuisenaire)

5. *Picture Word Match*
      (Lakeshore)
   Easy Picture Words
      (Frank Schaffer)
   Make-A-Word Spelling Games
   Singular and Plural Cards
      (Didax)
   Basic Sight Words
   More Sight Words
   Basic Picture Words
   More Picture Words
      (Trend)

SYMB.
SEARCH

Symbol Search

Short-Term Objectives

The learner will be able to

Instructional Level: 3-6

Materials

6. reproduce two and three dimensional patterns.

6. *Classroom Mosaic Playtile Set*
   Giant Crystal Climbers
   Build and Roll Raceway
   Slot-A-Rounds
   Magnashapes
      (Lakeshore)
   3-D Teaching Aids
      (Kids' Stuff)
   Mirror Game I and II
   DIME Build Up, Book I—An Approach
      to Thinking in Three Dimensions
   Tricubes Puzzles
   DIME Solids
   Pentacube Puzzles
   Polydron Shapes Starter Set
   Exploring with Polydron
      (Cuisenaire)

7. accurately match geometric shapes and designs within specified time limits.

7. *Geometric Shapes*
      (Didax)
   RelationShapes
      (Cuisenaire)
   Attribute Blocks Desk Set
      (Learning Resources)
   Symbol Discrimination Series
   Symbol Discrimination and Sequencing
      (Ann Arbor)

8. complete figure-ground exercises in timed activities.

8. *Perceptual Activities*
      (Ann Arbor)
   Figure-Ground Activity Cards
      (DLM)

9. reproduce designs using triangles, hexangles, and quadrilaterals.

9. *Polydron Shapes Starter Set*
   Exploring with Polydron
      (Cuisenaire)
   Triangles
      (Delta)
   Geometric Three-Sided Dominoes
      (Judy/Instructo)

322

Symbol Search

Short-Term Objectives

The learner will be able to

Instructional Level: 3-6

Materials

Geometry Problems and Projects—
  software
  (Sunburst)

10. create an original design for the class to reproduce using pegboards.

10. *Deluxe Pegboard Set*
  Pegboard Fun with Patterns, Group Set
    (Ideal)
  Pegboards, Pegs, and Pegboard
    Patterns
    (DLM)

11. reproduce designs drawn on paper or cards using manipulative materials such as colored cubes.

11. *Polydron Shapes Starter Set*
  Exploring with Polydron
    (Cuisenaire)
  Hands-On Manipulative Lab
    (Lakeshore)
  Picture Perfect Design Tiles
  Puzzle Tiles
  Puzzle Tiles Pattern Cards
    (Educational Insights)
  Pocket Parquetry Plus Patterns
    (Ideal)

12. reproduce spelling words with individual letters in timed activities.

12. *Lakeshore Letters Jar*
    (Lakeshore)
  Tub 'O Letters
  Letter Perfect
    (Educational Insights)
  Avalanche of Letters
    (Lauri)

13. build an animal or figure using building toys, pipe cleaners, or other materials.

13. *Heavy-Duty Construction Straws*
  People Builder
    (Lakeshore)
  Six Sticks
  Googolplex
    (Dale Seymour)
  Pipe cleaners
  Popsicle sticks

SYMB.
SEARCH

Symbol Search

Short-Term Objectives
The learner will be able to

Instructional Level: 3-6
Materials

14. find objects hidden in pictures.

14. *Where's Waldo*
The Great Waldo Search
(Little, Brown)
Figure-Ground Activity Cards
(DLM)

15. complete paper folding activities within specified time limits.

15. *Pholdit*
Spatial Problem Solving with Paper Folding
(Activity Resources)
Origami
Wings and Things: Origami That Flies
Paper Pandas and Jumping Frogs
Origami Paper
(Dale Seymour)
Origami Paper
(Bemiss-Jason)

16. complete jigsaw puzzles appropriate for age level with specific time limits.

16. *Word Puzzles*
(Instructional Fair)
Pyramid Puzzles
(Ideal)
Puzzles and Patterns
(Steck-Vaughn)
Boxed jigsaw puzzles purchased from variety stores

17. play games such as dominoes requiring the matching of designs and pictures.

17. *Geometric Shape Three-Sided Dominoes*
(Judy/Instructo)
Random Pattern Dominoes
Shadow Dominoes
Arrow Dominoes
Animal Dominoes
Color Dominoes
(Marvel)

18. identify missing letters in known words.

18. *Boxed Activity Cards: Short and Long Vowels*
(Frank Schaffer)

Symbol Search

Short-Term Objectives

The learner will be able to

Instructional Level: 3-6

Materials

Instant Spelling Words for Writing
(Curriculum Associates)
M-ss-ng L-nks—software
(Sunburst)
Wheel of Fortune Junior—software
(Fas-Track)

19. perform the operations of addition and subtraction using manipulative objects.

19. *Color Counters*
(Cuisenaire)
One-Inch Colored Cubes
(Ideal)
Dinosaur Counters
(Educational Insights)

20. complete weaving activities within specified time limits.

20. *Weave 'N Stitch Project Pack*
(Bemiss-Jason)
Weaving Mats
(Ideal)

21. type spelling words accurately.

21. *Type to Learn*—software
(Sunburst)
Typing Keys—software
Typing Keys
(ATP)
Hyper Typer—software
(EBSCO)

22. complete crossword and number puzzles appropriate for age level.

22. *Cross-Number Puzzles*
(Midwest)
Crozzzwords—Crossword Puzzles—
software
(Troll)
Crossword Puzzles
(EBSCO)

23. complete mazes appropriate for age level with specific time limits.

23. *Perceptual Activities Packets:*
   Mazes 1-4
ABC Mazes
The Maze Book
(Ann Arbor)
Algernon—software
(Sunburst)

SYMB.
SEARCH

Symbol Search

Short-Term Objectives

The learner will be able to

Instructional Level: 3-6

Materials

24. spell words by solving number/letter or geometric form/letter code in specified time limits.

24. *Challenging Codes: Riddles and Jokes*
    (Midwest)
    Plexers
    More Plexers
    Kid's Book of Secret Codes, Signals, and Ciphers
    (Dale Seymour)

25. locate cities, counties, rivers, highways, etc., on a map using the map legend.

25. *Basic Map Skills*
    (Educational Insights)
    Learning Map Skills
    (Milliken)
    Develop Map Skills, Books 1, 2
    (Hayes)
    Various state maps

26. complete exercises for practicing handwriting skills.

26. *Manuscript Writing (Letters)*
    Manuscript Writing (Words)
    Cursive Tracking
    Cursive Writing (Letters)
    Cursive Writing (Words)
    (Ann Arbor)

27. play games following specific rules such as Jacks, Pick-Up Sticks, Monopoly, etc.

28. circle the words in a list of real and nonsense words.

28. *Word Tracking: High Frequency Words*
    Sentence Tracking: High Frequency Words
    Sentence Tracking
    (Ann Arbor)
    Teacher-prepared word list

29. match parts of compound words using a master list for reference.

29. *Compound Word Puzzles*
    (Ideal)
    Everything for Language Arts
    (Carson-Dellosa)
    Teacher-prepared word list

Symbol Search

Short-Term Objectives
The learner will be able to

Instructional Level: 3-6
Materials

30. reproduce complex designs using multicolored blocks and puzzle pieces.

30. *Polydron Shapes*
    Exploring with Polydrons
    Tessellations
    Introduction to Tessellations
    (Cuisenaire)

31. fill in outlines of designs with small parquetry pieces.

31. *Parquetry Inlay Mosaics*
    (Learning Resources)
    Wooden Pattern Blocks
    Pattern Block Activities
    Tangrams 330 Puzzles
    (Cuisenaire)

32. match wooden tiles to the correct design displayed on a wooden strip.

32. *Sorting Box Combination for Counting and Color*
    (Marvel)
    Advanced Geometric Designs
    Advanced Color Matching
    (Constructive Playthings)

33. match random arrangements of designs with structural arrangements of the same designs.

33. *Large Geometric Plastic Forms*
    (Ideal)
    Colored Inch Cubes
    Colored Inch Cubes Designs
    Colored Inch Cube Designs in Perspective
    Lite Brite
    (DLM)

34. reproduce designs on a geoboard in timed activities.

34. *Geoboard Activity Books*
    Introducing Geoboards
    (Activity Resources)
    Cuisenaire Geoboards
    Geoboard Activity Cards— Intermediate Set
    (Cuisenaire)

35. type spelling or vocabulary lists in complete sentences.

35. *Type to Learn*—software
    (Sunburst)

SYMB.
SEARCH

327

Symbol Search

Short-Term Objectives
The learner will be able to

Instructional Level: 3-6
Materials

Typing Keys—software
Typing Keys
  (ATP)

36. create a drawing of a maze that can be solved by a classmate.

36. *The Maze Book*
  (Ann Arbor)
  Algernon—software
  (Sunburst)

37. circle correctly two letters or symbols which appear on a given line of a worksheet in a specified time limit.

37. *Symbol Discrimination Series*
  Symbol/Letter Tracking
  Symbol Discrimination and Sequencing
  (Ann Arbor)
  Keep on Tracking—software
  (EBSCO)

38. fill in the missing halves of a given design.

38. *Half 'n' Half Design and Color*
  (Ann Arbor)
  Part-Whole Puzzle Forms
  (Lakeshore)

39. complete sorting activities according to selected attributes (e.g., vowels, size, functions, etc.).

39. *Vowel Sorting and Word Cards*
  Sort and Sound Word-Making Puzzles
  Sort and Sound Digraph Puzzles
  (Didax)
  Sorting Box Combination for Counting and Color
  (Marvel)

40. assemble polyhedras in timed activities.

40. *Cut and Assemble 3-D Geometrical Shapes*
  (Cuisenaire)

Symbol Search

Short-Term Objectives

The learner will be able to

1. find the initials of a classmate in a row of letters.

2. locate a specific abstract symbol in a row of symbols.

3. use mnemonics to spell words or remember names.

4. reproduce a row of given patterns within a specific period of time.

5. produce a melody using a musical instrument following simple musical symbols.

6. reproduce from memory a series of symbols flashed in front of him.

7. complete dot-to-dot activities in a specified period of time.

8. identify the absence or presence of a symbol in a given row of symbols.

9. locate symbols and letters in tracking activities in a specified period of time.

Instructional Level: 6-12

Materials

2. *Symbol Discrimination and Sequencing*
   Symbol Discrimination Series
   Symbol/Letter Tracking
     (Ann Arbor)

3. *Demonic Mnemonics*
     (Dale Seymour)

4. *Lite Brite*
   Small Parquetry and Small Parquetry Designs I, II, III
     (DLM)
   Etch-A-Sketch
     (Ohio Art)

5. *Xylophone*
     (Fisher-Price)
   Chromatic Bell Set
     (Judy/Instructo)

6. *Visual Memory Cards*
   Visual Sequential Memory Exercises
     (DLM)

7. *Perceptual Activities Packets: Dot-to-Dot 1, 2*
     (Ann Arbor)

8. Teacher-prepared worksheets

9. *Symbol/Letter Tracking*
   Symbol Discrimination Series
   Symbol Discrimination and Sequencing
     (Ann Arbor)

SYMB. SEARCH

329

Symbol Search

Short-Term Objectives

The learner will be able to

Instructional Level: 6-12

Materials

10. identify a specific word in a line of printed material within a given time limit.

10. *Word Tracking: Proverbs*
    Word Tracking: High Frequency Words
    Sentence Tracking
    (Ann Arbor)

11. complete paper-folding exercises in a given period of time.

11. *Paper Folding with Origami Techniques*
    (Judy/Instructo)
    Complete Origami
    Origami Paper
    Wings and Things: Origami That Flies
    Paper Pandas and Jumping Frogs
    (Dale Seymour)
    Origami Paper
    (Bemiss-Jason)

12. play "Concentration" using a deck of cards.

12. *Touch 'N' See*—software
    (EBSCO)
    Memory Match—software
    (FasTrack)
    Memory Building Blocks—software
    Now You See It, Now You Don't—
    software
    (Sunburst)
    Playing cards or any set of cards with matching pairs

13. identify what is missing in pictures. (Increase the level of difficulty by imposing time limits of 15 seconds, 10 seconds, 5 seconds.)

13. *What's in a Frame?*—software
    Was It There? Was It Missing?—
    software
    (Sunburst)

14. identify what is different in pictures.

14. *Think, Compare, and Explain*
    Comparison Challenge
    (Academic Communication Associates)

Symbol Search

Short-Term Objectives	Instructional Level: 6-12

The learner will be able to

Materials

15. arrange jumbled letters into spelling or vocabulary words in a given period of time.

15. *Letter Perfect*
    Tub 'O Letters
    (Educational Insights)
    Avalanche of Letters
    (Lauri)

16. arrange jumbled words into complete sentences in timed activities.

16. *Build a Sentence Game*
    Super Sentence Game
    (Creative Teaching Associates)
    GrammaRummy
    Tub 'O Words
    (Educational Insights)
    Switchboard—software
    (Sunburst)
    Sentence Builder
    (Milton Bradley)
    Word and Phrase Sentence Builder
    (Kenworthy)

17. reproduce abstract designs using small tangram or parquetry pieces.

17. *Tangram Treasury, Book C*
    Tangrams ABC Kit
    The Fun With Tangrams Kit
    (Cuisenaire)
    Puzzlegrams
    Pocket Parquetry Plus Patterns
    Tangram
    Tangram Puzzles
    (Ideal)
    Tangoes
    Tangrams
    ESS Tangram Cards, Set III
    (Dale Seymour)
    Parquetry Inlay Mosaics
    Parquetry Blocks
    Parquetry Pattern Cards
    (Learning Resources)

18. assemble or complete three-dimensional puzzles.

18. *Spatial Problem Solving with Cuisenaire Rods*
    Polydrons

SYMB. SEARCH

Symbol Search

Short-Term Objectives
The learner will be able to

Instructional Level: 6-12
Materials

Exploring with Polydrons
  (Cuisenaire)
Cryptocube—software
  (Troll)

19. recognize similarities and differences between designs, words, and situations.

19. *Connector Vectors*
Word Benders
Figural Similarities
  (Midwest)
Symbol Discrimination Series
  (Ann Arbor)

20. complete hidden word puzzles.

20. *Wordzzzearch—Hidden Word Puzzles*
  —software
Crossword and Word-Search Wizard—
  software
  (Troll)
Word Works 1:
  Word Cross
  Word Search
  (EBSCO)

21. visually track two or three symbols at a time in timed activities. (Expand to five as student's ability increases.)

21. *Symbol Discrimination Series*
Symbol Discrimination and
  Sequencing
Symbol/Letter Tracking
  (Ann Arbor)

22. identify the presence or absence of a stimulus picture among a series of five pictures flashed before him.

22. *Consonants/Vowels Picture Card*
  Combo
Consonants/Vowels II Picture Card
  Combo
  (Judy/Instructo)

23. complete mosaic projects using mosaic kits or bits of colored paper.

23. *Parquetry Inlay Mosaics*
  (Learning Resources)

24. determine if a specific letter is present or absent in spelling words.

Symbol Search

Short-Term Objectives	Instructional Level: 6-12
The learner will be able to	**Materials**

25. solve mazes appropriate for age level within a specified time limit.

    25. *Think Quick*—software
        The Word Master Vocabulary Builder—
          software
          (Fas-Track)
        Algernon—software
          (Sunburst)
        The Maze Book
          (Ann Arbor)

26. decipher codes in timed activities.

    26. *Challenging Codes:*
        Riddles and Jokes
        Quips and Quotes
          (Midwest)
        Kids' Book of Secret Codes, Signals
         and Ciphers
        Plexers
        More Plexers
          (Dale Seymour)

27. complete a jigsaw puzzle of the United States within a specified time limit.

    27. *GeoPuzzle USA*—software
          (Fas-Track)
        State Flash Cards
          (Ideal)
        U.S. Map Woodboard Puzzle
          (Judy/Instructo)
         Fit-a-State
          (Lauri)

28. find objects, animals, or persons hidden in pictures.

    28. *The Great Waldo Search*
        Find Waldo Now
          (Little, Brown)
        Figure-Ground Activity Cards
          (DLM)

29. complete puzzles and activities involving visual perceptual and discrimination skills.

    29. *Eye-Cue Puzzles*
        Visual Thinking
          (Dale Seymour)
        Building Perspective—software
        The Right Turn—software
        Plane View—software
          (Sunburst)

SYMB.
SEARCH

Symbol Search

Short-Term Objectives

The learner will be able to

Instructional Level: 6-12

Materials

Mirror Game II
DIME Solids
DIME 3-D Sketching Project, Book 2
Tricubes Puzzles
   (Cuisenaire)

30. recall five of six words presented on cards for a period of 10 seconds and then hidden from view.

30. *Memory Jogger (Grades 4-6)*
   (EBSCO)
Basic Sight Words Flash Cards
More Sight Words Flash Cards
   (Trend)
Teacher-made word cards

31. fill in letters missing in words.

31. *M-ss-ng L-nks*—software
M-ss-ng L-nks Science Disk—software
   (Sunburst)
Wheel of Fortune—software
   (Fas-Track)
Scrabble
   (Selchow and Righter)
Word Works 2: Missing Vowels—
   software
Word Works 3: Missing Letters—
   software
   (EBSCO)

32. type spelling or vocabulary words in sentences.

33. circle the words in a list of real and nonsense words.

33. *Word Tracking: High Frequency Words*
Sentence Tracking
Word Tracking: Proverbs
Thought Tracking
   (Ann Arbor)

MAZES

Mazes

I. Purpose of the Subtest
To measure the ability to plan, use foresight, and perceptually organize according to a visual pattern.

II. Factors Affecting Subtest and Academic Performance
A. Attention skills
B. Visual-motor control
C. Speed and accuracy
D. Visualization
E. Spatial organization
F. Time
G. Foresight

III. Educational Significance
A. Additional time to complete tasks will be necessary for the student to succeed.
B. Be sure the student is giving attention to the instructions.
C. Include the student in planning activities for the class, in deciding objectives to be attained and how to attain them.
D. Assist the student in planning and organizing assignments by providing step-by-step instructions.
E. The auditory-vocal channel should be considered the student's primary modality for receiving information until visual skills improve.
F. The student's impulsive tendencies while manipulating paper-and-pencil tasks should be modified through behavior management techniques.

IV. Long-Term Goal
The learner will be able to plan, use foresight, and perceptually organize according to a visual plan.

MAZES

Mazes

Short-Term Objectives

The learner will be able to

1. complete worksheets designed by commercial companies to develop visual-perceptual skills.

2. trace pictures from coloring books, etc., of familiar objects with a crayon, staying on the lines of the pictures as much as possible.

3. string beads of various sizes, shapes and colors to match a given model.

Instructional Level: K-3

Materials

1. *Frostig Remediation Program*
   (Follett)
   Visual-Motor Readiness Skill Set
   (Continental Press)
   Perceptual Activities Packets
   Perceptual Activities
   ABC Mazes
   The Maze Book
   (Ann Arbor)

2. *Tracing Paper*
   (Bemiss-Jason)
   Visual-Motor Readiness Skill Set
   (Continental Press)
   Store-bought activity and coloring books

3. *Multivariant Sequencing Beads and Bead Patterns*
   (DLM)
   Colored Beads and Laces
   Beads and Laces Pattern Cards
   (Media Materials)
   Large Colored Beads and Patterns
   Laces for Stringing
   Plastic Beads
   (Ideal)
   Sequencing Beads and Design Cards
   (Incentives for Learning)
   Bigbeads
   Bigbeads Pattern Cards
   (Educational Insights)
   Beads of various colors, sizes and shapes
   String, shoelaces

Mazes

Short-Term Objectives
The learner will be able to

4. complete patterns and designs in lacing activities.

5. complete simple mazes gradually increasing in complexity.

6. identify and draw in the items that are missing in pictures.

7. use open stencils for tracing, coloring, and cutting activities.

Instructional Level: K-3
Materials

4. *Lacing Boards*
    (DLM)
    Lacing Shapes
    Lacing Bears
    (Lauri)
    Sewing Cards
    (Media Materials)
    Peg-N-Lace Board Set
    Sewing Cards Class Set
    (Ideal)

5. *Simple Mazes Wipe-Off Book*
    (Trend)
    Visual Tracking Cards
    (Ideal)
    The Maze Book
    ABC Mazes
    (Ann Arbor)
    Math Mazes, 2, 3
    Peanuts Maze Marathon—software
    (Opportunities for Learning)
    Visual-Motor Readiness Skill Set
    (Continental Press)
    Store-bought activity books

6. *Finish the Picture Wipe-Off Cards*
    (Trend)
    Visual Closure Cards
    (Ideal)
    Missing Parts Lotto
    (Media Materials)
    Half 'n' Half Design and Color
    (Ann Arbor)

7. *Clear Stencils*
    (DLM)
    Stencils
    (Highlights for Children)
    Stencil Shapes, Sets I, II, III
    (Learning Resources)

MAZES

339

Mazes

Short-Term Objectives	Instructional Level: K-3

The learner will be able to

Materials

8. place in correct order nesting toys and stacking toys that are graduated in size.

8. *Sort and Stack*
   Nesting Boxes
      (Constructive Playthings)
   Stacking Clown
      (Learning Resources)
   Shape Sorter and Stacker
      (Playskool)
   Color Stack
   Pile Up Cubes
   Sort and Stack
   Handy Boxes
      (Marvel)

9. match forms and shapes to similarly shaped holes in a board or to drawings of the shapes on paper.

9. *Coordination Board*
   Attribute Desk Blocks
      (Judy/Instructo)
   Montessori Shapes and Stencils
   Shape Form Board
      (Learning Resources)
   Geometric Inset Board
      (Marvel)
   Shape Squares
   Fit-a-Shape
      (Lauri)
   Geoboard Kit
      (Childcraft)

10. fit together various objects that open and close, or fit into another that are mounted on a board (e.g., latches, buttons and buttonholes, plugs, locks, screws and nuts, etc.).

10. *Fasteners*
      (Ideal)
   Teacher-made board

11. imitate or reproduce lines drawn by the teacher or found in printed exercises (e.g., vertical, horizontal, circles, ovals, etc.).

11. *Writing Readiness*
      (Hayes)

340

Mazes

Short-Term Objectives The learner will be able to	Instructional Level: K-3 Materials

12. trace simple designs and letters.	12. *Alphabet Mastery (Letters)*
	Manuscript Writing (Letters)
	Perceptual Activities
	  (Ann Arbor)
	Trace-A-Letter Cards
	Jumbo Alphabet Cards
	Alphabet Cards
	  (Zaner-Bloser)
	Stencil Factory
	Stencil Mini-Paks A-F
	  (Essential Learning Products)
	Alphabet Practice Cards
	Practice the Alphabet
	Perceptual Development Cards
	  (Ideal)
	Learn to Write—Manuscript Letters
	  (Media Materials)
	Follow the Path Wipe-Off Cards
	  (Trend)

13. complete and identify letters and numerals which are incompletely formed.	13. *Perceptual Activities*
	Manuscript Writing (Letters)
	Numbers and Numerals
	  (Ann Arbor)
	Lacing Boards
	  (DLM)
	Teacher-prepared worksheets

14. identify by feeling with eyes closed letters and numerals made of felt, sandpaper, etc.	14. *Super Alphabet Pack*
	  (Judy/Instructo)
	Tactile Sandpaper Numerals
	  (Didax)
	Flannel Board Numbers
	  (Media Materials)
	Beaded Alphabet Chart
	Foam Letters
	Foam Numbers
	Giant Beaded Number Cards

MAZES

Mazes

Short-Term Objectives

The learner will be able to

Instructional Level: K-3

Materials

Jumbo Alphabet:
  Capitals
  Lower Case
  (Ideal)
A-Z Panels
1-10 Panel
  (Lauri)

15. proceed in a required sequence through an obstacle course in the classroom using desks, chairs, dividers, etc.

15. *Aids to Psycholinguistic Teaching: Perceptual Motor Activities* (Charles E. Merrill)

16. move a toy car or train along a road or railroad track drawn on a mat, a large piece of paper, poster board, etc., departing from a designated spot and arriving at a designated spot without turning into blind alleys.

16. *Giant American Farm Scene Playmat American Town Playmat* (Heffernan) Teacher-prepared material

17. complete dot-to-dot pictures.

17. *Perceptual Activities Packets: Dot-to-Dot 1 & 2 Perceptual Activities* (Ann Arbor) *Teddy Bear Alphabet Dot-to-Dot Teddy Bear Numbers Dot-to-Dot Alphabet Dot-to-Dot Workbook Number Activity Workbook: Dot-to-Dot* (Frank Schaffer)

18. identify correctly simple words whose letters are incompletely formed.

18. *Manuscript Writing (Words) Perceptual Activities Perceptual Activities Packets: Find-the-Word 1 & 2* (Ann Arbor) *Manuscript Writing Manuscript Alphabet* (Instructional Fair)

19. complete paint or color by number activities and projects.

19. Paint-by-number kits Tempera paints and paper

Mazes

Short-Term Objectives

The learner will be able to

20. complete simple map and orientation activities.

Instructional Level: K-3

Materials

20. *Where I Am—Individual Map and Orientation Activities*
(DLM)
Map Skills
Maps, Charts, and Graphs
(Frank Schaffer)
Building Primary Maps
(Judy/Instructo)
Learning About Maps
(Milliken)
Developing Map Skills: Book 1
(Hayes)
Basic Map Skills
(Educational Insights)

MAZES

Mazes

Short-Term Objectives

The learner will be able to

1. draw lines on a map from city to city, illustrating a trip taken by one of the students on a make-believe tour.

2. trace highways on a map for traveling from hometown to another city.

3. complete mazes while verbalizing the directions taken to solve the maze.

4. fit various sizes of felt or rubber shapes inside each other in descending order of size.

Instructional Level: 3-6

Materials

1. *Map Skills*
   Maps, Charts, and Graphs
     (Frank Schaffer)
   Basic Map Skills
     (Educational Insights)
   Finding Your Way
     (Fearon)
   Map Skills
     (Instructional Fair)
   Developing Map Skills
     (Hayes)
   Various state maps

2. *Where I Am—Individual Map and Orientation Activities*
     (DLM)
   Finding Your Way
     (Fearon)
   Basic Map Skills
     (Instructional Fair)
   Various state maps

3. *The Maze Book*
   ABC Mazes
   Perceptual Activities Packets:
     Mazes 1-4
       (Ann Arbor)
   Puzzle Pals
     (Scholastic)
   Visual-Motor Readiness Skill Set
     (Continental Press)
   Math Mazes 2-6
     (Opportunities for Learning)
   Store-bought activity books

4. *Fit-a-Size*
     (Lauri)
   Various sizes and colors of felt or rubber shapes
   Felt board

Mazes

Short-Term Objectives

The learner will be able to

Instructional Level: 3-6

Materials

5. fold paper in a specific manner after watching a model demonstration.

5. *Paper Folding with Origami Techniques*
   (Judy/Instructo)
   Origami Paper
   (Bemiss-Jason)
   Origami Paper
   Origami, Sets A & B
   Wings and Things: Origami that Flies
   Complete Origami
   Paper Pandas and Jumping Frogs
   (Dale Seymour)

6. fold paper in a specific manner without a demonstration.

6. *Paper Animals*
   Paper Folding with Origami Techniques
   (Judy/Instructo)
   Origami Paper
   (Bemiss-Jason)
   Origami Paper
   Origami, Sets A & B
   Complete Origami
   Wings and Things: Origami that Flies
   Paper Pandas and Jumping Frogs
   (Dale Seymour)

7. prepare recipes observing health and safety rules (e.g., washing hands, touching hot oven, etc.).

7. *Cook and Learn*
   (Addison Wesley)
   A Special Picture Cookbook
   (Edmark)
   Bake and Taste
   (Cambridge Development Laboratory)
   Children's cookbooks

8. trace and retrace, with a finger, felt, rubber, or sandpaper letters, spelling simple words or words from the spelling lesson.

8. *Avalanche of Letters*
   (Lauri)
   Jumbo Alphabet:
   Capitals
   Lower Case
   Beaded Alphabet Cards

MAZES

Mazes

Short-Term Objectives

The learner will be able to

Instructional Level: 3-6

Materials

Foam Letters:
  Lower Case
  Upper Case
  (Ideal)
Kin-Tac Alphabet Cards
  (Zaner-Bloser)

9. trace several times, with a finger, difficult words which are written on the chalkboard; then write the words in the air several times.

10. write difficult words in the air and on paper correctly after viewing them written on the chalkboard.

11. draw lines in correct sequence in a given period of time between randomly placed numbers or letters.

11. Teacher-made worksheets

12. circle hidden words in word-hunt activities.

12. *Word Puzzles: Gr. 2-3, 3-4, 4-5, 5-6*
   (Milliken)
   Crosswords & Wordsearches: Gr. 2-3, 3-4, 4-5, 5-6
   (Opportunities for Learning)
   Crosswords and Wordsearches: Gr. 2-4
   Word Puzzles: Gr. 3-4, 4-5, 5-6
   (Instructional Fair)
   Store-bought activity books

13. draw lines in correct sequence between appropriate letters in a maze to spell a specific phrase or sentence.

13. *Sentence Tracking*
   (Ann Arbor)
   Teacher-made material

14. proceed through an obstacle course using classroom furniture, materials, etc. in a given period of time.

Mazes

Short-Term Objectives	Instructional Level: 3-6
The learner will be able to	**Materials**

15. identify the specific destination by hearing the route described.

15. *Building Primary Map Skills* (Judy/Instructo)

16. verbally describe how to get home from school or how to go from home to a friend's house using landmarks (e.g., stores, churches, homes of friends on the route, etc.).

16. *Building Primary Map Skills* (Judy/Instructo) Tape Tape recorder

17. describe how to get from a specific place to home or school.

17. *Building Primary Map Skills* (Judy/Instructo) *Finding Your Way* (Fearon)

18. trace exercises (letters and/or words) in cursive writing.

18. *Write-Better Kit* (Zaner-Bloser) *Drill-It Workbook: Handwriting Transition to Cursive (Bear)* (American Teaching Aids) *Practice Writing Series: Book 2, Let's Write Cursive Book 3, Let's Drill Cursive* (Hayes)

19. prepare a "contract" or a time schedule for completing a project or a group of activities.

20. bring three objects to class illustrating the attributes of taste, smell, and feel.

20. Three boxes labeled "Taste," "Smell," and "Feel"

21. maintain a daily assignment notebook.

MAZES

Mazes

Short-Term Objectives
The learner will be able to

1. keep a daily assignment notebook.

2. trace manuscript and cursive hand-writing activities.

3. trace spelling words provided by the teacher.

4. bring to class five objects to illustrate the attributes of taste, feel, smell, texture, and hear.

5. plan a party (e.g., invitations, refreshments, activities, etc.).

6. outline a short story.

7. play "Bingo" with different ways to win stated before the game begins (e.g., five in a row, the four outside rows and columns, Z shape, etc.).

Instructional Level: 6-12
Materials

2. *Write-Now Kit*
   Write-Better Kit
   Kin-Tac Alphabet Cards
   The 3-R Pack
   Desk-Top PracticeMats
      (Zaner Bloser)
   Manuscript Writing
   Cursive Writing
      (Instructional Fair)
   Developing Writing Skills:
      Book F Grade 6
   Practice Writing Series:
      Book 3, Let's Drill Cursive
      Book 4, Advanced Cursive Writing
      (Hayes)

3. *Tracing Paper*
      (Bemiss-Jason)

4. Five boxes labeled "Taste," "Feel," "Smell," "Texture," and "Hear"

6. *Outline Wizard*
      (Learning Works)
   Outlining, Note Taking, and Report Writing
      (Hayes)

7. *Bingo*
      (Milton Bradley)
   Sight Word Bingo
      (Frank Schaffer)
   Trend Bingo Games:
      USA
      Parts of Speech
      (Trend)

Mazes

Short-Term Objectives

The learner will be able to

Instructional Level: 6-12

Materials

8. solve mazes of greater complexity, appropriate to student's age and grade level.

8. *The Maze Book*
   Perceptual Activities
      (Ann Arbor)
   Maze Cube—software
   Math Mazes—software
   Math Mazes—Grades 2-7
      (Opportunities for Learning)
   Labrinth
      (Troll)
   Visual-Motor Readiness Skill Set
      (Continental Press)
   Quizzles
   More Quizzles
      (Dale Seymour)

9. complete a puzzle of the United States.

9. *U.S. Map Woodboard Puzzle*
   United States Floor Map Puzzle
      (Judy/Instructo)
   Large U.S. Map Puzzle
      (Bemiss-Jason)
   United States Map Floor Puzzle
      (Frank Schaffer)

10. map out alternate routes to well known locations within the community. (This activity may be expanded to outlining routes for short trips within a twenty-mile range.)

10. *Finding Your Way*
      (Fearon)
    Map Skills
      (Instructional Fair)
    Developing Map Skills
      (Hayes)
    Various city and state maps

11. trace a trip planned or taken on a map, indicating the highways from city to city and back to origination point.

11. Various maps

12. using a map legend,compute the mileage of a trip planned or taken and the number of days needed to make the trip.

12. *Maptime . . . USA*
      (Good Apple)
    Various maps
    Calculator

MAZES

349

Mazes

Short-Term Objectives	Instructional Level: 6-12
The learner will be able to	**Materials**

13. make a list of supplies needed for a planned trip (e.g., food, clothing, money, etc.).

14. determine where each night would be spent while taking a long trip by computing the time and mileage required.

    14. Various state maps

15. create and make a project with mosaic tiles such as trivets, trays, etc.

    15. Mosaic tiles
        Forms
        Mosaic kits

16. create and complete a project using rug hooking and tying techniques.

    16. Rug yarn
        Mesh wire
        Frames
        Hooked-rug kits

17. plan a meal for two people including buying and preparing the food and setting the table.

18. complete paint-by-number paintings.

    18. Paint-by-number kits

19. list in correct sequence the events that occur in a specific class period.

20. plan sequential activities in conjunction with the class for class projects or plays.

    20. *Stage: Creative Dramatics*
        (Opportunities for Learning)

21. list the sequential steps involved in finding a job.

    21. *Vocational Entry-Skills for*
        Secondary Students
        (ATP)
        Finding a Job
        (Fearon)
        Job Skills Programs
        Job Readiness Software Series
        The Job Hunter's Workbook
        Job Application Book Series
        (Opportunities for Learning)

Mazes

Short-Term Objectives

The learner will be able to

Instructional Level: 6-12

Materials

22. list the sequential rules for a well-known game (e.g., "Monopoly," checkers or chess).

23. create the rules of a new game.

24. determine the number of blocks in a presented design.

25. determine the number in a group of blocks.

26. assemble various abstract-shaped pieces into a design.

27. complete prepared activity sheets for the development of organizational skills.

24. *Colored Inch Cube Designs in Perspective*
    (DLM)
    Colored Cube Activity Cards
    (Summit Learning)

25. *Colored Inch Cubes*
    (DLM)
    Color Cubes
    (Judy/Instructo)
    Colored Cubes
    (Ideal)

26. *Tangram Puzzle*
    Tangram Patterns
    (Judy/Instructo)
    Tangram and Puzzle Cards
    (DLM)
    Tangram Treasury
    (Cuisenaire)
    Parquetry Inlay Mosaics
    Parquetry Blocks
    Parquetry Pattern Cards
    (Learning Resources)
    Tangram and Pattern Cards
    Pocket Parquetry plus Patterns
    (Ideal)

27. *Skills for School Success*
    Organization Skills
    Classification and Organization Skills—Developmental
    (Curriculum Associates)
    Study Skills Activity Pack
    (Opportunities for Learning)

MAZES

Mazes

Short-Term Objectives

The learner will be able to

28. trace a wiring diagram of an electric circuit to indicate which pair of terminals should be attached to a battery to make the circuit work.

29. create a drawing of a maze that can be solved by a classmate.

30. design and build an obstacle course in the classroom using the materials in the room (desks, dividers, etc.).

Instructional Level: 6-12

Materials

28. *Science Equipment Kit (Intermediate)*
    Mr. Wizard's 400 Experiments in Science
    Science Work-Texts
      (Opportunities for Learning)
    Science in Action: Electricity
      (Educational Insights)
    Science Shelf Activity Kits: Electricity
      (Ideal)
    Science Inquiry Labs: Lab II, Electricity
      (Weber Costello)